Second Edition

The Complete Guide to Writing Fiction and Nonfiction: And Getting It Published

Pat Kubis, Ph.D
Emeritus Professor of English, Orange Coast College

Robert M. Howland
President, HDL Publishing Company

Prentice Hall, Up̱ _____ _____ ___.__, New Jersey 07458

D0962900

Library of Congress Cataloging-in-Publication Data

Kubis, Patricia.
   The complete guide to writing fiction and nonfiction—and getting
   it published / Pat Kubis, Robert M. Howland.—2nd ed.
     p. cm.
   Includes index.
   ISBN 0-13-161019-8 : $16.95
   1. Authorship. I. Howland, Robert. II. Title.
PN145.K83 1990   88-34427
808'.02—dc19   CIP

Editorial/production supervision and
  interior design: Cyndy Lyle Rymer
Cover design: George Cornell
Manufacturing buyer: Ray Keating

©1990 by Prentice-Hall, Inc.
Upper Saddle River, NJ 07458

Printed in the United States of America
20 19 18 17 16

ISBN 0-13-161019-8

Prentice-Hall International (UK) Limited, *London*
Prentice-Hall of Australia Pty. Limited, *Sydney*
Prentice-Hall of Canada, Inc., *Toronto*
Prentice-Hall Hispanoamericana, S. A., *Mexico*
Prentice-Hall of India Private Limited, *New Delhi*
Prentice-Hall of Japan, Inc., *Tokyo*
Prentice-Hall Asia Pte. Ltd., *Singapore*
Editora Prentice-Hall do Brasil, Ltda., *Rio de Janeiro*

Contents

2   Viewpoint: The Magic Key to Publishing   *16*

3   How to Open a Short Story or Novel   *34*

4   The Art Of Creating Three-Dimensional Characters   *50*

5   How To Create Effective Dialogue   78

6 How To Develop A Good Style *91*

7 How To Create Settings *107*

10 Theme: What's It All About?   *137*

Do Titles Really Matter?   *146*

12 Research Made Easy   *154*

Fiction Writer's Bonus: Article/Nonfiction Section

13 Article Writing: How to Begin   *162*

14 How to Write the Query Letter for the Article *169*

15 Writing the Article   *182*

16 The Art of Magazine Characterization   *198*

Character Through Generalization *203*   Character Through Other
People's Remarks *204*   Character by Achievement/Background *204*

Summary, *204*

17 The Interview Article *206*

Interview Procedure: How to Start, *206*
Once You've Decided on a Particular Person,
    What Then? *207*
When You First Approach the Celebrity,
    What Do You Say? *207*
What to Do if the Celebrity Turns You Down, *208*
Do Your Homework Before the Interview, *208*
When the Interview Date Is Set, Send a Confirming Letter
    to the Interviewee Shortly Before the Interview, *209*
Arrive at the Specified Time, *209*
Relax and Enjoy the Interview, *209*
Be Sure to Dress Neatly, *210*
Know the Slant of Your Article Before You Begin
    the Interview, *210*
Make a List of Questions You Would Like Answered, *210*
Be Polite and Tactful, *211*
Is a Tape Recorder Necessary? *211*

What About Just Writing Things Down? *212*

Breaking the Ice, *212*
Don't Let the Interview "Get Away from You," *212*
Be a Responsible Reporter, *213*
Copywriting an Interview, *213*
Summary, *213*

18 Whom Are You Writing For—And Why? *215*

The Average Reader, *216*
Be Timely, *216*

19 How to Approach a Publishing House *226*

20 How To Develop the Nonfiction Book Query and Proposal and the Novel Package, Including the Synopsis *233*

21   Everything About Literary Agents   *270*

22 Whee! You Received a Book Contract—Now What? *277*

Index *288*

Preface

Why Do You Want to Write?

This question is important. It determines what you wish to accomplish through your writing. **Do you want to**

Tell stories?
See your name on a book jacket?
Be recognized by your friends and the world?
Travel, have an exciting life, meet interesting people?
Set your own schedule, be independent?
Be one of the leading artists/thinkers of your time?
Influence your culture, the world?
Write a bestseller, make money?
Write a fine novel, an artistic work?

All of these are valid reasons to be a writer. Yet whether you see writing as commercial or as purely artistic, the craft of writing is fundamental to both. In this sense writing is like music. Both Beethoven and the latest young pop composer use the same chords, but it's how they *use* those chords that determines the difference in their music. No matter which field of writing you choose, only a knowledge of craft will bring you the success you want. Editors in every field of writing know and respect craft. When they see it, they publish it. To write without a knowledge of craft is to write in a vacuum, to waste valuable time and energy.

If You Want to Publish, Do You Know How to

Evaluate subjects that are in demand?
Select the right subjects for you?
Identify your audience?

Identify and master the ten elements in fiction and nonfiction that cause most books to be rejected by agents or editors?
Prepare a cover letter?
Prepare a complete proposal?
"Hook" an editor into reading your manuscript?
Prepare a chapter outline?
Prepare a synopsis?
Handle multiple submissions?
Read, understand, and negotiate a contract?
Analyze royalties and advances?
Prepare and submit a final manuscript?

A professional knows all of these things before even submitting a project.

This Text Is Reality Therapy

This guide is designed for both the beginner and the professional. There is some duplication in the text so that nonfiction writers need not read through the fiction and publishing sections for pertinent reference material.

Both authors are specialists in their fields. Pat Kubis is a literary consultant, a prize-winning novelist, and a professor of English who has taught novel writing for more than twenty-three years. Bob Howland is the president and editor-in-chief of HDL Publishing Company. Together they explain *why* a manuscript is rejected by agents and publishers. They not only explain craft simply and directly, detailing the fundamentals every writer should know, but they also provide the writer with a method of preparing a complete manuscript proposal and a way of approaching a publisher. The text strips away the secrecy of the publishing industry, revealing how the writer can intelligently approach agents and publishers. It is a valuable handbook and guide that every writer who hopes to be a professional will find of value throughout his or her entire writing career.

Some Questions You Might Want to Ask

1. **Can any book about writing really help one to publish? Aren't the odds of publishing a first novel or a first work of nonfiction terribly high?**

Yes, the odds are high. But a knowledge of craft, which this book imparts, cuts those odds. Consider that more than half the material submitted to publishers is unpublishable simply because the authors do not know how to write.

2. Can a writer ever hope to make any money from a first novel?

Yes, and some writers have become unbelievable wealthy. Judith Krantz's first novel was so successful that she received $3.2 million for her second novel, *Princess Daisy*. William Safire's first novel, *Full Disclosure*, received $1.4 million, and Peter Benchley totted up a staggering $15 million in total earnings for *Jaws*, including movie and TV rights. Granted, becoming a bestselling novelist on your first book is like winning the Irish Sweepstakes, but you as a writer do have a chance in the lottery. Still, even if you don't make your first million on your first book, you will have the fulfillment of creating a work in which you really believe.

3. Should a writer think of money in relationship to writing? Shouldn't an artist just create (especially in a garret)?

An artist will always create but, like other people, has to pay bills and feed the family. To negate money in relationship to art is a negative mental equivalent. Didn't Balzac, Hemingway, Steinbeck, Faulkner, Mailer, Bellow, and many other writers do very well both commercially *and* artistically? After all, why shouldn't writers live well? They contribute the most precious commodities to the world: the ideas and values that shape society. Aren't professionals entitled to be paid for their work?

Note that I said "professional," not an amateur who sends what he or she believes to be a salable manuscript off to a publisher picked by trial and error out of a marketing guide. If you're going to be a professional, you have to think in professional terms. For example, did you know that many editors hardly, if ever, read unsolicited manuscripts? How then will your manuscript be read? The answer, of course, is that an agent should represent you. But before you think of approaching an agent, you must ask yourself the most important question: Is your writing truly professional? If it is not, then there's no use wasting an agent's time. As one prominent New York agent frankly commented: "Ten percent of nothing is nothing."

4. But what do I need to know to be a published writer? What exactly marks me as a professional?

A mastery of technique, for one thing. For example, do you understand the function of plot; do you know how to plot? Do you know why plot is essential in certain stories and most novels? In fact, do you know that although there are several types of plot, one particular plot is the bread and butter of the writing industry, both in serious and commercial writing? Are you aware that plot is not formula; do you know the difference between the two? Do you understand the intricacies of viewpoint: From whose point of view will you tell your story? Do you know how to open your novel, short story, article, or nonfiction work to hook the editor into reading further? Do you know the differences between the six ways of opening a fiction work?

Are you confident about your ability to create three-dimensional characters that walk right off the page? Do your characters speak believable dialogue; are they motivated to carry out the events you are dramatizing in your story or article? Is your style alive, dynamic, vital? Do you know how to develop a powerful style uniquely your own? Do you understand narration and scene and how to use them? Do you know how to create a setting so real that the reader is instantly transported to that locale? Can you create powerful, dramatic scenes, transitions that show the passage of time, and can you use flashbacks unobtrusively without confusing the reader as to time shifts? Can you work theme into your work gracefully? Do you know how to rewrite—to prune and polish? Can you honestly say you've mastered all these techniques? Until you have, you can't call yourself a professional. For just as a musician has to learn chords to play music, the writer must master these techniques to write professionally.

5. Is it necessary that a writer have a college education?

No. The purpose of an education is to enrich your life and to give you a broader perspective about a variety of things. Ideally, an education should enhance your appreciation of history, art, painting, literature, theatre, science, language, and philosophy; it opens the door into the world of ideas. Certainly it adds dimension to a writer's life. However, many famous writers are self-educated. What is absolutely needed, though, is a sensitivity toward life—an ability to see stories in everything about you.

Consider that Mark Twain, Ernest Hemingway, and Ray Bradbury never had a college education—yet they all fascinated their reading audience with their unusual perceptions. Writing excited them, and they followed their inner visions. If you have this kind of enthusiasm and belief in yourself, plus sensitivity and curiosity, you have exactly what a writer needs.

6. But what about creativity? Will my ideas really interest other people?

All of us share common experiences: growing up, falling in love, getting married, raising children, facing illnesses and death. We love excitement and seeing how other people face dangerous experiences in their lives. We are also touched by beautiful experiences in others' lives. If you can touch the truth of your own experience in your writing, you will touch a common chord in others who will be delighted to participate vicariously in your insights and your variation of the life drama.

7. Honestly, though, isn't talent necessary?

William Faulkner's reply to that question was that talent is 1 percent inspiration and 99 percent applying the seat of your pants to a chair.

Flaubert remarked succinctly, "Talent is long patience." It is absolutely true that no one can become a great writer without talent. But as most writing teachers have observed, often the most talented writers in a class do not become published writers. Why? It may be that down deep they do not really want to be writers. Or, it may be that they lack the golden quality of determination to become true professionals.

8. What are the characteristics of determined writers?

For one thing, they know they can write, and they study and practice techniques that will help them perfect their craft. (These techniques are detailed later in this book.) Determined writers write constantly, even if for only an hour a day, and they continually get better. They set a definite schedule for their writing and keep the commitment.

When the great French novelist Balzac first began to write, he was told by everyone—parents, editors, teachers, lawyers, writers—that he had absolutely no talent at all. Fortunately, Balzac was stubborn and refused to believe them. He wrote more than 175 novels, and at least 7 of them are considered great world masterpieces. So should you let anyone's opinion as to whether you have talent or not influence you? Definitely not. Remember Balzac.

9. Can writing be taught?

Speaking as the teaching partner of this writing team, I, Pat Kubis, can answer this question with authority. It has been my good fortune as a writing instructor to have had as students Clive Cussler, who wrote *Raise the Titanic*; Don Stanwood, who wrote *The Memory of Eva Ryker*; Barbara Conklin, who wrote *P.S. I Love You*; and Alex Thorleifson, who co-wrote *John Wayne: The Untold Story*—all bestsellers. Clive has said that after writing a first novel that didn't sell, he thought he should take a writing class to find out what he didn't know about writing. Each of these writers was determined to know everything possible about craft, and they wrote: they didn't talk about it. As a teacher, I have seen my students log more than 4000 publications, in every field of writing: novel, short story, articles, TV and screen writing, even poetry, and a number of them have won literary prizes. In a recent class, seven of my students published novels, and five were finalists in a national novel-writing contest. Yes, I know that writing can be taught. I also believe that a good writing teacher can save you anywhere from six months to twenty years of aimless, unpublished writing. Many times, a new writer has published within the first nine weeks of my beginning writing course; and this is not an unfamiliar story to anyone who teaches writing.

Last Words

If you feel that writing has nothing to do with publishing, then you do not need this book. Just write, put everything you write into a box, and store it under your bed; occasionally show it to your best friend, who will always tell you how good it is. But, if you want to see yourself in print, you will have to confront the editor. He or she is literate, knows the craft of writing, and, even more, expects *you* to know it. Magazine editors expect professional writing. Book editors generally have thousands of manuscripts to choose from and will publish the manuscript they feel is not only well written but also that has potential for commercial success. After all, they're in the business of publishing, and their company will go broke if they select "great" novels that no one buys.

Certainly, writing for publication should be a serious consideration for any writer who hopes to be a professional. But perhaps the greatest of all challenges, and the greatest task of all, is to write the absolute best you can, using all of the art and craft you know. And, if your craft is sound, your vision is true, and you have genuine determination, you will ultimately publish. Will you be great? We hope so, and what you find in this book will be a positive aid in that discovery. After you read and work with this book, we would be interested in your comments.

Pat Kubis
Bob Howland

Acknowledgments

We acknowledge our gratitude to Dr. Wirt Williams, Edward Dornan, and Lawrence Carlson for their analytical comments and suggestions.

We particularly acknowledge the many hours of discussion and direction given by Dr. Wirt Williams over the arduous craft of writing. We deeply value his encouragement and inspiration.

We also thank George, Robin, Bryan, and Sandy for their never-ending encouragement.

Credits

John Barth, "Lost in the Funhouse," from *Lost in the Funhouse* by John Barth. Copyright 1967 by John Barth. Reprinted by permission of Doubleday & Company, Inc.

Saul Bellow, "A Father-to-Be," from *Seize the Day*, by Saul Bellow, published by Viking Penguin Inc. Copyright 1951, 1954, 1955, 1956 by Saul Bellow. Copyright renewed © 1979, 1982, 1983 by Saul Bellow. Reprinted by permission of Viking Penguin Inc.

1

Dynamics of Plot

The Question Is, Why Plot?

Plot keeps the editor from writing rejection slips that ask, "Where is this book going, anyway? It's rambling all over the place." Yet new writers often reject plot because they feel that it immediately suggests certain limitations. Still, plot is an unsung hero, and only those who have been writing for some time really begin to appreciate it and then experiment with it to develop more complex plots.

Plot Defined

Simply, *plot* is the harmonic design of the action (the events) of a story. An imposed form on the narration, plot unites the various happenings and controls them. There is a cause-and-effect pattern. Each event causes another to happen until an ultimate climax and resolution complete the pattern. *Plot is the framework that holds the story together in a form.* It is, as Elizabeth Bowen remarked, "the knowing of a destination."

Does Every Story or Novel Have a Plot?

In general, yes, every story or novel has a plot. We as readers like plot for the same reason we like jokes. If someone tells you a long, rambling joke and goes on and on, we finally either walk away or fall asleep. We want to hear the end—and when the joke goes on too long we grit our teeth and say: "Get to the punchline!" So it is with story; we want to be built up to a psychological point and then reach a resolution that satisfies us.

Aristotle gave us many valuable insights on plot that are still relevant today. He said that plot has a *proper* beginning, middle, and end. That may sound simple, but most beginning writers do not know where to begin, some do not have a middle in their stories, and quite a few do not know how to end. In fact, Aristotle argued that it was impossible not to have a plot—because in every story there *has* to be some type of action. He also noticed that most new writers achieved competence in language and character development before they achieved competence in plot, and he held that given a choice between character and plot, plot was more important. Although contemporary writers of literature tend to dismiss plot, current writers of popular novels, biographies, and most TV, stage, and screenplays use plot heavily. So it seems a safe bet that plot will probably always be important to writing and will exist as long as books and scripts are written.

Relationship of Story to Plot

Aristotle said that tragedy—and we will interpose "story" here—is the imitation of life, of its happiness and misery. Plot, then, is the cause-and-effect structure used to depict the human condition. Plot has characters who carry out the action (events) in the story. Story is a narration of events that answers the question "What then?" Plot answers the question "*Why* did this happen?"

The Protagonist (The Hero)

Plot demands that a character *want* something that, Aristotle would say, brings him (or her) happiness; and this character (the protagonist) must try to achieve this goal through his or her own actions. In other words, someone else must not step in and *give* the protagonist what he or she wants. *The protagonist is often called "the hero" because he or she generally is required to do something brave, courageous, or clever to attain the things desired.* The protagonist confronts destiny—wrestles with destiny, if you will—to achieve something he or she believes is valuable. The protagonist is the main focus through which the story is seen. The way to determine the protagonist of a story is to ask, "Who wants this thing?" and "Who achieves it?" The person who achieves the goal is the true viewpoint character. For example, if a young gold miner is looking for treasure but his partner—a grizzled old prospector—finds it and fights off all intruders, the old prospector is the true protagonist. The young man didn't really do anything to get the gold. To be a true protagonist, the young gold miner would have to achieve the goal by himself, though the old prospector could help.

Intent

Significant in Aristotelian plot dynamics is that the character *want* something that will bring him or her happiness or misery—and this want or *intent* is the very beginning of plot. When one asks, "What does my character *want*?" one has begun to plot. Sometimes a writer will protest, "But my character doesn't want anything." The danger then might be that there really isn't any story. On the other hand, the character might *want* to want nothing—which is a story. For example, a young man who *wants* to drop out of society may have to struggle severely to be a societal drop-out.

Weak Plot

Aristotle defined *weak plot* as that which had a contrived mechanical ending in which outside forces step in and resolve the plot. Such an ending was called *deus ex machina*. In the Greek period, when a playwright could not resolve a plot logically and there was no possible way the protagonist could do it, the stone statue of a god was lowered onto the stage to indicate divine intervention—or, in contemporary terms, rich Aunt Mabel died and left the protagonist a fortune that extricated him from his problem. *Deus ex machina* is an unrealistic, fortunate intervention that solves all the hero's problems without any effort on his part.

Another use of unrealistic intervention is *reliance on coincidence* to solve various other plot problems. For example, two lovers break up and marry other people. Fifty years later, their respective mates dead, they meet on a cruise ship bound for Greece and now are free to marry. Neither knew that the other would be on the cruise ship. It's a heartwarming story, one that occasionally appears in publications like *The National Enquirer*. Yes, it does happen—once in a million times. But it's not the stuff of fiction that represents real life. A jaundiced reader would probably say, "Oh, come on now, I just can't believe this!" As Mark Twain once said, "Let miracles alone." If you do use them, try to make them as reasonable as possible, things that could possibly occur naturally.

On the other hand, if you properly *motivated* the incident between the two lovers who accidentally met on the cruise ship, you could change weak plot to strong plot. Perhaps your novel has an ESP theme, dealing with telepathy. One of your characters might be a psychiatrist who explains telepathy, that telepathic communication exists between people who are very close. In other words, you would *prepare* the reader for such a meeting. But now the meeting would not be coincidental; rather, it would be a natural occurrence with credibility that a reader can accept.

Weak plot is that which is unrealistic, unmotivated, and unbelievable.

Many new writers argue that as long as coincidences do occur in real life, they can be used to solve fictional situations. But readers respect characters who are strong and resourceful. They know how difficult it is to achieve a goal, and they don't really "believe" that destiny will just "hand" anyone something without any hard work. Readers like to see characters overcome obstacles through their own ingenuity. Coincidences do occur in the newspaper, but that's exactly why they're there—they're unusual. Rather, let *your* character create his or her own destiny.

Also, do not include any events, people, or things that are not essential to the plot. A sensational event included merely to catch the readers' attention acts as a "red herring" which fools readers into thinking that something is going to come of that event later, and they will be disappointed the "promise" is not kept. Sometimes, too, writers are carried away by ideas that interest them and they spend a great deal of time on those ideas, often to the boredom of the reader. At a critique session, one student spent seven pages on daffodils in a short story (that was not so short), and daffodils had nothing to do with the story. When asked why she spent so much time on them, she answered that she *liked* daffodils. However, the class had fallen asleep. The point is, if a shotgun is shown hanging on a wall in the beginning, then it must go off at the end.

Strong Plot

Aristotle held that strong plot resulted from a *character flaw* that produced the hero's problem. A good example is Shakespeare's Othello, whose tragic flaw of jealousy led him to murder his loyal wife—an act that destroyed him. Furthermore, the character should resolve the problem without having outside forces do it for him. In Shakespeare's play, Othello learns that Desdemona was a faithful wife, and he kills himself in expiation for his crime against her and the universe. The criterion that the hero should resolve his problem by himself is still true today.

Plot Structure

To Aristotle, plot represented a whole, complete action that moved from happiness to misery or vice-versa. He defined the parts of the story as:

1. Beginning: the initial action of a situation. Often a problem that has to be solved is introduced.
2. Middle: the part of the story that shows the hero's attempts to solve the problem.
3. Ending: the natural result of what has happened in the middle. At this point the hero either succeeds or fails at solving the problem.

Aristotle emphasized that each of these parts must have a *harmonic symmetry*. Just as there is a proper harmonic size for each part of the human body, so also is there a proper harmonic size for each part of the story. The length of the story must be sufficient to allow the development of the story to be harmonious with its parts; and all the parts in the story must be so integrated that if you removed or displaced a single element, the whole story would be destroyed.

Besides each part of the story being the proper size in relation to the whole, Aristotle is referring also to rhythm and pacing. The story must "feel" right. It should not "jerk" the reader along. Events should be contained in a smooth, rhythmic flow of action that satisfies the reader's aesthetic sense.

Classic Plot

Aristotle described complex plots as having specific elements:

1. Reversals: events occur in which the protagonist moves from bad situations to good ones or vice-versa.
2. Discoveries: certain revelations about events in the story lead the protagonist to unravel events, and in doing so he or she discovers something about his or her strengths and weaknesses; the protagonist moves from ignorance about him- or herself to self-knowledge.
3. The combined reversals and discoveries should produce strong emotions, such as pity and fear.
4. Complication: suspenseful incidents that occur from the beginning of a story up to a crucial point—a turning point followed by a change from apparent success to adversity.
5. Catastrophe: produced by a reversal, it is the lowest point of action in the story and shows the protagonist in his or her greatest despair.
6. Recognition scene: a key scene in which the protagonist understands the relationship of his or her character flaw to the problem and understands his or her moral responsibility and relationship to the universe.
7. Resolution: that which extends from the turning point to the end of the story.

Again, primary to classic plot is the harmonic form of the entire work, which encloses these elements.

Modern Dramatic Plot

Harold Weston, in his book *Form in Literature,* took the elements of classic plot and created a diagram of dramatic action that constitutes the "bread and butter" plot of the entire writing industry.

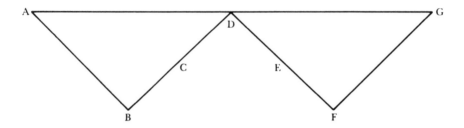

This *"W" Diagram, interpreted by novelist Wirt Williams, focalizes the Pivotal Points of Action.*

> AG: Intent—the protagonist *wants* to achieve something.
> AB: First Barrier—something stands in the protagonist's way.
> BC: First Barrier Reversal—the protagonist does something brave, noble, clever, or inventive to overcome the first barrier.
> CD: High Point of Action—it looks as if the protagonist is going to achieve his or her intent. *Things look good at this point.*
> DE: Second Reversal or Rug-Pulling—something happens that frustrates the protagonist's intent.
> EF: Catastrophe—the protagonist plunges to low point of action: He or she may be permanently thwarted or even killed at this point in the plot structure.
> FG: Resolution—the protagonist may go on and through strength, bravery, intelligence, or cunning achieve his or her intent.

Writers who become adept with dramatic plot often like to plot the "W" diagram for the major characters in their novel or screenplay, and the "W" diagram of each character intersects with the "W" diagram of the other characters. In other words, each major character has a "W" diagram that influences another character's diagram in some way. Remember, minor characters do not need a "W" diagram.

When analyzing a plot in a novel, short story, or script, it is important to notice the *pivotal points* of action, which are shown by AG, BC, CD, EF, and FG. Exactly *what* makes up the first barrier? At *what* place in the story does the high point occur? *What* happens to achieve the rug-pulling—the catastrophe, the resolution? You should be able to state these things in one sentence. (It's important to note that the form of the "W" diagram is not always symmetrical; one leg of the diagram may be longer or shorter than shown.)

The "W" Diagram of a Novel

In Ernest Hemingway's novel *The Old Man and the Sea*, the pivotal points of action are:

> AG: Intent—the old man wants to catch a truly big fish; as he says, "My big fish must be somewhere."
>
> AB: First Barrier—the fish aren't biting; he has gone eighty-four days without catching a fish.
>
> BC: Barrier Reversal—he goes out very far, farther than the other fishermen, to catch fish—and he does hook a fish. Complications occur when his hand cramps and there is an intimation that he may lose the fish.
>
> CD: High Point—but he keeps the fish on the line. The fish is so big it tows his boat; and when the fish surfaces, it is the biggest he has ever seen.
>
> DE: Rug-Pulling—but he has trouble harpooning the fish; a great battle ensues between him and the fish, and when he finally kills it, he is unable to put it in the boat—he must lash it to the boat so that it "rides" beside him in the water.
>
> EF: Catastrophe—the sharks move in and strip the fish to its skeleton.
>
> FG: Resolution—the old man does catch his big fish (the eighteen-foot skeleton proves it to the world); but after the sharks have finished with it, the fish isn't worth anything.

Other elements occur in the novel—a religious theme of the old man as a Christ figure, and perhaps an autobiographical portrait of Hemingway the writer too as he endeavors to "write/catch" the big book. But it is important to remember that plot deals only with the sequence of events that the protagonist acts out.

The "W" Diagram of a Short Story

In R. V. Cassill's short story "Happy Marriage," the "W" diagram appears more subtly. The movement is more shadowed, more oblique. The intent of the narrator is deliberately shrouded and becomes more apparent only late in the story.

> AG: Intent—the narrator wants to achieve "a balance," an attunement with the universe that will enable him to live without fear.

AB: First Barrier—the narrator is afraid to live; he fears death.

BC: Barrier Reversal—he marries—"the bare bones of cupid" (procreation, love) seem to annihilate death; his marriage provides a buffer between him and death, even though he discovers a mouse skull (symbol of death) in his cupboard.

CD: High Point—his wife gives him security ("yellow curtains in the window" and toast and eggs), solidity in the face of death; his fear is allayed.

DE: Rug-Pulling—but he leaves his wife and goes to Paris; in the bordellos of Paris, he sinks into eroticism and death—a *ménage à trois* with two suicidal Danish women who were born in the face of death.

EF: Catastrophe—with them, he plumbs the depths of hell and at last faces his fears of extinction.

FG: Resolution—he learns that no one is guaranteed immortality (there's no use "running," as his negative twin, Lynch, had told him); he comes back from death, his fear gone, and he has attained a balance—an attunement with the universe—he never had before.

The "W" Diagram of a Play/Script

In Tennessee Williams's play *A Streetcar Named Desire,* a "W" diagram is artfully crafted; and the individual "W" diagrams of the characters Blanche Du Bois and Stanley Kowalski interlock. The plot situation is this: Blanche is a southern aristocrat and a teacher who has been dismissed from her position on charges of immorality; she seeks a place to "rest." She decides to visit and stay with her sister Stella. Stella's husband, Stanley, is not happy with the arrangement and wants Blanche to leave.

Blanche's "W" Diagram

AG: Intent—Blanche wants a place to rest, a refuge.

AB: First Barrier—she tries to find refuge with her sister Stella, but Stanley doesn't want her there.

BC: Barrier Overcome—she tries to seduce Mitch, one of Stanley's friends, hoping Mitch will marry her and provide a refuge for her—and Mitch *is* taken with her.

CD: High Point—Mitch does think of marriage, and Blanche believes that her problem is solved.

DE: Rug-Pulling—but Stanley unearths Blanche's past, her promiscuity, and tells Mitch about it; Mitch refuses to marry her.

EF: Catastrophe—furthermore, when Stanley returns home from the hospital (Stella has just had a baby), he rapes Blanche. At this point in the "W" diagram Blanche is destroyed; she has a mental breakdown.

FG: Resolution—ironically, however, Blanche does achieve her intent; she is sent to a state mental institution; she has found a "place to rest."

Stanley's "W" Diagram

AG: Intent—Stanley wants to maintain his male supremacy and his marriage.

AB: First Barrier—Blanche is a threat to Stanley's masculinity; she keeps putting him down, calling him a Polack, her every move emphasizing her aristocratic superiority, and she is disrupting his marriage.

BC: Barrier Overcome—Stanley buys her a ticket to Laurel, where she came from.

CD: High Point—he ruins Blanche's chances to marry Mitch and is satisfied that Blanche will have to go back to Laurel.

DE: Rug-Pulling—but Stella goes to the hospital, and when Stanley returns home from the hospital he finds Blanche still there—and taunting him.

EF: Catastrophe—Blanche spoils his highest moment of being a father; she calls him a "swine."

FG: Resolution—Stanley does the one thing he knows to maintain his male supremacy—he rapes her; his act brings about his objective of getting rid of her: She has a nervous breakdown and has to be committed to a state mental hospital. He has achieved his intent.

Superimposed over these two diagrams is yet another thematic "W" diagram. Symbolically, Blanche also stands for the world of aristocracy, art, literature, imagination. Stanley stands for the animal world of eating, drinking, and procreation. Stanley's triumph over Blanche also represents the triumph of what Williams calls the "slob industrial culture" over the aristocratic culture.

Thematic "W" Diagram of *A Streetcar Named Desire*

AG: Intent—the aristocracy (Blanche) hopes to assert its supremacy over the industrial slob culture and maintain its rule as it did in earlier years (plantation symbol of Belle Reve)

AB: First Barrier—the slob culture (Stanley) has taken over.

BC: Barrier Overcome—the aristocracy (Blanche) tries to co-exist with the slob culture, maintaining its dreams.

CD: High Point—the now-decadent aristocracy, living in the imagination and drowning reality in whiskey (Blanche), believes it can live in its dreams.

DE: Rug-Pulling—but the industrial culture (Stanley) refuses to live in dreams; it wants material satisfactions and refuses to subsidize the aristocracy.

EF: Catastrophe—the industrial culture (Stanley) rapes the aristocratic culture (Blanche), destroying it.

FG: Resolution—the aristocratic culture (Blanche) is not capable of ruling the slob culture (Stanley), which is now more vital; and if it tries to exist in such a primitive culture, madness results. The only place the aristocracy (Blanche) *can* rule is in dreams of the past—the madhouse.

A similar thematic "W" diagram could be plotted out for Stanley as symbol of the slob culture.

Also, another plot factor is that Blanche's being a woman and Stanley's being a man create an additional thematic "W" diagram: the battle of the sexes, the problem of woman versus man and their eternal *struggle* for supremacy over each other.

The "W" diagram is often seen in films and in almost all genre writing such as romances, mystery writing, and suspense, and it can appear in conjunction with other plot forms. It is also a staple in biographies.

Subplot Motif

Occasionally, a plot may have a subplot. The most famous example is, of course, Shakespeare's *King Lear*, in which Lear and his three daughters —Goneril, Regan (both evil), and Cordelia (good)—are contrasted with the Duke of Gloucester and his two sons—Edmund (evil) and Edgar (good). The subplot of Gloucester within the main Lear plot emphasizes the parent–child relationship and variations of the situation. Often the subplot is an ironic comment on the situation of the main plot. Jane Austen's *Pride and Prejudice* has two subplots, that of Jane and Bingley and that of Lydia and Wickham, that counterpoint the main plotline of Elizabeth and Darcy. Each couple represents a different possibility of the love game. In essence, the subplot shows the reader two sides of the same coin.

Complication

An important element of plot is complication. Sometimes a character has a great deal of trouble in overcoming the first barrier in dramatic plot. He or she may succeed, only to be confronted by another obstacle and yet another until the character reaches the high point. We call these obstacles *complication*. Often complication occurs after the rug-pulling, on the downward slant of the "W" diagram. For example, a young man might want to be a doctor; he might overcome the financial barrier by getting a job to work his way through school—and so things look good (high point). But he might become involved with drugs and be arrested (rug-pulling); in jail he might be beaten up by other inmates and crippled, and perhaps he might even be mistakenly identified as a murderer and go to prison. In prison, he might have to fight other prisoners to stay alive.

Complication introduces new conflicts and new problems for the protagonist to solve. These conflicts increase suspense, and they also teach the protagonist something about his or her own character.

Is Dramatic Plot a Formula?

It's incorrect to think of dramatic plot as a formula; rather, dramatic plot is the "skeleton" of a story. These bones support the story, give it its shape. They hold the story together in a form just as your skeleton holds your body together. Consider that all of your friends have the same skeleton and yet none of them really *look* alike. Each one is different. One may be ugly, one beautiful, one fat, one thin. Without a skeleton we would all be shapeless amoeba-like creatures floundering around, going nowhere. Similarly, because many new writers do not understand plot, their stories often resemble amoebas.

A formula story is the *same* story written over and over again. A young man wants a girl; he struggles to win her and does. A writer who uses that "formula" in each of his or her books—a young doctor, a young lawyer, a young artist, a young composer—is exploiting his or her success with a particular formula.

The romance novel is formula. A young woman wants a particular man and goes through many obstacles to get him. Formula writing is not easy, particularly in romance writing. The field has been exhausted, and trying to come up with new plot twists to make the formula interesting is very difficult.

The trouble with formula is that if a writer once starts to write it, he or she may not grow as a writer or a craftsman. To be a true artist, one must continually work with new forms and master them. Great writers such as Balzac and Proust developed more and more intricate novels, developing more-complex plots. For example, Balzac's great series of novels *La Comedie Humaine* was a vast, interlocking design that depicted the entire French society; he created more than 2,472 characters and many of them appear throughout the entire series of novels. Balzac once said with a sweep of his hand, "I have created Paris." Marcel Proust, too, saw his *Remembrance of Things Past* as a vast design: the plot constructed architecturally in the shape of an actual cathedral. In this sense, plot becomes as artistically beautiful as Michelangelo's *David*. For plot is the *form* of the work.

When Should Dramatic Plot Be Used?

If you are contemplating a longer short story with much action, a novel, an action TV script, a biography, a western, a mystery, a romance, even a true confession, dramatic plot is probably your most effective choice. Its very structure has built-in suspense and conflict.

If you are writing any work that is long and many events occur, or if you wish a tightly compressed story that is action packed, dramatic plot is the most powerful plot. The novelist Wirt Williams contends that while other plots exist, the "W" is universal and can be found in all literature of dramatic and narrative nature. He suggests that other plots are simply *ways* of looking at a story from a different perspective.

Simple Plot

James Joyce referred to simple plot as the *epiphany plot*. It rises to a climax (the epiphany) and drops off. Joyce uses it extensively in his collection of short stories *The Dubliners*.

Simple plot is usually used for the short mood piece. Not enough action occurs in it to sustain a longer work. Simple plot builds to an insight that is enclosed in a mood (the epiphany). It is a realization story. Masters of this type of plot are Anton Chekhov, Katherine Mansfield, and Sherwood Anderson. If you want to study it, a good book to read is Anderson's *Winesburg, Ohio*. An exemplary plot can be seen in Anderson's short story "I Want to Know Why." The protagonist, a young boy, loves race horses and admires a trainer. Every day the boy watches the trainer work with the horses. Much detail is given to the color of the grass, sky, the description of the horses. Then one day the boy meanders down a strange road, and, coming up over a rise, he sees a house ahead; the window is open. Looking inside, he sees a prostitute sitting on the lap of the man he idolizes. The trainer is drunk. The boy's pain of discovery (the epiphany) is that same pain we, too, felt when we first discovered that someone we loved had feet of clay.

If you want to write a subtle, delicate mood piece that builds to an emotional realization, you will probably use simple plot.

Episodic Plot (Picaresque Plot)

Episodic plot doesn't have the great highs and lows of complex plot. It's a series of events or episodes, each of about the same magnitude. It lends itself well to comedy, the hero falling in and out of adventures. New writers often use it for their first novels; having written short stories previously, they link a series of short stories by a central character or situation common to all the stories. The name of the picaresque plot comes from a type of hero—a picaro, or rogue—who undergoes many adventures. The most famous picaro novel is Henry Fielding's *Tom Jones*, and Jack Kerouac's *On the Road* is a contemporary picaresque work.

Hourglass Plot

A favorite in many novels is the hourglass plot, and it deals with two people's lives that intersect.

Mark Twain's *The Prince and the Pauper* is such a story. In the novel, the child of the pauper is substituted for the child of the king and vice-versa. The true prince grows up as a pauper, and the pauper's son grows up as the prince. Equal time is spent on each character. Ultimately, the two meet and interact with each other. The hourglass plot is often used in love stories.

Circle Plot

Probably one of the most difficult plots to accomplish is the circle plot.

Here, the events or the subject of the novel/script is the protagonist: an earthquake, a revolution, an airplane in danger of crashing, a sinking cruise

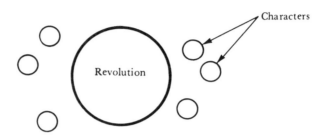

ship. This central event welds the characters together and we see the significance of the event in multi-focus. Each of the characters looks at the event through his or her own perspective. This treatment gives an in-depth study of the situation.

In Andre Malroux's *Man's Fate*, the conflict between the Nationalist Chinese and the Communists is the real protagonist of the story. A banker, a philosopher, a woman, two military leaders (one a Nationalist and one a Communist), and a spy act as viewpoints that focus on particular aspects of the war: the financial, philosophic, feminine, military, and political concerns.

Each character in a circle plot can also have a "W" diagram that interlocks with another character's "W" diagram.

Summary

Today, contemporary literary writing treats plot casually; however, plotted stories make up the bulk of commercial writing—and many serious writers still construct plots for their novels and scripts. Will we ever get away from plot? Probably not.

One reason we as human beings really enjoy plot is that plot is psychological. The hero is faced with problems which demand decisions. Plot is, in fact, a diagram of life. We have all wanted something intensely, and we've struggled to overcome the barriers preventing us from attaining that particular thing. Sometimes we've been defeated, and sometimes we've had the thrill of actually getting what we wanted. We've all hit the bottom of the "W" diagram, catastrophe, and we've all triumphed and we all know the wonderful feeling of reaching the high point—only to have what we've almost achieved slip through our fingers.

Many new writers love to write the story that ends in defeat, believing that the story which ends happily is sentimental. But most readers love success stories because they know how hard it is to achieve something difficult, and they admire the strong person who can move through all obstacles to obtain what he or she wants. This admiration for the "hero" (and the protagonist is traditionally referred to as the hero precisely because he or she is supposed to do something heroic) is one of the reasons why John Wayne movies are classics. Wayne's characters represented the man who could overcome, and that mythos made him a folk hero.

Most biographies use the "W" diagram. Vincent van Gogh wanted to be a great painter, Abraham Lincoln wanted to be president, Thomas Alva Edison wanted to invent the electric light. The greatest personalities all had obstacles in their way, overcame them, and achieved their goals. It may be that if you carry plot far enough, from God's perspective everyone's life is ultimately a "W" diagram—that each individual either achieves or fails at the life task he or she sets out to accomplish.

To Aristotle, action came first, character second. Perhaps Aristotle was one of the first existentialists, and he might well have said: *Character is defined by action.* What is important to see is that plot is not a mere literary convention. It is an "imitation of life." It may be that as we watch various plots unfold in literature and on the screen, we are really looking at archetypal adventures in time and space—that story telling is truly a divine play of consciousness that we, like the creator, enjoy.

Exercises

1. Read a novel or watch a movie or a dramatic TV series. See if you can correctly pinpoint the pivotal points of action in the "W" diagram of dramatic plot. Ask yourself, "What is the *first* barrier? How does the hero overcome it? At exactly what point in the work does the rug-pulling occur? What are the events of the rug-pulling? The events of the catastrophe? How does the hero achieve his or her intent? Write your analysis in an outline form, using one line for each pivotal point. Don't get sidetracked by complication. *Is the work you analyzed strong or weak plot?*

2. Read a collection of short stories and see if you can discover an epiphany short story. Can you pinpoint the epiphany that encloses the story?

3. Have you seen any contemporary films that use the circle plot? Write down the names of the characters and the aspect of the situation that they represent. Do they also have "W" diagrams?

4. Read any novel with a subplot and discuss the relationship of the subplot to the main plot.

2

Viewpoint: The Magic Key to Publishing

If there is one single reason why most new writers are unable to publish, it is because they do not understand viewpoint.

Few things are as terrifying—or exciting—as beginning to write a manuscript. The page is blank, waiting to be filled with your ideas. If you have a word processor, you find the blank screen waiting expectantly for the first sentence. But you face an immediate problem: Who is your main character?

How to Select Your Main Character

Once you have a story in mind and know the characters you want to use, you have to decide *who* will experience the events of the story (the protagonist) and *who* will record those events (the "viewpoint" or the angle of vision from which the story is told). It is important to remember that not all stories are told in the viewpoint of the main character—that is, *as experienced by* the protagonist. The choice of a main character and choice of viewpoint are both critical decisions. If the wrong character is chosen as the protagonist or if the story is told from the wrong viewpoint, the story will fail. Consequently, much thought must be given as to which character and which viewpoint will produce the strongest story.

Take, for example, the story "Snow White and the Seven Dwarfs." In the traditional version, an external storyteller tells us about the young girl Snow White. This storyteller is *omniscient;* like God, he knows all. He can focus on the young girl and tell us about her life and her dreams; he can focus on the evil queen and her machinations; and he can focus on the prince and the seven dwarfs. He can go into each character's body, mind, and emotions so that we see how each character acts, thinks, and feels. He can show us a scene in the queen's palace and, in simultaneous time, move to a scene in the woods with Snow White and the dwarfs. The mind of this omniscient narrator acts as a unifying device that holds all of the events together in a logical sequence of action.

Changing Viewpoint Changes the Story

However, change the viewpoint of the story, and the story itself changes. If Snow White became the viewpoint character, we would see events only through her eyes; we would not know what the evil queen was doing back at the castle or what the dwarfs were doing in the forest.

If the viewpoint character were changed to the evil queen, or the prince, or any one of the dwarfs, a different story would result. If the evil queen became the main character, *the protagonist,* we would see all events from *her* point of view. Alone, afraid, aging, the queen sees this stupid young girl as a threat to the throne and her kingdom. If the prince were the protagonist, the events of the story would concern his efforts to bring the beautiful young girl back to life. If one of the dwarfs were the protagonist, that dwarf would have particular character traits (as in the Disney version of the tale—Happy, Grumpy, Dopey, etc.), and the dwarf would concern himself with rescuing Snow White from the evil queen.

Choosing a Main Character

In deciding upon a main character, you have to ask yourself, Whom do I *sympathize* with the most? Also, *who* will achieve the goals set? Take the story of a young girl who falls in love with a very eligible man. She wants him very much. Her mother helps her to snare the young man by offering good advice—what kind of clothes and perfume to wear. Mother prepares a candlelit gourmet dinner for two, playing sensuous music. The girl gets the man, but it was *mother* who really solved the problem. Properly, it's the mother's story of all her efforts to help her young daughter land a husband.

Point of View and the Magic Camera

Think of the writer as a cameraman who possesses a magic camera that is able to perceive not only visual images but also sensory perceptions, feelings, and thoughts. Shifting the magic camera produces different viewpoints. There are three major ways the camera can be used:

1. the first-person narrator ("I" viewpoint)
2. the effaced narrator:
    a. second-person focus ("you" viewpoint)
    b. third-person focus ("he"/"she" viewpoint)
3. the omniscient narrator (God's viewpoint)

With first-person the character tells the story. With second-person and third-person a hidden narrator (the effaced narrator) tells it. With omniscient the author acts as an all-seeing god who intrudes personal observations into the work. It is important to remember that **once the writer has selected a particular viewpoint (camera focus), the writer must stay in that viewpoint.** Each of the viewpoints has its respective advantages and disadvantages.

The First-Person Narrator

Commonly called the "I" viewpoint, first person has two modes:

1. first-person fixed viewpoint
2. first-person agent narrator (peripheral narrator)

First-Person Fixed Viewpoint

When the hidden camera is locked to the mind of one person, recording his or her thoughts and feelings and all the events he or she perceives, the camera technique is called the "fixed point of view." In first person, the camera is locked to the "I" consciousness. An example of the "I" viewpoint is:

> I had just come out of Harry's Bar when I saw her. She looked very thin, and her long auburn hair blew in ringlets against her gaunt face. I waved. She hesitated, her eyes widening, then she walked to me. She seemed sad, I thought, very sad. I wanted to tell her I still loved her, but I knew she would not believe me.

Here the camera is locked on the "I" protagonist, who is the central narrator, the "center of action." Like any human being, the "I" protagonist has limitations. He can *know* only what is in his angle of vision. He perceives the girl, notices her reactions, and thinks particular thoughts. The viewpoint does not switch into the girl's mind and record her thoughts. Therefore, it is important to remember that when working in fixed viewpoint one can record the thoughts and emotions of the viewpoint character only. Also, if something is happening twenty miles away and the viewpoint character doesn't know about it, the author cannot introduce that material; it is something beyond the viewpoint character's knowledge.

First-Person Agent Narrator (Peripheral Narrator)

The first-person peripheral narrator is an eyewitness to the events of the story. Sometimes this camera position is called the "storyteller" viewpoint, the narrator indicating he or she is going to tell the reader a story. In this mode the narrator may be the second most important character in the story or merely an observer. He or she may be characterized in detail or very slightly. As the narrator observes the protagonist, he or she may make value judgments, predictions, and interpretations. He or she may also be an accurate, trustworthy observer or, in the case of many Russian novels, a fallible one. The narrator may even be a liar. Important, however, is that if you choose to have a narrator tell a story "about someone else," the narrator must have some relationship to the story, some "reason" for telling it. The narrator must be changed in some way by the events. He or she should have *learned* something from the situation—or else why would this individual be telling the story at all?

A good example of the peripheral narrator is F. Scott Fitzgerald's Nick Carraway in *The Great Gatsby*. Nick, a young midwesterner, is dazzled by the rich young racketeer Jay Gatsby and tells the story of Gatsby's life. Nick is drawn into Gatsby's world of money, parties, and women. But Gatsby dies tragically; the parties are over, and Nick, disillusioned, returns to his midwest home having "closed out" his interest "in the abortive sorrows and shortwinded elations of men." Still, *Nick is forever changed by Gatsby*.

Joseph Conrad also uses a first-person peripheral narrator in his novella *Heart of Darkness*. Aboard the cruising yawl *Nellie*, four men—including the first-person narrator—listen to Marlow spin a seaman's tale. Marlow tells of Kurtz, who epitomized the brightest light of civilization and who became a living incarnation of Satan. As Marlow finishes the tale, he reveals his relationship to Kurtz. Marlow too had "peeped over the edge" of that same black abyss of power and greed, and he understood Kurtz's temptation. Moreover, as a civilized white man he shares in Kurtz's infamy. The other four men on the *Nellie* are equally touched, and one of them (the director) expresses their communal guilt: "We have lost the first of the ebb . . . ." The director's remark is an acknowledgment that each of them had lost his innocence, that each of them knew too well "the heart of darkness."

Advantages of First-Person Fixed Viewpoint

Many new writers are attracted to the "I" viewpoint because:

1. It seems easiest to write directly in one's own voice.
2. It offers easy identification with the protagonist (the "I" of the character seems to equal the "me" of the writer).
3. It offers a chance to explore the inner consciousness of a single person who is restricted in time and space, as is the average human being.
4. It has a vitality, an immediacy of life, that no other viewpoint can offer. It is the voice of authority, seeming to record an actual true-life experience.

Disadvantages of First-Person Viewpoint

The very advantages of the "I" viewpoint are its dangers, for the "I" of the writer is *not* the "I" character. Consequently, the writer often:

1. overidentifies with the viewpoint
2. rambles
3. loses control of dramatic structure
4. writes the story "exactly as it happened"
5. includes irrelevant material and coincidences

What's Wrong with Writing a Story Exactly as It Happened?

The writer must be an *artist*, selectively arranging the events of a story into a harmonic art form; some of the events may be true, some not. He or she must use only those events that will produce the most powerful story. Usually, if one writes a story "exactly" the way it happened, the story will be dull. The writer may take too much time to develop trivial things that are unimportant to the story, events or occurrences that the author personally enjoys. Essentially, a writer must be conscious of *drama* and heighten events and even change them.

Avoid Coincidences

An incident that "really happened" may seem unbelievable. For example, a recent news item told of a man who, while sitting in a truck, was killed by a crane that fell on him. While the newspaper reader will accept this *coincidence*, the fiction reader will not accept such an unmotivated happening to resolve a story. If a character is handily disposed of without proper explanation, the reader will scoff that the events were too "pat," too "easy." What is "true" in life will not seem "true" in fiction.

First-Person Novels Tend to Be Less Salable

First-person narration is often used in romances, true confessions, and adventure stories because it evokes the authenticity of a true story—the feeling of "this actually happened to me." Yet many more novels are written—and sold—in third-person narration. Readers determine the market, and a sizable number of readers argue that the many "I's" the protagonist uses make the protagonist sound conceited. It is also a statistical fact that fewer books are published in first person. A large number of readers simply will not buy first-person novels. Ask readers why and they will often say they do not want to directly identify with the "I" character. After all, they are *not* the "I" character. They prefer "more distance." Editors are aware of these biases. Therefore, from a purely commercial viewpoint, if you choose first person, you may have less chance of publishing. From a literary perspective, however, first person is always a challenging viewpoint.

The Effaced Narrator

When the writer uses the invisible camera to move into any character's mind and to move from events happening in one place to events happening in another place, this technique is called "the effaced narrator" and sometimes "the roving narrator."

The effaced narrator is a hidden storyteller who acts as the substitute voice of the author; he or she is able to reveal the entire scope of the story and relate it authoritatively, with knowledge and objectivity. While the narrator does not let his or her personality directly *intrude* into the story, the narrator's *bias* is always there—for the narrator tells us only of particular incidents that have relevance to him or her as the teller of the tale.

In Casey Scott's *Ocean's Edge*, the third-person narrator intends to foreshadow a violent love in the life of the protagonist, Karen:

> She stared down the gravel incline. A splotch of red in the dry grass rimming the rock caught her eye. Fur and blood drying in the sun—a small hare. The swift dive of a passing hawk. She looked away, shivering, deliberately fixing her mind on the whiteness of the seagulls. Behind her, sheer rock walls rose out of sand. Everything about the land itself had a barbarous quality—bleak, stark; but very rich, sensual. Terribly bright, rapaciously so. A brilliant raw beauty—but death just underneath. Not brooding or melancholy—just red, sudden; like the small rabbit. Part of the landscape.

A few minutes later, Karen meets the man who becomes her destructive lover. She is the hare, he the hawk. The incident has been *orchestrated* by the narrator.

Never Confuse the Narrator with the Author

It is a mistake to confuse the narrator's bias with that of the author. The author may be using a fallible narrator, or one who is deliberately lying or slanting events (as Dostoyevski did). The author's reasons for writing the story, a creative process rooted in the unconscious, may be very different from the aims of the fictional narrator. Remember that the presence of the narrator is only a device to tell the story. Still, we do know the author by the themes, the value judgments, that he or she chooses to depict—and we are able to see the ideas that concern him or her.

Second Person

One mode of the effaced narrator is second person, the narrator speaking through the "you" viewpoint. The few books that have been published in second person remain literary curiosities. Michael Butor's novel *Change of Heart* is a rare example. Second person is more applicable in a short story, and then only for a short sequence. Second person may be used to make a character out of the reader:

> You walk out of Harry's Bar and you see her. She looks very thin, and her long auburn hair blows in ringlets around her face. You wave. She hesitates, her eyes widening. Then she walks to you. She seems sad, you think, very sad. You want to tell her you still love her, but you know she will not believe you.

Here, the reader is treated like a character in the story. However, second person may also be used to delineate a fictional character:

> Cindy Hawkins—will you always walk down that winding dusty road, blushing and sweaty in your red tee shirt and torn blue jeans, or will you grow up some day to be one of those pale creatures in flowing skirts and teetering in high-heeled, pointed shoes?

Occasionally, a writer uses second person to address remarks to the reader. John Hawkes uses this device in his novel *The Lime Twig:*

> Have you ever let lodgings in the winter? Was there a bed kept waiting, a corner room kept waiting for a gentleman? ... Or perhaps you yourself were once the lonely lodger.

The difficulty with second person is that it is very hard to sustain over a long period of time. The "you," like the "I," viewpoint, can get monotonous if not handled right. Again, readers may resent the direct identification with "you." Second person forces readers to accept this viewpoint as their own. There is always the protest: "But I'm *not* walking out of Harry's Bar, and I don't want to, either."

Third Person (the "He/She" Point of View)

When the story is told in third person, the point of view is inevitably that of either the effaced narrator or the omniscient narrator. The advantage of third person is that the "he" or "she" provides an artistic screen which encourages the writer to keep an artistic distance and more effectively control and illuminate the characters.

The effaced narrator can move the "camera of vision" from one mind to another mind and penetrate to the depths of each. The camera can also be pulled back so that all events are seen with an external objectivity. The effaced narrator can do all that needs to be done, go where ever it is necessary to go, so long as the narrator *knows* exactly what the camera is doing and where the camera is going. When the fictional camera is set in the effaced narrator's viewpoint, the writer can use the camera three ways:

1. effaced narrator as a fixed point of view focusing on one consciousness
2. effaced narrator as a fixed point of view focusing on externals alone
3. effaced narrator focusing on the consciousness of several characters and on simultaneous time sequences

Effaced Narrator as a Fixed Point of View: Focusing on One Consciousness

With the fixed point of view, the effaced narrator locks onto the consciousness of *one* character and records only what that character sees, thinks, and feels. The narrator objectively reports on all other characters and neither enters their minds nor interprets their thoughts. While the camera may microscopically analyze events, the effaced narrator will tell the story but will not intrude to make editorial comments:

> He had just walked out of Harry's Bar when he saw her. She looked very pretty, her long auburn hair blowing in ringlets about her tawny, oval face. He waved. She seemed sad, he thought, very sad. He wanted to tell her he still loved her, but he knew she would not believe him, and he felt himself trembling.

Here, the reader shares the main character's position of not knowing all and so *participates* with the character, groping toward understanding.

Central Intelligence

"Central intelligence," formulated by Henry James, is a variation of the effaced narrator. In this mode the effaced narrator moves the camera to a closeup, focusing on the *psyche* of the narrator; and what the narrator perceives is the story. The narrator/hero tells the story, comments on it, evaluates it, and makes moral judgments. However, while the camera primarily focuses on the narrator's consciousness, the camera is also able to penetrate the minds of others around the narrator—unlike the third-person fixed viewpoint, which cannot enter the minds of other characters. The hero's consciousness always remains in *center focus,* and the other characters' thoughts and actions are important only inasmuch as they impinge on his or her consciousness. The technique necessarily lends itself to introversion and introspection.

A good example of the technique is Henry James' short story "The Beast in the Jungle," in which John Marcher reflects:

> He had thought himself, so long as nobody knew, the most disinterested person in the world, carrying his concentrated burden, his perpetual suspense, ever so quietly, holding his tongue about it, giving others no glimpse of it nor of its effect on his life, asking of them no allowance and only making on his side all those that were asked. He had disturbed nobody with the queerness of having to know a haunted man, though he had moments of rather special temptation on hearing people say they were "unsettled." If they were as unsettled as he was—he who had never been settled for an hour in his life—they would know what it meant.

Note how the central intelligence reveals Marcher's consciousness, the psychology of his psyche. Marcher thinks of the woman who loves him, May Bartram, and the central intelligence delicately "shades" into her viewpoint:

> So, while they grew older together, she did watch with him, and so she let this association give shape and colour to her own existence. Beneath her forms as well detachment had learned to sit, and behaviour had become for her, in the social sense, a false account of herself. There was but one account of her that would have been true all the while, and that she could give, directly, to nobody, least of all to John Marcher.

Here, central intelligence reveals May's delicate relationship with Marcher but at no time enters her direct thoughts.

Stream of Consciousness

If the effaced narrator focuses entirely on the mind of the protagonist, *stream of consciousness* results:

> What was time? he wondered, staring at the television screen. Products —underarm deodorant.... Shattered fragments of splintered experiences. Shards of faces. Some loved, some detested. Moving pictures ... pictures of eyes assessing him. Outstretched arms fading in mists. Those faces .... Had they ever existed—or were they reflections of the private television set in his mind which he alone watched?

In stream of consciousness the camera records the workings of the mind, trying to capture the fragmented quality of thoughts. Often, outside stimuli—a doorbell, a child's cry, a television set—precipitate various thoughts. There is no effort to be grammatical, to use complete sentences, though the writer should strive for clarity.

Interior Monologue

The effaced narrator may also record *interior monologue,* the character talking to himself:

> Yes, I've been a fool. Everyone is a fool at eighteen. The world just waits for you with all its glories and unseen traps. I leaped into it all, leaped like any wild young animal, only to feel the bite of the steel jaws. But somehow I escaped— Yes, I was lucky to escape.

Note that this paragraph uses *direct thought.* If the effaced narrator had used *indirect thought,* the passage would have read:

> Yes, he had been a fool. Everyone is a fool at eighteen. The world is waiting with all its glories and unseen traps. He had leaped into it all, leaped like any wild young animal, only to feel the steel bite into his flesh. But he had somehow escaped— Yes, he had been lucky to escape.

Interior monologue is distinguished from stream of consciousness in that the character's thoughts are presented in complete sentences.

Effaced Narrator as a Fixed Point of View: Focusing on Externals Alone

The effaced narrator may also freeze the camera in a locked position, to view the characters externally only and objectively report on what is said and done. The narrator does not interpret thoughts, make reflections, or judge:

> The day was hot, sticky. Marie stopped in front of the boutique window, looking at the red dress. She hesitated. Reaching into her purse, she took out her wallet. She opened it, looked at the contents. Then, shaking her head, she put the wallet back into her purse and walked quickly away.

When the effaced narrator wields the camera in this fixed position, the reader can understand the character only through external actions and must *infer* what is going on in the character's mind. It's a good technique to use when you want to develop suspense. As the reader cannot enter the character's mind, he or she does not know what is going to happen. Mystery writers often prefer this mode as it enables them to withhold vital information from the reader. However, if you use this viewpoint, you will have to "clue" in impending action so that the reader isn't startled by events that seem implausible because they lack motivation.

Effaced Narrator Focusing on the Consciousness of Several Characters and on Simultaneous Time Sequences

Sometimes the effaced narrator focuses on several characters' consciousnesses and on simultaneous time sequences. This particular point of view is the most popular among contemporary novelists because it is the most flexible and sophisticated. The effaced narrator may use the camera to explore the consciousness of as many characters as he or she wishes, interpreting their thoughts and actions. The camera may also focus on scenes that occur simultaneously in time and that are beyond the main character's knowledge. The author may use the camera to span time—focusing telescopically, panoramically, or historically.

There are several ways to handle point-of-view shifts gracefully. One way of doing it is by the *hiatus*—leaving four white spaces between the shifts:

Joel worried about her; where was she going? What would she do now? He looked at Nancy, wanting to comfort her.

She drew her hand away, feeling sad. He was so protective; he just couldn't understand that she had to be alone, to solve this herself. Then she thought about Phil, alone in New York. Would he keep out of trouble or would it end up as it always did?

It was three o'clock when Phil went into the liquor store. He walked between the aisles of groceries as if he were looking for something. He saw his face in the curved mirror above. It looked white, scared. He saw the old man behind the counter, reading a newspaper. Now! he thought. But just then an old black woman hobbled in.

A hiatus can indicate a change of time, place, or viewpoint. Remember, however, that *many writers do not change viewpoint within the same paragraph or within the same sequence of action because the viewpoint shift might confuse the reader.*

Why Excessive Viewpoint Shifts Are Dangerous

Changing viewpoint in a short story is always a risk because the shift interrupts the unity of action. In novel writing, viewpoint shifts often occur at the chapter break—shifting from one character's mind to another or sometimes at strategic points within a chapter itself.

In contemporary mainstream writing, it is not unusual to have three or four viewpoint characters within a chapter. The Prologue of Sidney Sheldon's *The Other Side of Midnight* is a good example. Sheldon usually leaves a hiatus between each viewpoint character's section.

Occasionally at tense moments of emotion, particularly in sex scenes, the writer may elect to change viewpoint within a paragraph—from the woman to the man or vice-versa. The fact that both characters are involved in sex achieves a unity of action in which changing viewpoint is not disruptive if handled right. However, changing viewpoint within a paragraph is rarely done. Many writers avoid it altogether.

In the mystery novel, shifts of the camera are expected and occur frequently, from the police lieutenant to the murderer to the victim and into the minds of other related characters. On the other hand, in many romance novels the camera often remains focused on the heroine. However, the complex romance novel with a subplot may feature several viewpoint characters, among them the romantic hero.

Viewpoint Shifts Tend to Be Confusing

One of the major reasons new writers receive so many rejection slips is *excessive* viewpoint shifts. Examine this incorrect passage:

> Jeremy wanted to tell her he loved her but he could not. It was better that she just forget about him. He saw Ann watching him. She felt hurt, wanted to cry. Why was he always so distant? She remembered her father—Jeremy had that same coldness. He decided this would be the last time he was going to see her. No, she would never accept a convict for a husband. She knew something was bothering him, but what?

The constant shifting back and forth between the two minds is not only confusing but distracting. You do not have to enter another character's mind to know what he or she is thinking. The main character can infer a great deal. Note how much more clear the passage is in one viewpoint:

> Jeremy wanted to tell her he loved her, but he could not. It was better that she just forget about him. He saw Ann watching him. He knew she felt hurt, wanted to cry. He saw the reproach in her eyes, that he was "distant," like her father. He decided this would be the last time he was going to see her—she

would never accept a convict for a husband. He realized she knew something was bothering him, but he also understood that she did not have the courage to ask him what it was.

Jeremy can *notice* facial features and expressions. He can "know," can "realize" things about Ann. When we know a person well, we often know what a person is thinking. Even if we don't know a person well, we can tell by facial expressions and body language what that person is thinking. Words like he *understood, intuited, surmised* enable the protagonist to reveal another character's mind. Also phrases like *she seemed troubled, seemed as if she were about to cry, looked downcast* enable the writer to reveal a character's thought without changing viewpoint.

Always ask yourself, "Is this viewpoint shift necessary?" In general, you will probably do your strongest and most powerful writing within sequences of a single viewpoint. While literary writers like to experiment with viewpoint shifts, commercial writers who write for a mass market audience are aware that the average reader is confused by the shifts, and so they often opt to write more conventionally.

Omniscient Viewpoint (God's Viewpoint)

If the author intrudes into the story with mock conversations, editorial comments, making moral judgments and forecasts of the future, the viewpoint technique is called "omniscient." Eighteenth- and nineteenth-century writers such as Fielding, Thackeray, and Trollope often stopped the action in their novels to directly address the reader with their "Dear Reader" remarks.

Like the effaced narrator/roving narrator, the omniscient narrator can enter any character's mind at will, interpreting the thoughts and actions of the characters. The author may use the camera as a device to span time and to focus on scenes that are beyond the main character's knowledge. Editorially omniscient, the author may tell the reader what to think, intruding to voice judgments and universal truths. He or she can combine all these devices with objective reporting.

Omniscient viewpoint is often called "God's viewpoint" because the author, like God, can enter anybody's mind at will. Remember, however, that the reader tends to identify with one character and to experience events through that character's mind. If you switch viewpoints at will, the reader is often distracted and loses track of the story line. Also, omniscient viewpoint kills suspense. If you go into *every* character's mind, the reader no longer looks forward to the coming action; rather, he or she *knows* what is going to happen.

Writers often use the omniscient viewpoint to open a short story or novel because it is the easiest way to set a scene or describe a character. For, once in viewpoint, it is difficult for a character to think of himself in the terms that the omniscient observer might use: "He was a handsome, susceptible man, extraordinarily attractive to women, dashing, witty, and totally fascinating."

Most writers generally open with the effaced narrator describing a scene, introducing and describing a character. Then the narrator slips into the character's mind, into third-person fixed point of view, and continues the story. Tolstoy used the omniscient viewpoint in his novel *War and Peace*, interrupting the story with essays on war:

> The first fifteen years of the nineteenth century in Europe present an extraordinary movement of millions of people. Men leave their customary pursuits, hasten from one end of Europe to the other, plunder and slaughter one another, triumph and are plunged into despair, and for some years the whole course of life is altered . . . . What was the cause of this movement, by what laws was it governed?

This device of the author intruding to philosophize, reflect, and give historical background is not fashionable in twentieth-century writing because contemporary writers prefer the dramatic form of writing and do not like to interrupt the action of the story. Herman Wouk in his novel *The Winds of War* uses a variation on omniscient viewpoint. He interposes the chapters of his novels with "chapters" of a novel written by a general. The general's account gives a voluminous amount of background, but many readers elect to skip the general's chapters and read the action chapters instead.

Try to give background information actively through a character, either through thought or dialogue, using his or her own vocabulary and thought pattern. To avoid a stilted, dull summary of facts, ask yourself, *How would my character say this—how* would he or she think it?

The main difference between the omniscient viewpoint and the effaced narrator is author intrusion.

Types of Novels That Use Other Viewpoint Techniques

The Epistolary Novel

In the epistolary novel, the narrative is achieved by a series of letters written to someone or by letters written back and forth between two or more characters. Samuel Richardson's *Pamela* is considered the first of this genre. A contemporary epistolary novel is Elizabeth Forsythe Hailey's *A Woman of Independent Means*. The novel begins:

December 10, 1899
Honey Grove, Texas

Dear Rob,

I have just asked Miss Appleton to put us on the same team for the spelling bee. Since we're the only two people in the fourth grade who can spell *perspicacious*, our team is sure to win. Can you come over after school? The gardener is clearing the hollyhock bed so there will be more room to play tag. It was my idea.

Bess

As the letters flow, a plot and a very empathetic heroine emerge.

The Monologue Novel

The writer may use a character to address the reader in a long monologue that forms the novel. In Albert Camus' *The Fall*, the main character introduces himself as Jean-Baptiste Clamence and says:

> Pleased to know you. You are in business, no doubt? In a way? Excellent reply! Judicious too: in all things we are merely "in a way." But a cultured bourgeois! Smiling at the use of the subjunctive, in fact, proves your culture twice over because you recognize it to begin with and then because you feel superior to it.

The entire book is made up of Clamence's monologue; no other characters dramatically interact with Clamence, although he tells the reader about various people. Interestingly enough, Clamence finally reveals he is the Devil and his hell is Amsterdam. Ultimately, the reader realizes that he or she—like Clamence—is a fallen angel.

The Journal/Diary Novel

Often a ruse of the journal/diary novel—the *confessional* novel—is a Preface which explains that the *journal* or *diary* was found in an ancient castle or monastery. Sholem Asch's narrator in *The Nazarene* is shown a "document which has been hidden from the world for nineteen hundred years . . . ." and which "contains the complete truth concerning that world-tragedy which was enacted in Jerusalem." The narrator translates the ancient document, and the translation is the novel.

One of the most famous diary novels is Dostoyevski's *Notes from Underground,* which begins:

> I am a sick man . . . . I am a spiteful man. I am an unattractive man. I believe my liver is diseased. However, I know nothing at all about my disease, and do not know for certain what ails me. I don't consult a doctor for it, and never have . . . . I know better than anyone that ... I am only injuring myself . . . . But still, if I don't consult a doctor it is from spite. My liver is bad, well—let it get worse!

Some Do's and Don'ts

1. Don't switch from one character's mind to another indiscriminately or carelessly. It confuses the reader. The main character can *infer* what others are thinking. If you need to switch, don't do it in the same paragraph or the same sequence of action unless you have very compelling circumstances.
2. Consider using a hiatus (four lines of space) to signal camera shifts, or shifting at the chapter break.
3. Don't stop the action of your story to put in large blocks of facts or historical background. Try to work these things in gracefully in thoughts, dialogue, letters, newspaper headlines, or radio/TV announcements.
4. Don't have your characters *know* things they could not possibly know. For example, if something is happening twenty miles away, how could they be aware of it?
5. Once you choose a viewpoint strategy, stick with it. Be consistent.
6. Avoid author intrusion, making editorial comments and value judgments.

Basic Elements to Consider in Choosing a Viewpoint

Some questions you need to answer when choosing a viewpoint are:

1. Does the viewpoint you have chosen tell the story from the most sympathetic angle of vision?
2. Will the choice of this particular viewpoint enable you to write the most scenes you really want to write?
3. Does this viewpoint permit the character to make the major decisions in attaining the goals you've set?
4. Does this viewpoint enable you to write the story without backtracking a lot to give information: Does it afford a minimum of narration (straight telling)? Will this viewpoint allow you to get right into the action?
5. Do you *know* this character to the point that he or she will not lead you into areas that you know nothing about? For example, you may want to use a neurosurgeon as a viewpoint character in your novel; but if you don't know anything about neurosurgery you may find yourself unable to complete the book.
6. Which viewpoint offers you the most *satisfaction* in telling your story?

Summary

Choosing the correct viewpoint in your story is a crucial decision. You have to decide who your main character is and through whose eyes the events will be perceived. For, although the main character is usually the viewpoint character, occasionally he or she is not. You may choose to use:

1. first-person fixed (the "I" viewpoint) or the first-person peripheral narrator
2. The effaced narrator (hidden narrator who tells the story):
    a. second person ("you" viewpoint):
        i. reader as "you" character
        ii. fictional character as "you"
    b. third person ("he/she" viewpoint):
        i. effaced narrator, fixed viewpoint, entering only one character's mind and reporting about all other characters
        ii. effaced narrator focusing on central intelligence (psyche of character) and penetrating minds of others only as they impinge on the character's consciousness
        iii. effaced narrator, camera frozen in a fixed position and recording only external features and movements
        iv. effaced narrator/roving narrator, allowing simultaneous time sequences and switching into other characters' viewpoints
3. the omniscient narrator who knows everything (God's viewpoint) and who intrudes to make comments, reflections, and value judgments. This viewpoint is rarely used in contemporary writing.

Exercises

1. Using the Fred Muir diagram (see accompanying illustration) and choosing any character, write a sketch of that character in third person, focusing on one consciousness.
2. Write a love scene consciously using the effaced narrator in any one of the third-person modes.
3. Using the Fred Muir diagram, write a scene from the omniscient viewpoint, going into as many viewpoints as you wish, and include a universal truth that you as author wish to convey.
4. Write a one-page sketch, consciously using first-person central intelligence. An interesting viewpoint might be that of the corpse in the Fred Muir diagram.
5. Using the Fred Muir diagram, write a sketch from the effaced narrator's point of view, focusing on externals only.
6. Write one paragraph of stream of consciousness and one paragraph of interior monologue. Note the difference.

VIEWPOINT POSSIBILITIES

Plot: Fred Muir has just killed his wife. Unknown to him, he is watched by a large audience. Each has a different perspective.

The Writer

Drunk

Idiot

Liar

Fred's Best Friend

Philosopher

Psychologist

Fred's Sister

Doctor

Sociologist

Artist

Police Lieutenant

Family pet

Wife (corpse)

Convict

Minister

Fred

Omniscient (God)

Fred's Mistress

Wife's Mother

Historian

Wife's Sister

3

How to Open a Short Story or Novel

Probably the most important element that determines whether your manuscript will be read by an editor is the *first page*. In short fiction, the editor rarely reads further. Novelists are generally given a little more latitude—three pages—but the novel writer, too, usually tries to "hook" the reader on the first page. Years ago, editors used to read the first fifty pages of a novel. Today, they generally read a short synopsis and a chapter. But the first page of the novel is very influential in their judgment. Many editors concur that if the first page is bad, the rest of the book will be bad also. The reason for this assumption is that the first page is a *showcase* of your writing technique. The point is, do you know how to hook the reader's attention—to develop his interest in your story so he can't put the book down, so he *has* to turn the page?

The Narrative Hook

The opening of a story is often referred to as the narrative hook, and traditionally it contained the journalistic elements of the five W's and an H: Who, What, Where, When, Why, and How:

1. Who is the character?
2. What is the situation (the problem)?
3. Where is this story taking place (locale)?
4. When is this story taking place (which time frame)?
5. Why did this situation happen?
6. How did it happen (what is the background)?

Sometimes the writer tries to achieve the hook elements in a few sentences. Note the following three compressed hooks:

1. They were new patients to me, all I had was the name Olson. Please come down as soon as you can, my daughter is very sick. (William Carlos Williams, "The Use of Force")
2. Paul stepped off the curb and got hit by a truck. He didn't know what it was that hit him at first, but now, here on his back, under the truck, there could be no doubt. Is it me? he wondered. Have I walked the earth and come here? (Robert Coover, "A Pedestrian Accident")
3. As Gregor Samsa awoke one morning from uneasy dreams he found himself transformed into a gigantic insect. (Franz Kafka, "The Metamorphosis")

In all three hooks, a main character is introduced, and we know the situation, the problem. The time frame is now, and the locale is a contemporary one. In Williams's story, the protagonist is a country doctor who makes house calls—for city doctors rarely do. In Coover's short story the locale seems to be the city, and Kafka's locale is a bedroom.

While few writers attempt the compressed hook any more, most writers do try to achieve some hook elements within the first 250 words to create an engrossing situation and a believable, empathetic character. However, two things every writer should strive to do in the hook are:

1. create an overwhelming curiosity about what is going to happen in the story
2. pose a question that has to be answered

The Beginning Versus the Opening

The beginning of a story is not necessarily its opening. A story generally doesn't open at the "beginning" of a situation; rather, it usually opens at a high point of action. If you decided to write the life of any exciting movie star with a flamboyant lifestyle, you probably wouldn't write it chronologically from birth and include every boring detail up to the present—that would be a diary account. More likely, you would start at the most exciting point in the star's life to "catch" the reader, then flash back and fill in significant details, and then move from exciting incident to exciting incident. If you wrote the story chronologically, including every fact you'd gathered, the book would be terribly dull even though the movie star is a fascinating person. In this sense, art is *not* like life. The artist skillfully *arranges* life into an artistic form. If you insist on writing a story "exactly the way it happened," you probably will never be published. You *can* use real-life incidents, but you have to artfully change them so that they can be used for fiction. Sometimes a totally different ending has to occur, or the character must be changed, or the locale, or the chronology of events.

In a recent critique seminar, a new writer turned in a story about a truck driver who had a heavy load that exceeded the safety code. The driver stopped at each weigh station and retightened the load. After fifty pages, he finally arrived at his destination. By the end of the story everyone in the seminar had fallen asleep. When the writing teacher tried to explain how dull the story was, the student argued: "But that's the way it *really* happened!" Well, perhaps it did—but the point is, *who cares?* On the other hand, if some of the ropes had broken and the truck was careening down a treacherous mountain road and the driver was fighting to save himself and his truck—that's another story, but a vital and successful one.

The Opening

The opening of your story should *promise* that something different is going to happen. Life may have gone on the same for the last couple of years, but today is different. Otherwise, why write this story? The opening should indicate that a problem is going to occur, is occurring right now, or has just occurred, and the hero will have to do something about it.

Generally speaking, the hook excites the reader in one of six ways:

1. by presenting compelling events
2. by presenting an unusual character
3. by presenting a vivid setting
4. by using striking language
5. by an unusual presentation of ideas
6. by using striking technical devices

In most short stories and novels, several of these elements may occur.

Another pertinent consideration, particularly in commercial writing, is that the "stakes" should be high. Anybody playing poker doesn't take a penny ante as seriously as a $500 ante. Similarly, in a story, the more crucial the events, the more reader interest is heightened. Frankly, the fact that Rebecca lost her doll in the meadow can hardly compare with Frank's situation: His rope broke while he was mountain climbing, catapulting him to an icy ledge; and now, with a broken ankle, he has to try to make his way to safety while a snowstorm is brewing.

The Hook of Compelling Events

The primary ingredient of this hook is action. Pat Kubis's novel *Burn Baby Burn* begins:

> Reverend Daniel Beverly rounded the corner, his long legs stretching out in an even rhythm. A bunch of kids screeched past him. He sighed, envying their energy; he was not only turning grey, but his lanky, athletic body had developed an unmistakable bulge at his belt buckle. The neighborhood was changing. He turned into the alley leading home. Too late he saw the six parked motorcycles—the sunken-chested teenagers stepping from the shadows, long greasy hair, T shirts stamped with "Coors." His stomach kicked. He saw the garbage cans standing in rows along the garages as the strutting bodies closed in on him. No smart mouthing—just the knowing white grins they were going to get him—for fun. He stopped, seeing the twenty-two in the wiry boy's hand. The leader jerked his thumb. The boy hesitated, his soft lips pulling back in a grimace of fear and uncertainty. "Don't," Daniel said as the bullet slammed into his abdomen. He fell, writhing, clutching his stomach. A boot smashed into his face, grinding his glasses into his skin. He saw the barrel of the gun pointing down at him, stared up into the grins, felt the bullet tearing into him and then he sank gratefully into the black velvet haze.

In this compressed hook, Reverend Daniel Beverly stumbles into a gang that is initiating a new member (the "what" and "why"). The time is now, and the locale is any place where the neighborhood has changed. A theme of the nonviolent man (a minister) confronted by violence is posed. Later, at the hospital, when Daniel regains consciousness, he is asked to identify his assailants, and his identification may send a young boy without any previous record to prison. This decision prompts Daniel to recall the past events of his life.

The Hook of Unusual Characters

The object of the hook of unusual characters is to involve the reader with an interesting personality. Eudora Welty's description of the old black woman Phoenix Jackson in her short story "A Worn Path" offers an excellent example:

> It was December—a bright frozen day in the early morning. Far out in the country there was an old Negro woman with her head tied in a red rag,

coming along a path through the pinewoods. Her name was Phoenix Jackson. She was very old and small and she walked slowly in the dark pine shadows, moving a little from side to side in her steps, with the balanced heaviness and lightness of a pendulum in a grandfather clock. She carried a thin, small cane made from an umbrella, and with this she kept tapping the frozen earth in front of her. This made a grave and persistent noise in the still air, that seemed meditative, like the chirping of a solitary little bird. She wore a dark striped dress reaching down to her shoetops and an equally long apron of bleached sugar sacks, with a full pocket, all neat and tidy, but every time she took a step she might have fallen over her shoe-laces, which dragged from her unlaced shoes. She looked straight ahead. Her eyes were blue with age. Her skin had a pattern all its own of numberless branching wrinkles and as though a whole little tree stood in the middle of her forehead, but a golden color run underneath, and the two knobs of her cheeks were illuminated by a yellow burning under the dark. Under the red rag her hair came down on her neck in the frailest of ringlets, still black, and with an odor like copper.

Now and then there was a quivering in the thicket. Old Phoenix said, "Out of my way, all you foxes, owls, beetles, jack rabbits, bobwhites . . . . Keep the big wild hogs out of my path. Don't let none of those come running in my direction. I got a long way." Under her small black-freckled hand her cane, limber as a buggy whip, would switch at the brush as if to rouse up any hiding things.

On she went. The woods were deep and still. The sun made the pine needles almost too bright to look at, up where the wind rocked. The cones dropped as light as feathers. Down in the hollow was the mourning dove—it was not too late for him.

Phoenix is the protagonist; what's happening?—she's on her way somewhere; the locale is the country; and the time could be now or the recent past. While the hook doesn't tell us *why* such an old woman is making such an extraordinary journey through the woods, the rest of the journey will reveal the why—to get medicine from the doctor in the city for her small nephew who swallowed lye. Welty's detailed description of the old woman involves our emotions, and we admire this brave old lady who is not afraid to face wild hogs with only her cane. We see her switching her cane at the wildlife in the thicket, and we understand from the last line that time is running out for her. The difficulties of her hazardous journey touch us, and we want to know what's going to happen to her.

The Hook of Setting/Atmosphere

An opening image sets the scene and mood. One of the great all-time atmospheric hooks was written by Raymond Chandler in his story "Red Wind":

There was a desert wind blowing that night. It was one of those hot dry Santa Anas that come down through mountain passes and curl your hair and make your nerves jump and your skin itch. On nights like that every booze party ends up in a fight. Meek little wives feel the edge of the carving knife and study their husbands' necks. Anything can happen.

In Chandler's hook, locale is set, the time is now, the weather is what's happening, and there's a promise of violence.

A very subtle hook that revolves around setting is John Steinbeck's opening to "The Chrysanthemums":

> The high grey-flannel fog of winter closed off the Salinas Valley from the sky and from all the rest of the world. On every side it sat like a lid on the mountains and made of the great valley a closed pot. On the broad, level land floor the gang ploughs bit deep and left the black earth shining like metal where the shares had cut. On the foothill ranches across the Salinas River, the yellow stubble seemed to be bathed in pale cold sunshine, but there was no sunshine in the valley now in December. The thick willow scrub along the river flamed with sharp and positive yellow leaves.
>
> It was a time of quiet and waiting. The air was cold and tender. A light wind blew up from the southwest so that the farmers were mildly hopeful of a good rain before long, but fog and rain do not go together.

Steinbeck's next paragraph introduces Henry Allen's foothill ranch and the protagonist, Elisa Allen:

> She was thirty-five. Her face was lean and strong and her eyes were as clear as water. Her figure looked blocked and heavy in her gardening costume, a man's black hat pulled low down over her eyes, clod-hopper shoes, a figured print dress almost completely covered by a big corduroy apron with four big pockets to hold the snips, the trowel and scratcher, the seeds and the knife she worked with. She wore heavy leather gloves to protect her hands while she worked.

Steinbeck combines setting and character in the hook. His opening image presents the ranchland as a closed pot with a lid; when such pots come to a boil, they explode—which is what happens to Elisa when she meets a peddler who magnetically attracts her. *She* is the boiling pot, symbolized by the closed valley, and her womanliness is hidden by her bulky, mannish clothing. Like the valley, she is closed off from the world, from life. Steinbeck uses sexual imagery when he writes of the gang ploughs biting deep into the earth; she, too, is a fallow field waiting to be ploughed. Also, she's in the winter of her years (the December image) and at a time in her life when there will be one last "flaming." For her, it is "a time of quiet and waiting." The hook, then, uses an image that not only gives us an insight to Elisa but that also foreshadows the action of the story. The imagery of the hook combined with the description of Elisa achieves the Who, What, Where, When, Why, and How elements. Who?—Elisa Allen. What's the problem?—Elisa is hungry for life, but she's growing older.

Where's the locale?—Salinas Valley. When?—now. Why is this situation taking place?—she's closed off from life. How did this happen?—she married a rancher. While Steinbeck uses the atmospheric hook to "catch" the reader, he also interweaves the conventional hook elements, using the opening image as a symbolic device to analyze character. In so doing, he avoids the trap of merely using a nice piece of description in a random way.

The Hook of Striking Language

In the hook of striking language, the juxtaposition of words is important. The writer has a poetic interest in words and says something in a new, fresh way. Certainly James Joyce's novels *Ulysses* and *Finnegans Wake* use this type of hook; but in a simpler way, so does John Updike's "A & P":

> In walks these three girls in nothing but bathing suits. I'm in the third checkout slot, with my back to the door, so I don't see them until they're over by the bread. The one that caught my eye first was the one in the plaid green two-piece. She was a chunky kid, with a good tan and a sweet broad soft-looking can with those two crescents of white just under it, where the sun never seems to hit, at the top of the backs of her legs. I stood there with my hand on a box of HiHo crackers trying to remember if I rang it up or not. I ring it up again and the customer starts giving me hell. She's one of those cash-register-watchers, a witch about fifty with rouge on her cheekbones and no eye-brows, and I know it made her day to trip me up. She'd been watching cash registers for fifty years and probably never seen a mistake before.

Updike's hook achieves originality through the freshness of his word choices: "third checkout slot," "a sweet broad soft-looking can with those two crescents of white just under it, where the sun never seems to hit . . . ." Specific detail such as the checker standing there with his hand "on a box of HiHo crackers" gives the reader a sense of place, the supermarket. Also, the details emphasized give us an insight into the checker's mind: His daily work with products and his consciousness of them achieves characterization. Updike doesn't tell us the checker is a young man, but his insights and vocabulary reveal it. Again, most of the hook elements are achieved. Who?—the checker. What's the problem?—three good-looking girls walk into the supermarket. Where are we?—the A & P. When does this take place?—now. Why the fuss?—the girls are clad only in bathing suits, which probably shocks the older customers. The young checker's breezy tone, his slang (*witch, can*), his insights, and his sense of detail are all characterizing elements in this hook that achieves uniqueness through a fresh way of saying things.

The Hook of Ideas

In the hook of ideas, the writer involves the reader through philosophic concepts. C. S. Lewis's opening chapter of *The Screwtape Letters* is a good example. The devil Screwtape is writing to his young protegé devil, Wormword, and Screwtape's advice is an analysis of what is good and evil. Screwtape offers expert advice on how to tempt a human from God (the Enemy) and the path of goodness:

> My dear Wormwood,
>
> I note what you say about guiding your patient's reading and taking care that he sees a good deal of his materialist friend. But are you not being a trifle *naif?* It sounds as if you supposed that *argument* was the way to keep him out of the Enemy's clutches. That might have been so if he had lived a few centuries earlier. At that time the humans still knew pretty well when a thing was proved and when it was not; and if it was proved they really believed it. They still connected thinking with doing and were prepared to alter their way of life as a result of a chain of reasoning. But what with the weekly press and other such weapons, we have largely altered that. Your man has been accustomed, ever since he was a boy, to having a dozen incompatible philosophies dancing about together in his head. He doesn't think of doctrines as primarily "true" or "false," but as "academic" or "practical," "outworn" or "contemporary," "conventional" or "ruthless." Jargon is your best ally in keeping him from the church. Don't waste time trying to make him think that materialism is *true!* Make him think it is strong or stark or courageous—that it is the philosophy of the future. That's the sort of thing he cares about.

In the hook of ideas, the reader is caught by the philosophic observations the narrator poses. Here Screwtape points out that the average individual is seduced not by what is really true but rather by current jargon that makes the individual believe that he or she is in the mainstream of contemporary thought.

In *The Screwtape Letters*, Lewis has a protagonist—the devil Screwtape. What is happening, the situation, is that Screwtape is telling his young assistant devil, Wormwood, how to seduce a human. The time is the eternal now, and the place is here on earth. Why are the devils tormenting humans? Because it's part of the cosmic scheme. So, even though the hook is a philosophic one, there are still characters in a story and the characters are involved in action.

A danger one must always face when writing the philosophic novel is that the novel of ideas is still fiction and not philosophy. A protagonist is required, as is a situation, and problems must occur and be solved in a fictional sense. Too often, new writers attempting the philosophic novel get lost in their ideas and present them in a straight argument, as if they were writing philosophy. In this type of novel the protagonist is the searcher for a particular truth and moves through certain events that reveal that truth; whereas in philosophy, one can argue various points without the necessity of having a characterized individual experience a sequence of events. Fiction—whether philosophical or not—always demands a living, breathing character involved in a particular life experience.

The Hook of Striking Technical Devices

What attracts the reader to the hook of striking technical devices is an unconventional approach to writing: experimentation in literary technique. John Barth's "Lost in the Funhouse" is an example of a conscious effort to break conventional short-story form:

> For whom is the funhouse fun? Perhaps for lovers. For Ambrose it is *a place of fear and confusion. He has come to the seashore with his family for the holiday, the occasion of their visit is Independence Day, the most important secular holiday of the United States of America.* A single straight underline is the manuscript mark for italic type, *which in turn* is the printed equivalent to oral emphasis of words and phrases as well as the customary type for titles of complete works, not to mention. Italics are also employed, in fiction stories especially, for "outside," intrusive, or artificial voices, such as radio announcements, the texts of telegrams and newspaper articles, et cetera. They should be used *sparingly.* If passages originally in roman type are italicized by someone repeating them, it's customary to acknowledge the face. *(Italics mine.)*

Note that Barth does not conventionally present his protagonist as shown by an unseen author. Barth interrupts his narrative to give a small lesson on italics, thus signaling that he will be interrupting the course of his story from time to time to directly address the reader. While the "realistic" writer tries to create the illusion of life by having the reader crawl into the skin of a character and live the character's experiences, experimental writers such as Barth often invite the reader to get into the very mechanics of writing the story, to share in the creation aspect. He invites the reader to look at the story from the artist's perspective. Although Barth's opening is unconventional and experimental, he does contrive to introduce the hook elements: who?—Ambrose; what's happening?—a day at a seashore amusement park; where?—the funhouse; when?—now; why?—his family comes here every Independence Day.

Other writers such as Alain Robbe-Grillet and Joyce Carol Oates use the elements of fiction in a different way. Robbe-Grillet creates startling images juxtaposed against one another that enable you to see and experience what his narrator does. In *The Voyeur,* the reader experiences a series of images and finally realizes that he or she is in the mind of the protagonist, Mathias, a homicidal maniac. Through these carefully joined images the whole history of a possible rape and murder is revealed. Joyce Carol Oates in her story "How I Contemplated the World from the Detroit House of Correction and Began My Life Over Again" breaks the structure of her story into segments: I. Events; II. Characters; III. World Events; IV. People and Circumstances Contributing to This Delinquency; V. Sioux Drive; VI. Detroit; VII. Events; VIII. Character; IX. That Night; X. Detroit; XI. Characters We Are Forever Entwined With; XII. Events. The short story emerges from this "outline" of life.

Literary writers are those who experiment with form and theme. There are no rules in experimental writing; no one can tell you how to do it. These frontier writers consciously break the rules that the realistic writer follows, but it is also true that the experimental writer does *know* what the rules are. He or she is not a beginner, writing in a slapdash fashion. The great danger of experimental writing is that it often confuses the reader. It always demands more participation from the reader, who often does not want to expend that much effort. In general, experimental writing is cerebral; and because it rarely touches the reader's emotions the audience for this type of fiction remains small, under two percent of the people in the world. Yet it is a most important kind of literary form, for literary writers introduce us to new ways of writing. In the main, if you hope to write for a large audience you will probably choose to use more conventional techniques.

Does the Opening Always Have to Be So Contrived?

The answer to this question demands that you be perfectly honest with yourself. When you are in a doctor's office and pick up a *Reader's Digest,* what attracts you first to an article or story? Isn't it the title? Then, after you turn to the article, don't you read the first paragraph? If you don't like that first paragraph, don't you turn to another article? It's a great curiosity that new writers expect *other* people to act differently from the way they themselves act—new writers expect other people to put up with a dull beginning and continue reading their article or story when they would refuse to do it themselves. If you mean that the opening of a story must be contrived to be interesting—yes, *that* is true.

But the point is that the writer must learn to write openings so gracefully that they do not seem contrived: They must in fact seem artlessly graceful.

A Classic Hook

An artfully crafted hook can be timeless. One of the most beautiful classic hooks occurs in Ernest Hemingway's *The Old Man and the Sea*, and it is worth studying to see how effortlessly Hemingway has achieved the five W's and an H of the traditional hook in the first 380 words of the novel:

> He was an old man who fished alone in a skiff in the Gulf stream and he had gone eighty-four days now without taking a fish. In the first forty days a boy had been with him. But after forty days without a fish the boy's parents had told him that the old man was now definitely and finally *salao*, which is the worst form of unlucky, and the boy had gone at their orders in another boat which caught three good fish the first week. It made the boy sad to see the old man come in each day with his skiff empty and he always went down to help him carry either the coiled lines or the gaff and harpoon and the sail that was furled around the mast. The sail was patched with flour sacks and, furled, it looked like the flag of permanent defeat. *[Situation sketched in 147 words.]*
>
> The old man was thin and gaunt with deep wrinkles in the back of his neck. The brown blotches of the benevolent skin cancer the sun brings from its reflection on the tropic sea were on his cheeks. The blotches ran well down the sides of his face and his hands had the deep-creased scars from handling heavy fish on the cords. But none of these scars were fresh. They were as old as erosions in a fishless desert. *[Description of the old man is sketched in 80 words.]*
>
> Everything about him was old except his eyes and they were the same color as the sea and were cheerful and undefeated. *[Main traits emphasized in 22 words.]*
>
> "Santiago," the boy said to him as they climbed the bank from where the skiff was hauled up. "I could go with you again. We've made some money." *[Name of old man is introduced.]*
>
> "No," the old man said. "You're with a lucky boat. Stay with them." *[Old man's first line of dialogue enforces traits of kindness, nobility.]*
>
> "But remember how you went eighty-seven days without fish and then we caught big ones every day for three weeks." *[Reinforcement of old man's main trait of being undefeated, enduring.]*
>
> "I remember," the old man said. "I know you did not leave me because you doubted."
>
> "It was Papa made me leave. I am a boy and I must obey him."
>
> "I know," the old man said. "It is quite normal." *[Old man is forgiving and understanding of human nature.]*
>
> "He hasn't much faith."
>
> "No," the old man said. "But we have. Haven't we?" *[Introduction of theme of faith that shapes the novel.]*

Actually, the first line of the first paragraph achieves an abbreviated narrative hook: "He was an old man who fished alone in a skiff in the Gulf stream and he had gone eighty-four days now without taking a fish." Who is the character?—the old man, a fisherman. What is the problem?—he hasn't caught a fish in eighty-four days. When is the time?—now. Where does the story take place?—in a geographic location situated around the

Gulf stream. Why did this situation occur?—the old man is unlucky. How did this situation occur (what is the background)?—the old man had been fishing for many weeks; others had caught fish, but he had not. In 147 words the whole background of the situation has been sketched and the requirements of the narrative hook met.

In that first paragraph Hemingway also conveys the *feeling* of the fisherman's life through specific detail: the skiff, the coiled lines, the gaff and harpoon, the sail furled around the mast. The image of the patched sail that "looked like the flag of permanent defeat" reinforces the old man's dauntless courage despite his lack of success in fishing. Moreover, the image sets a "tone" to the first paragraph that tells the reader that this book will be a serious novel; it tells the reader what type of story to expect.

In the second paragraph, Hemingway personalizes the old man so that the reader sees him vividly. Hemingway avoids such stereotyped description as "he was six feet tall with blue eyes." Rather, Hemingway focuses on *unusual physical characteristics:* deep wrinkles on the back of the neck, brown blotches of skin cancer on the cheeks, deep-creased scars on the hands from handling fish. This description does more than randomly describe; it tells us a great deal about the personality of the old man. Hemingway at no time *directly states* that the old man is tough, but we gain that information *indirectly from the description.* The last line about the scars being as "old as erosions in a fishless desert" is an image that leads us into the mythic—the old man isn't *any* old man; he's more than that: He is *the* old man of the sea.

After Hemingway describes the old man, we see him and feel him as a person. Note how Hemingway directly states the main character traits of this old man: *undefeated* and *cheerful.* Even though the sea has continually defeated him, he remains cheerful and undefeated. Next, Hemingway names his characters. Names are extremely important because they add to character. Consider the names *Scrooge, King Lear,* and *Mary Poppins* and the feelings those names convey. Zola once said that picking the right name for a character was a definite sign of genius in an author; and he advocated looking through the street directory (we would say telephone directory today). *Santiago*, a very musical name with dignity, fits this old man very well. Also, the prefix of *sant* means "saint" or "holy," and this "fisherman" is indeed in symbolic terms a sainted person or holy man who lives in the universe. Many critics have found a theme of Christ in Hemingway's novel, and the name of the old man certainly supports that concept.

The boy speaks to Santiago, offering to go with him again even if the old man is unsuccessful. But the old man's first lines of dialogue reveal his traits of kindness, nobility, forgiveness, and understanding of human nature. He refuses to share his bad luck with the boy, who has a chance of making money. Then the boy gives us further background on Santiago's past—reminding the old man that while they had gone a long time without catching fish once before, they had caught big ones after all. The boy's dialogue reinforces the old man's key trait of being undefeated. Then the boy's remarks introduce the theme of the novel. The boy speaks of his father, who does not want the boy to fish with the old man—the father has no "faith." The old man affirms, "… but we have. Haven't we?" Now the theme of faith is introduced—some men have faith in the universe, and others do not.

NOTE THE ELEMENTS IN HEMINGWAY'S HOOK

1. who, what, where, when, why, how
2. images that establish character traits
3. images that set tone of book
4. specific nouns (*harpoon, gaff, coiled lines*) that achieve a description of character's occupation, which also help to create a setting
5. image that reveals mythic quality of old man
6. specific description highlighting unusual physical characteristics that reveal trait
7. direct statement of key traits
8. excellent name choice for character; name points to theme of novel
9. first lines of dialogue reveal character traits
10. first lines of dialogue reveal theme of novel

Format of Camera Positions That the Effaced Narrator May Use to Open a Story or Book

New writers often create very "jerky" openings, and they also often forget to describe their characters. Being aware of various ways of handling the viewpoint camera enables a writer to move into the story more gracefully. Note *the sequence of development* in this opening, how the setting is introduced, then the character and a brief description of character, moving into peripheral thought and direct thought, and finally into dialogue.

CAMERA POSITIONS THE EFFACED NARRATOR MAY USE

1. **Panoramic View: A Wide Lens Shot of the Setting**

   Wind rippled the lake's surface into gray wavelets. Wet red leaves spattered the yellow grass. The cold white sun moved behind scudding thick gray clouds. The air was damp and chill from the early-morning rain.

2. **External Long Shot: Move in with Camera and Focus on Subject (Target), Viewing the Subject from a Distance**

   A boy slipped from the birch woods, walked to the edge of the water. He knelt at the water's edge.

3. **External Medium Shot: Focusing on Subject (Target). Move camera in closer to see more detail, such as clothing and body build**

   He wore a red windbreaker zipped to his chin and blue jogging pants with a stripe down the side. He was a slender boy, about fifteen, and he carried a long stick, which he poked into the water.

4. **External Closeup: Focusing on Subject (Target) so camera reveals fine detail, such as facial features and expressions**

   His long dark hair fell into almond-shaped brown eyes. His skin was pale gold, and his high forehead ridged as he poked the water; his face wrinkled with intensity. Then he sat back on his heels, smiling.

5. **Moving into Subject's Peripheral Consciousness; camera now enters the subject's mind, but only enough to reveal his or her state of mind**

   He was satisfied now. The gun was there. But he felt the fear, too. He knew the murderer.

6. **Moving into Subject's Direct Thoughts**

   If they find out I know, he thought, they'll kill me too. What should I do? If I go to the police, they'll know for sure. If I don't go to the police, they'll kill again ... and again. I can stop it. And what about Mom and Dad? They're in as much danger as I am . . . .

7. **Recording Dialogue**

   "Dammit—why did this happen to me! If only I'd never met her. If only I'd never walked into Shelley's that night—"

By practicing these various camera shots of the effaced narrator, one can develop the ability to move gracefully into the story. Many writers use this format. Note the difference between indirect (peripheral) thought and direct thought.

What Is the Strongest Type of Hook?

A hook that involves you with action—either physical or psychological—is generally the most powerful. Remember that the reader tends to identify with the first person brought on stage; for this reason, most writers get their protagonist on stage right away and involve him or her in some type of serious problem. The protagonist could be fighting some element of nature (as is the old man), could be facing with a difficult decision, or could be facing a profound emotional dilemma. The hook should always hint at a problem even if it doesn't directly show one occurring; sometimes *the way* a writer describes a setting indicates that a problem is about to occur, and the tone of the writer, the writer's choice of words, indicates the nature of the problem and its seriousness.

THINGS TO AVOID IN HOOKS

1. Promising a situation you really can't carry through or resolve. Some hooks are so flamboyant (the sixty-foot black widow spider behind the door) that you really can't go anywhere from there. The hook should gracefully lead into an involving situation that becomes more and more interesting.
2. Hooks beginning with dialogue; remember, however, that experimental writers will try anything.
3. Long descriptions that go nowhere.
4. An exciting opener that doesn't really have anything to do with the story.
5. Introducing an interesting character who doesn't have much to do with the story (remember, the reader tends to identify with the first character introduced).
6. Philosophic arguments presented without character involvement.

SUMMARY

Get your main character on stage as soon as possible and involve him or her in a serious problem (remember, psychological problems are as good as action situations). Try to gracefully work in as many of the five W's and an H as possible, considering the structure of your story and your intent. Be as original as you can in your hook, striving for a fresh choice of words and images. Strive to be original in describing your character and see that the dialogue the character speaks reveals his or her major traits. Promise that something has happened, is happening now, or will happen. Keep the stakes high. If you do all these things, you will have created an excellent hook.

Exercises

1. Examine the second paragraph of Ernest Hemingway's hook from *The Old Man and the Sea*, the old man's description. Write down all the things you *know* about the old man just from Hemingway's description (tough, brave). Analyze *why* you know these things. What particular things in the description evoke your reactions?
2. Go to the supermarket, drugstore, bookstore or library and read at least five openings to current bestsellers. How many elements of the hook do you find in them? Outline the hook elements or underline them in book.
3. Write a narrative hook, double spaced, typed on one page only:
   a. Try to achieve as many of the five W's and an H as you can.
   b. Introduce and *describe* your main character, involving him or her in a problem; be sure that the first line of dialogue reveals trait.
4. Write a one-paragraph hook of each of the six types.
5. Using the effaced narrator, and the format of camera shots as a guide,

write a hook. Follow the sequence in the format exactly: Panoramic View (setting); External Long Shot (focusing on target); External Medium Shot (focusing on clothes and body build); External Closeup (focusing on facial features); Moving into Subject's Peripheral Consciousness; Moving into Subject's *direct* Thoughts; Recording Target's Dialogue.

4

The Art of Creating Three-Dimensional Characters

One of the most common criticisms an editor makes of a new writer's story or novel is: "I just don't believe it. The action isn't credible." Studying the rejection slip, the writer finds the editor's remark perplexing and wonders what it means—why *can't* the editor believe it?

Credibility

In plain, simple terms, the editor doesn't believe the book is credible because the writer hasn't created a three-dimensional character who believably wants to carry out the action the writer has determined. Often the plot is sound, but it just doesn't seem believable that *this* particular character wants to achieve that particular goal. For example, let's say you're writing a story and your character, a man, is supposed to rob a bank. You say, "Well, he just does—and that's that." Sorry, it's not that easy. Look around you, at the hundreds of people you know. How many of them have robbed a bank? And many of them need the money, too. It takes a special personality to do something so dangerous and criminal as rob a bank. The question you have to ask is: **What is there in this one man's nature that** makes him *want* to rob a bank? The answer to this question is motivation, and it is **motivation** that makes a character credible.

How Are Characters Motivated?

You want to create in your writing a character who is so *real*, so human, it seems inevitable that he or she do the thing you've determined he or she must do—in fact, if your motivation is handled properly, the character could not have acted in any other way. You can't "push" a paper-doll character through a plot, and you can't build a strong story around a faceless, emotionless *he or she*. A strong story results from a character who really *wants* something. To understand those wants, we have to know many things about the character.

Motivation begins with a description of the character that includes specific traits, clothing, speech, and action; and the writer reveals that character through physical makeup, background, and psychological nature—the way the character thinks. All of these elements artfully combined produce a three-dimensional character.

Why Do Characters Need to Be Described?

Description makes the reader *identify* with the protagonist. How many times at the breakfast table have you picked up the paper and read: "Five People Killed in Earthquake." You probably kept sipping your orange juice and turned to the comics section. But perhaps you saw a picture of a pretty nineteen-year-old woman beside that article and read the interview with her grieving mother. The photo reveals a slender young woman wearing glasses, long hair waving to her shoulders, an honor student, engaged to be married in June, who volunteered her time to tutor disabled students. Then maybe you noticed that the police described one of the unidentified as a young man, about twenty years old, six feet two inches tall, with curly brown hair and green eyes, a tattoo of a rose on his right arm. At this point, you may have found that you've stopped sipping your orange juice. The point is that the moment we see details, we begin to get interested. Details impress on us that this is a person. The *human quality* reaches us. We read the article now because suddenly we realize that it could happen to us.

In fiction, readers want to build an image of the protagonist in their minds, to crawl into the hero's skin and vicariously experience the hero's life. But it's impossible for readers to construct such images if the writer hasn't given any guidelines. For example, you may be reading along and think you're in the mind of a forty-year-old man only to discover you're in the mind of an eight-year-old boy.

Or you may visualize the hero as a handsome blond surfer type and then discover you're in the mind of a thirty-year-old woman, which can occur if the writer has used the first-person ("I") viewpoint. Such discoveries jolt the reader right out of the illusion of life that the author has been trying so hard to create; and when you destroy that illusion, the reader may very well put the book down and never pick it up again. The object of writing well is to keep the reader entranced in the book until the very end. *Get readers into the skin of your protagonist and keep them there.*

Flat Description

Some new writers grudgingly condescend to describe their character in a cursory way: "He was six foot two with blond hair and blue eyes." Inevitably one of them might add: "He looked like a Greek god." Aside from the fact that this is clichéd description, I would also like to remind you that a minister, a college professor, a junkie, a gambler, a cop, a dentist, and a pervert could fit that description. The point is, with such flat description you haven't said anything at all significant about the character to set him apart from anybody else.

Physical description is not only necessary from the reader's viewpoint, as a visualization, but it is also the first step in the motivational process. Physical appearance is the colored glasses through which your particular character views the world. If she is too tall or short, too fat or thin, these physical characteristics perhaps distort her attitude; she may feel inferior and be timid and shy as a result. Basic things we should know about the character are: sex, age, and general body build. Color of hair and eyes are important. They tell us about the character, evoke certain attitudes. If you say that your heroine has honey blonde hair and *soft* brown eyes, the feeling is different from what it would be if you say she has carrot red hair and *snapping* blue eyes—or she has jet black hair with a widow's point that cuts into her forehead, *malicious* brown eyes, and very white teeth. (Note that the adjectives have added additional meaning). Yes, there definitely *are* certain preconceived notions about hair colors and body types, and writers do use those attitudes to advantage.

But Isn't That Stereotyping?

Stereotyping comes from using flat surface description that does not *individualize* the character in any way. To avoid stereotyping, try to find some physical feature that is unique. Hemingway's "old man" is distinctive because he has "brown blotches of benevolent skin cancer" on his cheeks.

Importance of Description

Often when you read a book, your response may be your own
and does not go back to the person who originated the message.

If an author does not describe a character or describes the character superficially, the reader
will not have a clear picture of the character in mind. *Specific description* is necessary to create
an accurate physical portrait.

Chaucer spoke of the miller's wart, which had "a soft tuft of hairs, red as the bristles in a sow's ear ..." growing from it. Steinbeck described Juan Chicoy as having the third finger of his left hand amputated at the joint. Remember, however, that these birthmarks or scars must reveal character in some way. Hemingway's old man is a fisherman who is daily exposed to the sun. The image of the sow's ear coupled to Chaucer's miller indicates that the miller is a dirty old man; and Juan Chicoy's ring finger is a mutilated stump and so we know that because he wears his wedding ring on the stump, his marriage is "amputated" too.

Focusing on Details

A writer works with some common stereotypes but transforms them either by zeroing in on unusual physical features or by closely examining the character and focusing on specific details. Notice how John Steinbeck avoids the stereotype of the neighborhood garage mechanic in his treatment of his protagonist:

> Juan Chicoy carried his lantern to the garage, took a bunch of keys from his overalls pocket, found the one that unlocked the padlock, and opened the wide doors. Juan picked a striped mechanic's cap from his workbench. He wore Headlight overalls with big brass buttons on bib and side latches, and over this he wore a black horsehide jacket with black knitted wristlets and neck. His shoes were roundtoed and hard, with soles so thick that they seemed swollen. An old scar on his cheek beside his large nose shows as a shadow in the overhead light. He ran fingers through his thick, black hair to get it all in the mechanic's cap. His hands were short and wide and strong, with square fingers and nails flattened by work and grooved and twisted from having been hammered and hurt.
>
> ... A pencil and a ruler and a tire pressure gauge protruded from a slot in his overalls bib. Juan was clean-shaven, but not since yesterday, and along the corners of his chin and on his neck the coming whiskers were grizzled and white like those of an old Airedale.
>
> This was the more apparent because the rest of his beard was so intensely black. His black eyes were squinting and humorous, the way a man's eyes squint when he is smoking and cannot take the cigarette from his mouth, the underlip slightly protruding—not in petulance but in humor and self-confidence—the upper lip well formed except left of center where a deep scar was almost white against the pink tissue. The lip must have been cut through at one time, and now this thin taut band of white was a strain on the fullness of the lip and made it bunch in tiny tucks on either side .... His movements were sure, even when he was not doing anything that required sureness. He walked as though he were going to some exact spot. His hands moved with speed and precision and never fiddled with matches or with nails. His teeth were long and the edges were framed with gold, which gave his smile a little fierceness.

Note in the passage that Steinbeck uses a facial scar and a scarred lip to individualize Juan's character. But the scars also indicate that Juan is "tough," which Steinbeck suggests by his use of the image of Juan's Airedale-like beard and by telling us that Juan's smile had a little fierceness. By careful attention to detail, Steinbeck avoids the flat description that produces stereotype.

Stereotype results from not taking the time to really *look* at a character and record what you see.

One of the things that make Hemingway a great writer was his incisive use of detail. He spent many afternoons in cafés, sketching people in words, writing what he *saw*. He described a girl at a nearby table:

> She was very pretty with a face fresh as a newly minted coin if they minted coins in smooth flesh with rain-freshened skin, and her hair was black as a crow's wing and cut sharply and diagonally across her cheeks.

In these lines, Hemingway takes the cliché of "she was pretty as a newly minted coin" and transforms it into something fresh through his precise observations. *Seeing*, as Joseph Conrad pointed out in his Preface to *The Nigger of the Narcissus*, is the great task that every writer must achieve.

Essentially good description enables the reader to "see" the character visually and the portrait the author draws is as well delineated and emotive as that which any good portrait painter renders. The purpose of good description is to give us a distinct feel of personality. Another way to evoke this keynote of personality is to see the character in terms of particular traits.

Creating Character Through Trait

Examining character in terms of specific traits is psychological. We do it with all our friends. Don't we say things like "Doris is such a catty person"? Or "Robert is all mind"? Or "Jane is so caring"? Or "Dave is really selfish"? If you think out it, don't you have a particular word to sum up each friend? Writers, too, often search for that one magic word which catches the essence of personality and which gives a key to the identity of the character. As the great French writer Flaubert told his nephew De Maupassant:

> There are not two grains of sand, two flies, two hands, or two noses absolutely alike in the world. When you pass a grocer smoking his pipe, or a cabstand, let me see that grocer and that porter, their attitude and their whole appearance, with an indication of their whole moral nature, in such a fashion that I could not mistake them for any other grocer or porter; and by one word make me comprehend wherein one cab-horse differs from fifty others in front or behind it.

Flaubert emphasizes looking for the one word that is the heart of your character. For example, consider the grocer Flaubert mentions. Some delineating words might be: *kind, cheating, explosive, selfish, melancholy, sympathetic*. Each of these words would produce a different kind of grocer.

I'm not suggesting that you characterize only in terms of one word, for a personality has many facets; but I am suggesting that you should know this key word and use it to focus your characterization. If you say, "That's so mechanical!"—I would like to remind you that Scrooge was a miser, Hamlet was indecisive, and King Lear would not have been fleeced of his goods if he hadn't been so vain; and all of these characters came from great world masterpieces.

In fact, Tolstoy used one word in an enchanting way to characterize Anna Karenina when she danced with her lover, Vronsky:

> Anna smiled and her smile was reflected by him. She grew thoughtful, and he became serious. Some supernatural force drew Kitty's eyes to Anna's face. She was fascinating in her simple black dress, fascinating were her round arms with their bracelets, fascinating was her firm neck with its thread of pearls, fascinating the straying curl of her loose hair, fascinating the graceful, light movements of her little feet and hands, fascinating was that lovely face in its eagerness, but there was something terrible and cruel in her fascination.

If you missed the point that Anna is fascinating, it wasn't Tolstoy's fault!

However, Tolstoy did use more than one-word characterizations to complete his portrait of Anna. The point is, though, that if you find the "right" word that "catches" your character, it will evoke other traits for you. For example, take the word *miserly*. Some other words that tie in psychologically might be:

1. *cold* (thinks only of one's own interests)
2. *selfish*
3. *calculating*
4. *manipulating*
5. *unfriendly*
6. *greedy*
7. *dislikes borrowers*
8. *fears robbers, suspicious*

You could go on and on with such a list; and as you do, you begin to get distinct feelings about your character.

After you have selected the trait you believe to be your character's main trait, then select two corollary traits that seem to accompany it. (Study your friends for examples.) You might see this miserly character as vain, pompous, conceited, or stubborn. These corollary traits modify the main trait, and the combination creates a particular type of individuality.

If you examine the main trait of *miserly*, and the various feelings evoked by synonyms and other evocative words, you might begin to feel your description growing out of the trait. Such a character might have bad teeth because he didn't want to waste money at the dentist's office. He might shop at the local thrift shop and feel that the clothes he bought there were just as good as those at his neighboring clothing store. He might be thin because he hated to spend money for food. He might live in a cheap apartment to avoid high rent. He might even have bars on his windows to protect him from thieves. He might choose to walk or ride the bus rather than assume the upkeep and expense of a car. He might decide not to marry because he doesn't want some spendthrift woman spending his money—and if he does marry, he probably resentfully doles out money to his wife and quarrels over how she spends it. **Remember the key word is a focus through which to view character.**

Note how John Steinbeck presents Pa Joad in *The Grapes of Wrath* and how he uses that magic one word:

> Across the yard came four people. Grampa was ahead, a lean, ragged, quick old man, jumping with quick steps and favoring his right leg—the side that came out of joint. He was buttoning his fly as he came, and his old hands were having trouble finding the buttons, for he had buttoned the top button into the second buttonhole, and that threw the whole sequence off. He wore dark ragged pants and a torn blue shirt all the way down, and showing long gray underwear, also unbuttoned. His lean white chest, fuzzed with white hair, was visible through the opening in his underwear. He gave up the fly and left it open and fumbled with the underwear buttons, then gave the whole thing up and hitched his brown suspenders. His was a lean excitable face with little bright eyes as evil as a frantic child's eyes. A cantankerous, complaining, mischievous face. He fought and argued and told dirty stories. He was as lecherous as always. Vicious and cruel and impatient, like a frantic child, and the whole structure overlaid with amusement. He drank too much when he could get it, ate too much when it was there, talked too much all the time.

First, Steinbeck uses the word *quick* to reveal the key to Pa Joad's personality.

Note the Main Trait Accompanied by Related Corollary Traits

QUICK	CANTANKEROUS	CHILD
(main trait)	(corollary)	(corollary)
jumping	complaining	mischievous
fumbling	fighting	frantic child's eyes
excitable	arguing	laughing
frantic	vicious	talking too much
impatient	cruel	drinking too much
		underlaid with amusement

Steinbeck also *shows* us the main trait of being quick in action: Pa Joad is too impatient to button his clothes properly and just leaves them undone. His description, too, relates to the main trait: Pa is lean—anyone who hops around that much isn't going to put on weight. The corollary trait of being a child is expressed in Pa's having the eyes of a "frantic child."

The corollary traits give more dimension to Pa Joad's character. Study the relationship between the main trait and the corollary traits and see how they all tie together in Pa Joad—that frantic, quick, immoderate child of a man; and note, too, how the opposing corollaries of cruel/vicious and mischievous/laughing work to make Pa's cruelty childlike and, therefore, harmless. We don't believe Pa to be really "vicious," but we certainly understand that he's a handful of a child-man. Most important, however, is that Steinbeck has in 195 words created a powerful character.

We know how Pa Joad will act if threatened. We know he'll pick up his shotgun and run us off his land, chortling all the while. He's not peaceful, given to reflection, or philosophic thoughts. We know that wherever he shows up, he's going to be a troublesome character.

Seeing When Characterizing

When the novelist Nikos Kazantzakis interviewed Mussolini, Kazantzakis not only delineated a persuasive portrait of the dictator in the setting of the Cicci Palace, but he also brilliantly evoked fascist Italy. Kazantzakis catches Mussolini's dominant traits in his description:

> I could see him clearly now: long torsoed and short-legged, hypertrophied head with blunt features, all chin and forehead, all angles, as though hewn out of hard wood. Huge primitive jaw, cold conceited eye. The expression of the face tight and belligerent.

Creating Character Through Description

Description of character, as Steinbeck shows, has a great deal to do with the central trait. Many people in the "new thought" movement would agree with that statement. (Many people today believe that we are what we think. In fact, people who read physiognomy claim that every feature of our body is an outward manifestation of our deepest thoughts and attitudes, that the body is the mirror of the mind.) Notice how Steinbeck's description of Ma Joad evolves from her main trait, which we have italicized:

> Ma was *heavy, but not fat*; thick with child bearing and work. She wore a loose Mother Hubbard of gray cloth in which there had once been colored flowers, but the color was washed out now, so that the small flowered pattern was only

Note specific details and use of key trait words in Nikos Kazantzakis' Interview with Mussolini.

a little lighter gray than the background. The dress came down to her ankles, and her *strong*, broad, bare feet moved quickly and deftly over the floor. Her thin steel-gray hair was gathered in a sparse wispy knot at the back of her head. *Strong*, freckled arms were bare to the elbow, and her hands were chubby and delicate, like those of a plump little girl. She looked out into the sunshine. Her full face was not soft; it was controlled, kindly. Her hazel eyes seemed to have experienced all possible tragedy and to have mounted pain and suffering like steps into a high calm and a superhuman understanding. She seemed to know, to accept, to welcome her position, the citadel of the family, the *strong* place that could not be taken. And since old Tom and the children could not know hurt or fear unless she acknowledged hurt and fear, she had practiced denying them in herself. And since, when a joyful thing happened, they looked to see whether joy was on it, it was her habit to build up laughter out of inadequate materials. But better than joy was calm. Imperturbability could be depended upon. And from her great and humble position in the family she had taken dignity and a clean, calm beauty. From her position as healer, her hands had grown sure and cool and quiet; from her position as arbiter she had become as remote and faultless in judgment as a goddess. She seemed to know that if she swayed the family shook, and if she ever really deeply wavered or despaired the family would fall, the family will to function would be gone.

TRAIT	DESCRIPTION	COROLLARY	COROLLARY
strong	not soft	goddess	joy
citadel of family	steel-gray hair	arbiter kind	laughter
strong place	gray dress (steel color)	healer	
controlled			
denial of hurt	strong, freckled arms	understanding	
denial of fear	heavy	superhuman	
calm	calm, clean beauty	great/humble	
imperturbable	strong, broad, bare feet	healer dignity	

Ma Joad is more than a woman; she is a goddess. Her description goes beyond that of a mortal woman. She is Mother Earth herself, but a worn goddess—the flowers have washed out of her dress. The care Steinbeck has taken to characterize Ma Joad shows us that description should not be random. It must give us insight into the character, and it should be related to the character's central traits.

Note that Ma and Pa Joad's character traits are in *opposition*. She is controlled; he is impatient and immoderate. This technique of using character oppositions to produce conflict is called *orchestration*. In fact, if a writer can create strong characters using orchestration, the characters themselves will create plot all by themselves. For example, think of a Christian Scientist practitioner who falls in love with a surgeon; a minister with a chorus girl; a yachtsman with a woman who is afraid of the water.

Developing Character Through Image

Sometimes using an image, a word picture, is an effective way to make us see and feel the character. Kazantzakis calls his character Zorba "a living heart, a large voracious mouth, a great brute soul, not yet severed from mother earth." Anaïs Nin describes her character Sabina in image:

> Dressed in red and silver, she evoked the sounds and imagery of fire engines as they tore through the streets of New York, alarming the heart with the violent gong of *catastrophe*; all dressed in red and silver, the tearing red and silver cutting a pathway through the flesh. The first time he looked at her he felt: "Everything will burn."

Nin's description of Sabina is powerful, but isn't it just another way of saying Sabina is a *femme fatale*? A plain, direct statement such as "Sabina wore red and silver and had a fiery personality" wouldn't have been half as effective.

Kazantzakis creates an unforgettable Madame Hortense through image. First he describes her vividly:

> A dumpy, plump little woman, with bleached flax-colored hair ... waddling along on her bandy legs. A beauty spot, from which sprang sow bristles, adorned her chin. She was wearing a red-velvet ribbon round her neck, and her withered cheeks were plastered with mauve powder. A gay little lock of hair danced on her brow . . . .

Then he compares her to:

> ... an old frigate who had known victory and defeat, her hatches battered in, her masts broken, her sails torn—and who now, scored with furrows which she had caulked with powder and cream, had retired to this coast and was waiting.

Madame Hortense is waiting for another man to be her captain, and who is that but Zorba! Image gives a depth to characterization that mere straight description cannot equal. It touches a deeper chord in the reader and evokes more emotion.

Developing Character Through Setting

Balzac was perhaps a master of the technique of developing character through setting. He often began a novel describing a city, a particular street, a particular house; then he took you inside the house, described the furniture, and finally you met the character. Steinbeck does this in *The Wayward Bus*. He opens the book, describing a bus stop called Rebel Corners: "Forty-two miles below San Ysidro, on a great north-south highway in California, there is a crossroad which for eighty-odd years has been called Rebel Corners." He describes Rebel Corners, gives its history, then mentions that Juan Chicoy and his wife bought the original blacksmith shop that had been built there and converted it into a store restaurant-garage. Steinbeck goes on to describe the lunchroom where Alice Chicoy worked:

> There was a little lunchroom in back of the gas pumps, a lunchroom with a counter and round, fixed stools, and three tables for those who wanted to eat in some style. These were not used often for it was customary to tip Mrs. Chicoy when she served you at a table and not to if she served you at the counter. On the first shelf behind the counter were sweet rolls, snails, dough-nuts; on the second, canned soups, oranges and bananas; on the third, individual boxes of cornflakes, riceflakes, grapenuts, and other tortured cereals. There

Characterizing by Furnishings and Setting

was a grill at one end behind the counter and a sink beside it, beer and soda spouts beside that, ice-cream units beside those, and on the counter itself, between the units of paper-napkin containers, juke-box coin slits, salt, pepper, and ketchup, the cakes were displayed under large plastic covers. The walls, where there was room, were well decorated with calendars and posters showing bright improbable girls with pumped up breasts and no hips—blondes, brunettes and redheads, but always with this bust development . . . .

Alice Chicoy ... who worked among the shining girls, was wide hipped and sag chested and she walked well back on her heels. She was not in the least jealous of the calendar girls and the Coca-Cola girls. She had never seen anyone like them and she didn't think anyone else had either. She fried her eggs and hamburgers, heated her canned soup, drew beer, scooped ice cream, and toward evening her feet hurt and that made her cross and snappish. And as the day went on the flat curl went out of her hair so that it hung damp and stringy beside her face, and at first she would brush it aside with her hand and finally she would blow it out of her eyes.

By seeing the isolated location of Rebel Corners, and moving inside the little lunchroom, the reader understands Alice's life. Her world is canned soup and hamburgers, and she's tired and grumpy at the end of the day. Nothing very exciting happens to Alice, nor does she expect anything exciting either. We understand Alice very well, through the device of seeing her in her everyday environment.

Developing Character Through Symbol

Sometimes a writer may wish to use a particular symbol to develop character. John Fowles' novel *The Magus* uses this device. *The Magus* happens to be the number-one card in the Tarot deck, and it signifies the magician—a man who has the power to transform things. Fowles presents the character Concis (a play on "consciousness"), who is a psychiatrist, standing in the symbolic pose of the Magus as depicted in the Tarot deck:

> He was nearly completely bald, brown as old leather, short and spare, a man whose age was impossible to tell; perhaps sixty, perhaps seventy; dressed in a navy-blue shirt, knee length shorts, and a pair of salt-stained gym-shoes. The most striking thing about him was the intensity of his eyes; very dark brown, staring, with a simian penetration emphasized by the remarkably clear whites; eyes that seemed not quite human. He raised his left hand briefly in a kind of silent salutation, then strode to the corner of the colonnade, leaving me with my formed words unspoken.
> … "You …" I began, as he turned. But he raised his left hand again, this time to silence me; took my arm and led me to the edge of the colonnade. He had an authority, an abrupt decisiveness, that caught me off balance.

Concis, the psychiatrist, *is* the Magus—and he does have the power to transform; for he transforms Nick, the narrating character. Important, too, are Concis' eyes. As a psychiatrist, he is able to *see* through you, but Fowles indicates that Concis seems to be more than human ("eyes that seemed not quite human"); whatever Concis knows, he seems to have gone beyond the human's limitation.

Kazantzakis uses symbol in a different way. He shows Zorba the Greek taking out his beloved instrument, his fingers caressing it as though undressing a woman. He

> opened the sack and drew out an *old santuri*, polished by the years. It had many strings, it was adorned with brass and ivory and a red silk tassel. Those big fingers caressed it, slowly, passionately, all over, as if caressing a woman. Then they wrapped it up again, as if clothing the body of the beloved lest it should catch cold.

The *santuri* symbolizes Zorba's passionate self. He loves music as ardently as if it were a woman. Although Zorba is a workman with cracked, gnarled hands, he has a passionate soul.

Developing Character Through Allusion

An interesting way to create character is through allusion, perhaps to a mythic character. Hemingway's old man is mythic, and we know that because Hemingway describes him as having scars "as old as erosions in a fishless desert." The old man is not any old man—he's *the* old man of the sea. Kazantzakis has Zorba's first dialogue mentioning the devil in various expressions: "the devil took a hand in it … the poor devil had even handed out cigarettes." In fact, Zorba first shows up when the protagonist is reading *Dante's Inferno*. Finally Zorba remarks that his nickname is "Mildew," which happens to be the devil's nickname. Obviously in the novel *Zorba the Greek*, the devil in Zorba's skin has appeared to show the narrator a lesson in devilment. John Fowles depicts the psychiatrist Concis as the Magus, but he also spends much time in comparing Concis to the great god Dionysus. Concis lives on the island Phraxos and like the god Dionysus appears in summer and goes away in winter; on his estate Bourani grow the pine and olive trees, sacred to the god. A satyr statue, a bronzed Priapus with a grotesque phallus, is enshrined in rock, marking this the home of the great fertility god Dionysus. Concis is a psychiatrist, but he is also a magician who has the powers of Dionysus.

Developing Character Through Background

One of the most important ways to characterize is by seeing characters through their background—their home life, their education, their place in society, their race, their amusements or hobbies. In my novel *One More Time*, I used this type of characterization for a black musician named Sully:

> He was never pretty. His daddy, Jake Hawkins, had a face that looked three-quarters gorilla and a body almost that big, and Sully wasn't much different. He just sort of grew up by himself in the small cabin right at the edge of Knoxford Swamp. He had five brothers and seven sisters, he was the thirteenth—lucky or unlucky as that may be, he never figured it out.... He stayed at home till he was twelve—picking cotton, pushing along the rows, all bent over, dragging his sack across the sun baked dirt, his fingers pulling at the fluffy white stuff till he ached so he could hardly sleep at night. Then he cut out hiring out to the work gangs along the Mississippi. He stood as tall as his daddy, Jake, and he passed for eighteen. The company brought in women to keep the men from getting itchy feet. He was thirteen when he had his first woman. He fell into the life. Drinking and dancing on Saturday night. Life was cheap. If a man got killed, they just hauled him back out of the way. Then the feeling came on him that he had to get a horn. He got to standing around, watching the musicians and he knew it was the life he wanted. He started burying his coins in a jar out under a tree, letting them grow till he saved enough to buy his first clarinet, ten dollars, from the widow of a musician who'd just died. He finally got good enough with his clarinet to get into a four piece combo that played for dances and picnics, and he worked around railroad camps, living in boxcars, filling his belly with beans and chicken on Sunday.... Then, when he was nineteen, he walked into Coy Jingo's place.

Even professional cartoonists need to establish background for their characters.

The point about showing background is that environment *shapes* a person's life. By knowing a person's background, the reader is able to understand *from which perspective* the character is viewing life. In *The Magus*, Fowles presents his protagonist Nicholas d'Urfe through background also. The narrator, Nick, tells the reader he was born in 1927, his parents were middle class, Victorian, his father a brigadier with a choleric temper. Nick wrote poetry, was good at English, and attended Oxford. He modeled himself after the existentialists, living in literature rather than life. He was "affected," "green," and "handsomely equipped to fail" when he finally went out into life. Fowles spends three full pages giving us all this information about Nick so that we understand Nick and his *need* to be transformed into a complete human being. Nick has been stifled by his Victorian parents, his ivory-tower education.

Knowing the background of both Sully and Nick, you have an understanding of both characters, and you understand the particular kind of "colored glasses" they are wearing through which they view the world.

Developing Character Through Self-Revelation

When we know a man's environment and his temperament, we have an insight into his mind and are able to look at his attitudes, ambitions, and complexes. The Russians are masters of psychological characterization. In Tolstoy's *Anna Karenina*, Stepan Oblonsky (Stiva) is presented psychologically. Tolstoy describes him as a soft, indulgent man who likes to sleep with his face buried in a pillow, dreaming of parties and women. When Stiva wakes he remembers that he's had an affair with the governess, and his wife, Dolly, has found out about it. Stiva reflects, "Yes, she won't forgive me, and she can't forgive me. And the most awful thing about it is that it's all my fault—all my fault, though I'm not to blame." He remembers returning home and bringing his Dolly a pear only to be confronted with the "unlucky" letter that revealed everything. Pondering his situation, he tells himself that he is

> ... a truthful man in his relations with himself. He was incapable of deceiving himself and persuading himself that he repented of his conduct. He could not at this date repent of the fact that he, a handsome, susceptible man of thirty-four, was not in love with his wife, the mother of five living and two dead children, and only a year younger than himself. All he repented of was that he had not succeeded better in hiding it from his wife .... Possibly he might have managed to conceal his sins better from his wife if he had anticipated that the knowledge of them would have had such an effect on her .... He had even supposed that she, a worn-out woman no longer young or good looking, and in no way remarkable or interesting, merely a good mother, ought from a sense of fairness to take an indulgent view.

Stiva thinks the escapade with the governess is a terrible situation, but, on the other hand, she was really worth it—although, unfortunately, she's pregnant. "Ill luck," he despairs and wishes he could go back to sleep to the music and the lovely ladies of the night.

While Tolstoy does describe Stiva as a stout man and depicts him as wearing a gray robe lined with blue silk (which emphasizes his sensuality), the real revelation of character comes through Stiva's thoughts about himself. Even more interesting is that his thoughts about himself are not *true* at all. While he regards himself as being "truthful," the reader is aware that he continually lies to himself. The reader surmises that Stiva isn't as handsome as he thinks he is—he's more likely one of the bores who are always trying to seduce women at cocktail parties—and that his wife, Dolly, who is approximately his own age, is probably not worn out at all. Psychological revealing of character is particularly powerful, for no matter how much the writer tells the reader what the character is like, the reader will believe only what the character reveals through thought and action. Stiva is a consistent character. We know that he isn't hurt, that he isn't going to beg for forgiveness, and we also know he's probably going to do the same thing again. Even though Tolstoy hasn't said any of these things, we know Stiva very well from his thoughts about himself, and we understand his *psychology*. At no time does Tolstoy directly characterize by saying as author that Stiva is morally wrong, that he is a cheat and a liar. Rather, Tolstoy lets *you* realize it through his indirect presentation of character.

Developing Characterization Through Action

People reveal themselves through their actions. The man who says, "I love animals" and then refuses to feed a stray is a liar. People reveal their true nature by facial expressions, gestures, unconscious movements, and physical reactions to emotional and physical stress. Note this protagonist:

> Paul missed the red light at the corner, swore irritably, and smashed his fist against his palm. The whole morning was shot. Harry the paper vendor waved at him and Paul ignored him, stepping down hard on the gas when the light changed. He saw the pigeon ahead and veered directly at it, knowing it would probably fly away in the last possible second; then, looking back in the rear-view mirror, he saw the small bloody mound lying there and he felt the satisfaction.

We don't need to be told directly that Paul has a rotten temper and is vengeful. The incident does it in an economical way. In fact, one cardinal rule about writing is: **Don't tell the reader about a character. Show the character in action!**

Developing Characterization Through Speech

The way people talk reveals a great deal about personality. Consider these two men who enter a café at the same time; both tell the waitress they want immediate service:

> First man: "Pancakes and coffee, please, Miss. I'd appreciate it if you could hurry up my order; I'm rather late for an appointment."
>
> Second man: "Stack of wheats and some java—make it snappy, babe, I gotta split."

Just from the dialogue, which man is wearing the suit and which the leather jacket? Which man carries the briefcase? Which man is more likely to punch you in the jaw? Which man wears a very expensive watch? Just by the dialogue, you should be able to answer the questions.

One very important point about dialogue is that the very first words a protagonist speaks should reveal character in some way.

Developing Characterization Through Clothing

If you wear a teeny bikini and lead a white Russian wolfhound down Hollywood Boulevard, I know a great deal about you. If you wear a dark brown polyester suit with a brown striped tie, I surmise you're rather conservative. If you wear a green flowered house dress, carry a full shopping bag, and push a baby buggy, I know pretty much about you, too. The clothes we give our protagonists add to the other characterization methods. Consider Sportin' Life in *Porgy and Bess*—in his green suit and yellow tie, would you trust him with your life's savings?

Developing Characterization Through Consciousness

Today the big movement in writing is away from externals and into consciousness. The writer reveals self through an exploration of consciousness. Wirt Williams in his novel *The Far Side* gives us a peek into the mind of a university professor, Walter Munday. A close friend has just given Walter a copy of his new book, *Tiberius*, and inscribed on the flyleaf is: "For Walter, who made me do it. In gratitude, Dick." Munday reflects:

CHARACTERIZATION

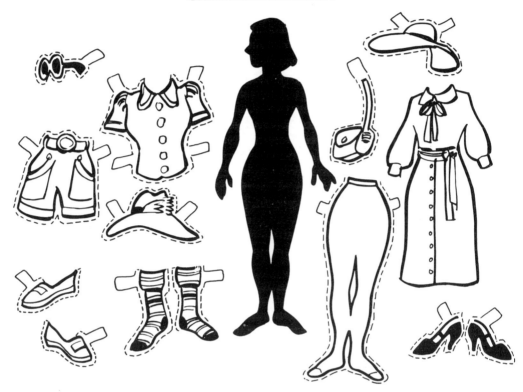

Characterizing by Clothes

> And he had to drink the hemlock mixture of reaction to a successful effort by a close friend and professional colleague: honest delight, profound jealousy, and stern self-reproach for the jealousy. It was more painful to have a friend surpass you than an enemy . . . . With an enemy you could give yourself to bitterness and enjoy it.

The passage evokes the competition of university life, the scholarship, and the professorial reactions of one man in response to the success of another man he's helped. We see Walter as a man of considerable intellect, aware of the subtlety of his own emotions, a man who strives for emotional balance and who refuses to give into jealousy but is piqued by it. His last line reveals an ironic sense of humor.

John Updike, too, uses an examination of consciousness in his short story "Leaves." He looks into the mind of a man whose wife is divorcing him:

> In nervousness, I rise and walk across the floor. A spider like a white asterisk hangs in air in front of my face. I look at the ceiling and cannot see where its

thread is attached. The ceiling is smooth plasterboard. The spider hesitates. It feels a huge alien presence. Its exquisite white legs spread warily and of its own dead weight twirls on its invisible thread. I catch myself in the quaint and antique pose of the fabulist seeking to draw a lesson from a spider, and become self-conscious. I dismiss self-consciousness and do earnestly attend to this minute articulated star hung so pointedly before my face; and am unable to read the lesson. The spider and I inhabit contiguous but incompatible cosmoses. Across the gulf we feel only fear. The telephone remains silent.

Updike's character is not described externally, but through examining the images evoked in his consciousness we feel his perplexity at the universe, his loneliness and confusion. He, like the spider, is alone and unprotected in an alien world.

Characterization in the Commercial Novel

In the contemporary commercial novel, writers often like to present a character very quickly in a *block* description. *Remember that a character should be described as soon as he or she is brought on stage.* Note the characterization elements in Sidney Sheldon's novel *The Other Side of Midnight:*

Dr. Israel Katz was flying to Athens from Capetown, where he was the resident neurosurgeon and chief of staff at Groote Schur, the large new hospital that had just been built. Israel Katz was recognized as one of the leading neurosurgeons in the world. Medical journals were filled with his innovations. His patients included a prime minister, a president and a king.
He leaned back in the seat of the BOAC plane, a man of medium height, with a strong, intelligent face, deep-set brown eyes and long, slender, restless hands. Dr. Katz was tired, and because of that he began to feel the familiar pain in a leg that was no longer there, a leg amputated six years earlier by a giant with an ax.

We know that Dr. Katz is an important person, world famous. World leaders seek him out. We know his profession and that he is highly respected in his field. His whole description indicates brilliance. He is not an "ordinary" man. A key to the bestselling novel is to use characters who are "bigger than life," "more successful," "rich," "powerful." Dr. Katz's character traits are "intelligence" and "restlessness." Sheldon piques our curiosity with Katz's amputated leg. Like Steinbeck's Juan Chicoy, Katz has suffered a mutilation, and this mutilation is very visual and sets him apart from other characters. The blunt statement that his leg was "amputated ... by a giant with an ax" acts, too, as a hook. The reader wants to read on and see what had happened to Katz.

In *Rage of Angels*, Sheldon quickly sketches his female protagonist:

It was Jennifer Parker's first day at the trial.... She ... was a slender, dark-haired girl of twenty-four with a pale skin, an intelligent, mobile face, and green, thoughtful eyes. It was a face that reflected pride and courage and sensitivity, a face that would be hard to forget. She sat ramrod straight, as though bracing herself against unseen ghosts of the past.

Sheldon's protagonist is a young woman, designed to attract the young female reader. Jennifer's character traits are intelligence, pride, courage, and sensitivity. Her traits suggest a thoughtful, ethical nature—a person who will fight being victimized. Sheldon's enigmatic statement that she braces "herself against unseen ghosts of the past" acts as a hook in that we must read further to see what those "ghosts" were.

One of Sheldon's most interesting characterizations, and one done in a humorous vein, is that of Detective Max Hornung in *Bloodline*. Sheldon describes him as:

> ... a dumpy, wistful-looking man, egg-bald with a face that had been put together by an absent-minded prankster. His head was too large, his ears were too small, and his mouth was a raisin stuck in the middle of a pudding face. Detective Max Hornung was six inches too short to meet the rigid standards of the Zurich Kriminal Polizei, fifteen pounds too light, and hopelessly nearsighted. To top it off, he was arrogant. All the men on the force felt unanimously about Detective Hornung: they hated him.

Note Sheldon's characterization signature of making the description a hook. How did such an improbable man *get* on the police force? He obviously didn't pass the police physical. *Why* do the other policemen hate Hornung?

Sometimes, new writers ask, "How much time should I spend to describe and characterize my character?" Most current novels spend a paragraph or two in specific description. But in the case of Max Hornung, Sheldon spends at least ten pages developing his character and has a lot of fun with the intrepid detective. *Characterizing depends on how much time you want to spend on it—and how good you are.* The point is, can you keep your reader interested as you describe?

Developing Characterization Woven in Through the Book

Sometimes the writer doesn't want to use a block description on the first page. The writer may feel that certain events, or background, are more important. Still, the writer should give some type of brief description that will give the reader the "feel" of the character. An initial brief description of a protagonist might be: "A stocky, red-haired man in an ice-cream suit stood in the doorway." Then, a few paragraphs later, another description might read: "He had a high, broad forehead with three wrinkles and a firm, well-shaped mouth and vivid blue eyes. When he smiled the sun shone."

Still later there might be another descriptive reference: "The light glanced from his hair, turning it burnished copper."

When you intersperse description throughout, make sure that you use enough description to make the character *real*. It isn't enough to describe a character once in the beginning of the book. Sixty pages later, the reader may forget what your character looked like. So refer again to various physical attributes: "his blue eyes darkened," "his red hair curled into his forehead," "three wrinkles ridged his forehead."

First-Person Characterization

One question often asked is how to do in-depth characterization in first person. Saul Bellow describes his character Henderson in *Henderson the Rain King* in great detail.

> When I think of my condition at the age of fifty-five ... all is grief .... A disorderly rush begins—my parents, my wives, my girls, my children, my farm, my animals, my habits, my money, my music lessons, my drunkenness, my prejudices, my brutality, my teeth, my face, my soul! I have to cry, "No, no, get back, curse you, let me alone!" But how can they let me alone? They belong to me. They are mine. And they pile into me from all sides. It turns to chaos .... I must face up to the facts. I might as well start with the money. I am rich. From my old man I inherited three million dollars after taxes, but I thought myself a bum and had my reasons, the main reason being that I behaved like a bum .... I am a graduate of an Ivy League university .... At birth I weighed fourteen pounds and it was a tough delivery. Then I grew up. Six feet four inches tall. Two hundred and thirty pounds. An enormous head, rugged, with hair like Persian lamb's fur. Suspicious eyes, usually narrowed. Blustering ways. A great nose. I was one of three children and the only survivor. It took all of my father's charity to forgive me and I don't think he ever made it altogether .... I got into brawls in the country saloons near my farm and the troopers locked me up. I offered to take them all on, and they would have worked me over if I hadn't been so prominent in the country .... Then I had a fight with the vet over one of my pigs, and another with the driver of a snowplow on US 7 when he tried to force me off the road. Then I fell off a tractor while drunk and ran myself over and broke my leg. For months I was on crutches, hitting everyone who crossed my path, man or beast .... With the bulk of a football player and the color of a gypsy, swearing and crying out and showing my teeth and shaking my head—no wonder people got out of my way.

Bellow gives us a compendium of facts about Henderson, wild, conflicting facts. He has a pig farm and he takes music lessons, he's rich and he quarrels with everybody, he's a graduate of an Ivy League university—he exudes *chaos;* and Henderson *is* chaotic, chaos and madness being his main traits.

Characterizing the Minor Character—One-Liners

One problem that troubles the new writer is how to handle the character who walks in and out of a scene and never appears again. The danger is that if too much time is spent on the character, he or she may begin to take on a life of his or her own and thus detract from the protagonist. A good idea to handle the minor character is the "one-liner," one succinct line of description that makes this character real. The trick is to zero in on a key quality or a specific feature of description:

> The secretary sat at the desk, her slender legs crossed, her blood-red fingernails tapping her typewriter.
>
> The detective stared at her, his quick brown eyes instantly veiling, leaving her wriggling on the pin of his glance.
>
> He saw the girl sitting on the dock, talking to her boyfriend; loneliness shone from her face, then refracted at his too-loud laugh.
>
> The waiter had a sophisticated boyishness that startled her with its seriousness.
>
> The receptionist looked like Snow White without the dwarfs.
>
> The bartender was a great chunk of a man with a Hitler lock of hair that fell into his eyes.
>
> He had a pinkish Greek face that spoke of money and wryness.
>
> The boy was as lanky and gawky as Lincoln; and in his blue checked shirt he looked as if he should have been hewing logs in the woods.

Actually, one-liners are fun to construct, and it's a good idea to carry a notebook and do them on buses or in cafeteria lines. The main idea is to give the minor character a feeling of personality; and this treatment also gives the protagonist a chance to make what might be some witty or penetrating observations that give us an insight into him or her too.

Summary

In playwriting and TV writing, the audience *sees* the character "live" on stage or on screen. In fiction, however, the writer has to create the character through words. Yet even playwrights and TV scriptwriters are meticulous in describing their characters so that producers and directors will select the right person for the part.

Characterization awakens emotion in readers, makes them feel that they *know* this man or woman—that they *know* how this character will act in all situations. Aristotle praised the quality of "consistency," that in creating a character the character will act in accordance with the traits that have been set up by the author. A new writer often protests, "But my character is inconsistent! After all, isn't life inconsistent?" Yes, life is inconsistent, but fiction isn't. Coincidences happen in life, but when they happen in fiction readers just don't believe it. As far as having an inconsistent character, the inconsistency may be a trait—which would make your character consistent in his or her inconsistency. But if the character acts randomly, without purpose, you had better consider motivating him or her.

We have given you ways to characterize—and there may be yet more ways. But these are the principal ones most writers use. As to which is *best*, that you will have to decide for yourself; it seems that each story determines its own mode of telling. Some writers spend a great deal of time describing their characters, and some writers work characterization in between action. If you describe your character in long blocks of description, the book will tend to be static unless you have the verve of a Steinbeck or a Bellow. In general, there's more life to your writing if you feed your description in between action. Instead of saying that a character wore blue slacks, you might use a line like "He brushed a piece of lint from his blue slacks." The main thing, however, is to study these various modes of characterization and experiment with them so that when you write a story you won't always handle your characters in the same old way. Techniques, as we've said before, are like chords to the musician—and your mastery of chords will produce more variation in your writing.

No matter which type of characterization you choose, though, we suggest that you *do* understand your character's main traits and that they act as a unifying force that shapes your character's external description, your images, your symbols and allusions. **Know your character's background, environment, how your character thinks, feels, talks, and acts under stress.** Know what kind of clothes your character wears, what kind of books and magazines he or she reads, what his or her hobbies and talents are. See your character standing before you with his or her scars, birthmarks, and mannerisms. If you really know all these things *before you write*, you'll find that your character is three-dimensional—in fact, your character will probably begin to start spinning his or her own story and you'll be running behind, pen in hand. And when your book or script is over, you will find that you feel as if a good friend had died.

If your character is believable, your plot will be believable, and your story will be believable—and your check will be believable—because publishers love believable stories. And not only that: You'll probably receive bushels of mail from readers who "cried all the way through your story" because it was *so real*.

Exercises

1. Write a character sketch, no longer than one page, developing character from a main trait and two corollary traits. Show these traits in action.
2. Describe the character, keeping the traits in mind, and have at least one line of dialogue that reflects the main trait.
3. In less than half a page, show your character through an image or symbol.
4. Write a one-page character sketch revealing your character, using the technique of exploration of consciousness.
5. In one page, create a setting and show your character through that setting. Remember that books, furnishings, records, and pets are also things that characterize.
6. Do a block characterization in one to two paragraphs. Be sure to work in the main traits.
7. Write several pages in which you intersperse description. Compare this exercise with the block characterization exercise. Which is stronger?
8. Write a character sketch from the first person ("I") viewpoint, giving physical description, thoughts, and revealing traits. Write the same sketch from the third person and note the difference.
9. Write as many one-liners as you can in half an hour.

Create a Character Portrait Chart to Know Your Character.

Three-Dimensional Character Chart

Minor/Major Character _____   Novel _____

Name _____   Date _____

Name _____ Sex _____ Age _____ Birthdate _____
Birthplace _____ Nationality _____
Religion _____ Feelings about Religion _____
Languages spoken _____
Political Party _____
Class in Society   Lower _____ Middle _____ Upper _____
Morals _____
Ambitions _____
Education _____ Date Graduated _____ Major _____
Name of School _____ Where _____
Married _____ Divorced _____ Single _____

Family Background ▊▊▊▊▊▊▊▊▊▊▊▊▊▊▊▊▊▊▊▊▊▊▊▊▊▊▊▊▊▊

Father _____ Profession _____ Living or dead _____
Mother _____ Profession _____ Living or dead _____
Parents Divorced _____
Parents Happily Married _____
Brothers (number) _____ Sisters _____
Happy Home Life? _____
Interesting Information Regarding Family _____
_____
_____

Physical Appearance ▊▊▊▊▊▊▊▊▊▊▊▊▊▊▊▊▊▊▊▊▊▊▊▊▊▊

Height _____ Weight _____ Eyes _____ Hair _____ Forehead _____
Jawline _____ Lips _____ Mouth _____ Eyebrows _____
Hands _____ Fingers _____ Shoulders _____
Limbs _____ Complexion _____ Face _____
Breasts _____ Waist _____ Hips _____
Neck _____ Ears _____ Nose _____ Teeth _____
Type of Body _____
Any Birthmarks or Scars _____
Posture _____ Appearance _____

Occupation/Profession ▊▊▊▊▊▊▊▊▊▊▊▊▊▊▊▊▊▊▊▊▊

Profession _____ Union _____
Education in Work _____ Favorite Subjects (School) _____
Poorest Subjects _____ Grades (School) _____
Quality of Work Performed _____ Reputation _____
Hours worked _____ Income _____

Military Service ▊▊▊▊▊▊▊▊▊▊▊▊▊▊▊

Branch _____ Nationality _____
Enlisted rank _____ Highest Rank Achieved _____
Service Dates _____ Unit or Legion _____
Served under what ruler _____
Campaigns _____
Decorations if applicable _____
Official Opinion of Protagonist as soldier _____

Character-Trait Analysis

Major Traits _____

Minor Traits _____

Outstanding Qualities _____

Character Flaws _____

Habitual Expressions _____

_____

_____

_____

Habitual Mannerisms _____

_____

_____

_____

Fears _____ Frustrations _____

Complexes _____

Temperament _____

_____

Emotions _____

_____

_____

Attitude Toward Life _____

Leader _____ Follower _____ Dropout _____

■■■■■■■■■■■■■■■■■■■■■■■■■■■ Personal Information ■■■■■■■■■■■■■■■■■■■■■■■■■

Hobbies or favorite pastimes _____

Favorite Books _____ Favorite Magazines _____

Favorite Newspaper _____ Favorite Records _____

Taste in jewelry _____ Favorite Colors _____

Type of men preferred _____

Type of women preferred _____

Favorite Entertainment _____

Favorite foods _____

_____

Favorite drinks _____

Favorite clothes _____

House (type) _____ (Apartment) _____

City background _____ Country background _____

Describe furnishings (use colors & materials) _____

_____

_____

5

How to Create Effective Dialogue

One of the most important things every writer must master is dialogue. It reveals character, gives necessary plot information, builds emotion in scenes, and develops local color. Dialogue adds "freshness" and life to the page. It enables the writer to convey information in a lifelike way, rather than bore the reader with long narrative passages.

How Can You Learn to Write Good Dialogue?

No one can teach you how to write good dialogue. Basically, it takes a perceptive ear. If you want to be a good writer, sit back and listen to people talk. You will notice that most people do not speak in complete sentences. For example, few people say, "Where are you going?" Most say, "Where you going?" Don't worry about being grammatically correct; don't worry about splitting infinitives in dialogue or ending a sentence with a preposition.

Be observant: on the bus, in a cafeteria or movie line, in a doctor's or dentist's office, in a supermarket. Of course, you know that a lawyer or teacher speaks differently from a truck driver. But can you *pinpoint* those differences?

Be aware of *cadences*. Listen to a German, a Frenchman, a Jew, an Italian, an Irishman, or a Scot speak. Can you catch in words the rolling rhythms of those languages? If your character is of a nationality other than English, you should be able to write dialogue that reveals nationality without misspelling any words. In writing dialect, think of rhythms and word placement. Intersperse a few foreign words for effect. A key to writing good dialogue is always to speak your lines aloud as you write them. In this way, you will notice whether you have written unreal or *stilted* dialogue.

Strive to Be Natural

It's true you won't be able to write dialogue *exactly* as people talk, because many people stammer or clutter up their language with "You know what I mean," or "uh," and assorted bleeps and bloops. Yet those very mannerisms give you, the writer, valuable insights into dialogue, for you may wish to characterize certain characters as speaking this way.

Some characters will speak in clichés; it's part of their personality pattern. Take Sinclair Lewis' Babbit, for instance:

> I was saying to my son just the other night—it's a fellow's duty to share the things of this world with his neighbors, and it gets my goat when a fellow gets stuck on himself and goes around tooting his horn merely because he's charitable.

The clichés show the extent of Babbit's mind, his limited viewpoint of the world.

One of the reasons Mark Twain is still read so widely today is that his characters Tom Sawyer and Huck Finn spoke so simply and well that children and adults in the twentieth century can understand and identify with the dialogue. Huck says:

> Well, I went fooling along in the deep woods till I judged I warn't far from the foot of the island. I had my gun along, but I hadn't shot nothing.

However, if Twain had written in the involuted prose of the time in which he lived, Huck would have sounded like this:

> Well, I meandered among the thick virgin timber till I ascertained I was nearing the extremity of the island. I had my fowling piece along, but I had not killed any game.

Twain, in his short story "Buck Fanshaw's Funeral," points up the exasperation the reader feels when exposed to unnatural dialogue. Twain's character Scotty Briggs is talking to a minister who uses jawbreaker words:

SCOTTY: You see, one of the boys has gone up flume—
MINISTER: Gone where?
SCOTTY: Up the flume ... kicked the bucket—
MINISTER: Ah—has departed to the mysterious country from whose bourn no traveler returns.
SCOTTY: Returns! I reckon not. Why, pard, he's *dead!*

Though Twain is making fun of ornate, grammatical dialogue, he *has* characterized the minister as being the type of person who would logically use such involuted language. But in general, avoid having your characters speak in such a stilted manner.

Be Sure That Your Dialogue Is Appropriate for Your Character

When you write dialogue for a specific character, make sure that your character is the type of person who would use such dialogue. A lawyer isn't too likely to say, "What's up, babe?" nor is a child likely to say, "In the early morning, the willows were inexplicably green, and sunlight glazed the windowpanes." In both cases, the dialogue is inappropriate for the characters depicted. In the first example, the dialogue is too crude; we expect more sophistication from the lawyer. In the second case, the vocabulary is too "adult" to be believable. You may argue that you know a child or lawyer who speaks this way, but it will be difficult to make a reader believe it.

In the event you insist on writing a character who uses dialogue that is seemingly inappropriate, you will have to spend a great deal of time *motivating* why he or she really does speak this way. You might characterize the lawyer as having worked his way up from the streets and so he retained his vocabulary of street language, or the child as having an I.Q. of 180.

If you're going to write children's stories or use a child as a character, you should listen to children speak. Many writers fall into the trap of having children use language that was current when the writer was a child. For example, a child of today would hardly say: "Horrors!" Also, many slang expressions *date* a contemporary story and are best avoided. Also consider that today, with television, computers, tapes, and movies, children have some advanced learning concepts, and if you want to be *timely*, you should know what subjects interest children of particular age groups. While children may be somewhat more sophisticated in certain areas than they were years ago, it's preferable to keep language simple.

How to Avoid the "He Said"/"She Said" Problem

In dialogue, the "he said" or the "she said" is called a *tag*. A tag is the material that introduces a quote or clarifies it. You will need to use a few "he said"/"she said" tags in a long interchange so that the reader knows who is speaking, but strive for balance. Several lines may not need any tags at all. Overuse of the "he said"/"she said" tag becomes monotonous.

However, better than "he said" or "she said" is the *action tag*. *Action tags* show body motions, facial expressions, voice intonations—any physical action of the character. Action tags produce stronger writing by giving the dialogue impact:

> "John." She touched his arm. "I want to talk with you."
> His mouth twisted. "Really? You never worried about that before."
> "Please."
> He walked to the window, then turned. "I just want to forget everything that ever happened between us."
> "John—"
> He strode to the door. "Goodbye, Susan. Try those tricks on someone else. I've had enough." The door slammed behind him.

When it is apparent who is speaking, a tag may not be necessary. In the line "John—" it is clear that Susan is speaking and that she has been interrupted.

Often the "he said"/"she said" can be deleted to produce a stronger tag:

> First draft: "I want to go to the party," she said, avoiding her mother's eyes.
>
> Edited version: "I want to go to the party." She avoided her mother's eyes.
>
> First draft: "You've always hated me," Ann said in a cutting voice.
>
> Edited version: Ann spoke in a cutting voice. "You've always hated me."
>
> First draft: "I want a divorce," Harry said angrily. Then he put his newspaper down on the table.
>
> Edited version: "I want a divorce." Harry slammed the newspaper down on the table.

Stagger Your Tags

If you use a tag before the first line of dialogue, then put a tag either in the middle of the next line of dialogue or after it:

She turned to him. "Andy, I love you."
"I love you, too," he said. "But I have things to work out."
"What things?" she asked, her hands trembling.

Avoid Overuse of Adverb Tags

Adverbs are modifiers, words which usually end in *-ly: wonderingly, seemingly, angrily, softly.*

Both Mark Twain and Ernest Hemingway felt that writing with nouns and verbs produced the strongest prose. Adverbs can become a crutch. They tell the reader *what to feel* rather than let the reader directly experience what is being said. If the dialogue is written correctly, the emotions of the speaker are usually evident. Also, adverbs slow dialogue.

The purpose of the adverb tag is to clarify ambiguous dialogue: " 'I know you want to sell the house,' Will said sarcastically." Here, the actual line of dialogue denotes no emotion; the adverb tag is *needed* to reveal Will's feelings. On the other hand an adverb tag is not needed in the line: " 'Oh, Joe, I'm so happy to see you!' she said joyfully." In this case, the dialogue expresses the emotion, and the tag is superfluous.

Overuse of adverb tags produces unbelievable and often comic dialogue:

> "Don't shoot!" he said fearfully.
> She released the safety and said threateningly, "I've wanted to do this for years."
> "I know." He smiled wonderingly. "It's always amazed me."
> Her eyes glinted vengefully. "Has it?"
> "Don't you care about me at all?" he asked feelingly.
> "No," she said murderously. And she pulled the trigger.

Avoid Excessive Use of Tags

Overuse of tags also tends to produce a comic effect. The reader inevitably begins to focus on the tags themselves instead of the dialogue:

> The window opened, and the young man looked up, startled, as she swung inside. "Hello," he gasped.
> She laughed. "We meet again."
> "Yes," he trembled, white-faced. "I thought—" he began.
> "We all think," she murmured.
> "No," he growled, "I didn't mean that."
> "Of course you did," she hissed.
> "Please," he whimpered.
> "Be quiet," she whispered, taking the German Mauser from her purse.
> "You're going to kill me!" he shrieked.
> "What makes you think so?" she chortled.
> "Good grief," he coughed (he had a cold). "Please, I want to live," he faltered.
> "You should have thought of that before!" she shouted.

"Just kill me and stop the screaming," he grunted.

"Ah, Henry, it's come to this," she sighed.

Seeing her hesitate, he grabbed the Mauser from her hand and it went off, killing the pound of pork chops on the table. "Bang," banged the Mauser.

"Oh, my lunch," he groaned.

"It's over, isn't it?" she moaned.

"Yes," he intoned, "it really is—especially my lunch."

Avoid Irrelevant Dialogue

When you are building a dramatic scene, only use dialogue that effectively forwards the action. Don't interrupt building action:

"My God—the fire is starting to spread! Get that hose over there."

"Right away. Say, did I tell you I won twenty bucks at poker last night?"

"No kidding? What kind of hand you have?"

"Four jacks."

"Lucky guy."

All of the *drama and tension* of the scene has been killed by the irrelevant dialogue, which produces a comic effect. Yet, if the dialogue of the characters had reflected the frantic action to put out the fire, the scene would have had greater dramatic impact.

On the other hand, irrelevant dialogue *is* often used in comedy. The firemen bantering about cards while they are putting out a fire points up the funny and irrational side of life. This technique was often seen in the TV comedy "M*A*S*H," when the medics performed critical surgery while telling jokes.

Avoid Ping-Pong Dialogue

Ping-pong dialogue is dialogue that shows no emotional reactions to what is being said. The result is an unnatural sequence of dialogue. Playwrights and scriptwriters most often fall into the trap of using Ping-Pong dialogue when writing novels because they are not used to using tags to signal the characters' emotions. Actors convey these emotions. But the novelist does not have the advantage of a living actor who is visually seen; instead, the novelist must indicate the emotions that the characters feel. Observe the unnaturalness in the following example of Ping-Pong dialogue:

"Edith, I wish I didn't have to be the one to tell you. My dear, your husband has just been killed in an automobile accident."

"I can't believe it."

"It's a terrible thing."

"But I just talked to him—only a few minutes ago. On the phone."

"Yes, that's what makes it so awful."

"What am I going to do now?"

"Somehow, you'll come through this."

To make this dialogue more lifelike, have the characters *react* to each other:

> Dr. Harris put down the telephone receiver and raised his head sadly. He turned to his receptionist. In spite of his shock, he tried to keep his voice level, supportive. "Edith, I wish I didn't have to be the one to tell you. Edith, my dear, your husband has just been killed in an automobile accident."
> She stared at him. "I can't believe it."
> "It's a terrible thing." He realized what he'd said was trite, but all he could do was murmur useless things.
> She stood there, shaking her head. "But we just talked, only a few minutes ago. On the phone." She looked at him as if he could do something, could return her husband to life—as he had with so many other patients.
> "Yes," he said, feeling her pain. "That's what makes it so awful."
> "What am I going to do?" she whispered.
> He put his arm around her. "Somehow, you'll come through this."

Now the reader understands the emotions that the characters are feeling. Reactions are particularly needed when the characters are involved in traumatic situations. For example, if a character said, "I'm going to kill you," the other character would hardly give a simple response of "Don't, please." Emotion must be shown. What visceral feelings are both characters experiencing? These enhance the dialogue, make it real.

To avoid Ping-Pong dialogue, read the dialogue aloud, and as you say it note the kind of feelings you experience. *Act out your dialogue and reflect your feelings in your tags.*

Avoid Contrived Dialogue

Contrived dialogue is unnatural dialogue that conveys excessive amounts of information. You should use dialogue to give information which will help move the plot forward, but don't overdo it:

> "Why, Leonard, I haven't seen you since high school—right after your parents were killed in that air crash in San Diego, when a navy jet flew into that 747 and 250 people died, and you had to go to work selling vacuum cleaners and so were prevented from going to medical school."
> "Yes," said Leonard, "it was terrible I could not pursue my education at Johns Hopkins, to specialize in pediatrics. I lost my job selling vacuum cleaners and ended up in sewing machines. But I was fortunate to marry Susie Edwards and have four fine children, and we now have a nice home in Brentwood, a new Datsun, and two Irish setters."

The point is, of course, no one talks like this. Yet many writers are guilty of packing so many facts into dialogue that conversation which should be natural sounds artificial and mechanical.

Don't Use Dialogue to Show Off
Your Oversize Vocabulary

A reader who has to reread what you've said two or three times to figure out the meaning, will likely just put the book down in disgust. Even if you're writing science fiction, don't have your character say:

> "Consequently, exploration of the outer planetoidal bodies is certainly feasible because of the supermicrominiaturization of wave-length patterns in the communicational configuration of space craft."

A little technical jargon may be necessary, but don't become incomprehensible.

Avoid Meaningless Dialogue

Dialogue should characterize, give information, or advance the action of the plot in some way. Avoid dialogue that does not have a purpose:

> "Hello, Jim—how are you?"
> "Fine. And you?"
> "Oh, getting along."
> "Well, nice to see you."
> "Sure, you too."

This kind of dialogue tells the reader nothing. Notice how the dialogue could be pointed to show the reader much more about the situation and even build suspense.

> "Jim, I—I never figured you'd still be working here at the old hardware store. How you doing?"
> "Fine. Been here over twenty years now. And you?"
> "Oh—I ... I'm getting along. Money's tight, though. I lost my job."
> "You need a loan to tide you over, Bill?"
> "No—I got plans. Big plans. I—I didn't know you were still working here. Look, I've got to run along. It was good to see you."
> "Sure, you too. But remember what I said about the money. Hell, we're old friends. Stay out of trouble, okay?"

Reading the more pointed dialogue, we've learned that:

1. Jim is very stable in occupation, working at the hardware store for more than twenty years.
2. Bill is out of a job and needs money. His "big plans" sound phony.
3. Jim is generous, and he is concerned about Bill.

If actions are added to the dialogue, the situation becomes more clear.

> Jim saw the unshaven man sidling up to the counter between the aisles of nails, screws, and chains, saw the man's hand inside his windbreaker, as if he had a gun hidden there. The fellow looked at him, startled.
>
> "Jim—I … I never figured you'd still be working here at the old hardware store. How you doing?" He pulled his hand awkwardly from his jacket.
>
> The voice took Jim back to his high school days—Bill Steele! "Fine. Been here over twenty years now. And you?"
>
> "Oh—I … I'm getting along. Money's tight, though. I lost my job."
>
> Jim saw the deep lines in his face, the dark shadows under his eyes. "You need a loan to tide you over, Bill?"
>
> "No—I got plans. Big plans." He patted his jacket, then he flushed. "I—I just didn't know you were still working here." He turned evasively. "Look, I've got to run along. It was good to see you."
>
> "Sure, you too," said Jim uneasily. "But remember what I said about the money. Hell, we're old friends. You stay out of trouble, okay?"

The added "action" makes it fairly certain that Bill was going to hold up the hardware store but did not because the clerk was his old friend. Jim realizes what Bill had intended to do and not only tries to help him, but also warns him.

Use Dialogue to Punctuate Action

Dialogue gives life, realism, a sense of human presence, and tension to action scenes:

> The truck careened into the intersection, smashed into a white Toyota, then spun off toward the curb. Amy saw it coming toward them. "Jump!" she screamed, pushing her sister. "Oh, my God—it's going to get us!"

Use Dialogue for Ironic Counterpoint

Sometimes you can use dialogue to ironically counterpoint a situation or a thought passage:

> He had felt so desolate since Karen died. The world was gray, absolutely gray. Even the birds had stopped singing. The hours seemed as heavy as anvils. "Good morning, Mr. Graham," he heard someone say. "Isn't it a lovely day, so green and fresh."

The mundane, cheerful remarks ironically contrast with the character's gloomy mood.

Use Dialogue Repetitively with Variation

You can also use dialogue *repetitively* to emphasize ideas, places, and situations and to establish characterization.

> "What do you want to do, Sal?
> "I don't know what I want to do."
> "Well, we've got to do something."
> "Like what?"
> "Look, you just can't let the kid take the fall when you know who killed the old man."
> "Why can't I?"
> "It isn't right."
> "Who says it isn't right?"
> "I'm not God, but I know when something isn't right."

Repetitive dialogue is an often-used technique, so be very careful in using it. Many contemporary writers avoid it.

Use Dialogue as a Transition

You can use dialogue to bridge scenes:

> "I met Harry at three, just before they found his body. He was standing at the corner, near the street sign. He looked terribly worried. He said he was going to meet a woman named Rose. We talked a moment, and then I left. I waved and saw a lovely brunette crossing the street, walking toward him. How can I tell the police about the woman? Harry's wife will take it badly."
> "You don't have any choice. The police lieutenant is waiting."

Here, the first character recounts what's just happened: Harry's death. His friend's remarks act as a transition to the next scene, the meeting with the police lieutenant.

Use Contrapuntal Dialogue to Build Suspense

Contrapuntal dialogue is a dialogue sequence in which two or more characters talk about different things at the same time. It is an excellent technique to use in big scenes. Shakespeare often used it in his mad scenes. Lillian Hellman used it to advantage in "The Little Foxes" to show Birdie's emotional alienation from her family. While Ben, Regina, and Oscar discuss Regina's future, Birdie thinks about the family manor, Lionnet:

BIRDIE:	I should like to have Lionnet back. I know you own it now, but I should like to see it fixed up again, the way Mama and Papa had it. Every year it used to get a nice coat of paint—Papa was so very particular about the paint—and the lawn was so smooth all the way down to the river, with the trims of zinnias and red-feather plush. And the figs and blue little plums . . . .
BEN:	That's a pretty picture, Birdie. Might be a pleasant way to live. (Dismissing Birdie) What do you want, Regina?
BIRDIE (happily):	I could have a cutting garden. Just where Mama's used to be. Oh, I do think we could be happier there . . . . "
BEN:	What do you want, Regina?
REGINA:	I'm going to Chicago. And when I'm settled there and know the right people and the right things to buy—because I certainly don't know now—I shall go to Paris and buy them . . . .
BIRDIE:	Oscar, please let me have Lionnet back.
OSCAR (to Regina):	You are serious about moving to Chicago?
BEN:	She is going to see the great world and leave us in the little one. Well, we'll come and visit you and meet all the great and be proud you are our sister.
REGINA:	Certainly. And you won't even have to learn to be subtle, Ben. Stay as you are. You will be rich, and the rich don't have to be subtle.
OSCAR:	But what about Alexandra? She's seventeen. Old enough to be thinking about marrying.
BIRDIE:	And Oscar, I have one more wish. Just one more wish.
OSCAR:	What is it, Birdie? What are you saying?
BIRDIE:	I want you to stop shooting. I mean, so much. I don't like to see animals and birds killed just for the killing. You only throw them away.
BEN (to Regina):	It'll take a great deal of money to live as you're planning, Regina.
REGINA:	Certainly. But there'll be plenty of money. You have estimated the profits very high.

It's obvious in this dialogue sequence that Birdie is not involved in the conversation of the others; and the dialogue reveals her gentle, withdrawn nature in contrast to the more dominating personalities of Ben, Regina, and Oscar, who control her.

Beside revealing character, contrapuntal dialogue creates suspense. The reader is interested in Birdie's attempt to "get Lionnet back." Only everyone keeps ignoring her and they talk about everything else but that.

Use Dialogue to Enliven Static, Narrative Pages of Writing

Dialogue freshens a manuscript, gives it the breath of life. Juice up pages of narrative with *scenettes,* miniature scenes that use a few lines of dialogue. It's a good rule of thumb to have at least a line of dialogue on every page or to use thoughts which act as dialogue.

The scenette can be very brief:

> He thought about Hong Kong, the slender tour guide with black, straight cut hair. "Are you going to Guilin?" she asked.
>
> "No," he replied. Now he wished he'd gone. Coming home had been a mistake.

Summary

1. Avoid stilted, unnatural dialogue. Don't worry about being grammatically incorrect.
2. When writing dialect, try to capture cadence and rhythm rather than misspell words. If you're trying to evoke a particular nationality or race, use a few interspersed foreign words. However, don't overuse them, for you may become incomprehensible to the reader.
3. Be sure your dialogue is *appropriate* for your character.
4. Avoid overuse of the "he said"/"she said" tag by using action tags or by not using a tag at all.
5. Stagger your tags.
6. Avoid overuse of adverb tags.
7. Avoid excess tags. Strive to let the dialogue speak for itself.
8. Don't use irrelevant dialogue that distracts the reader from the action.
9. Avoid Ping-Pong dialogue.
10. Avoid contrived dialogue.
11. Don't try to show off your vocabulary.
12. Avoid meaningless dialogue that doesn't advance the action in some way, give information, or characterize.
13. Do use dialogue to punctuate action.
14. Use dialogue for ironic counterpoint.
15. Don't forget that dialogue can be used as a transition.
16. Enliven static pages of narrative with interspersed lines of dialogue or thoughts that act as dialogue.
17. Strive to develop nuance.

Exercises

1. Go to a cafeteria, a restaurant, and listen to people talking. Notice the cadence in people of different ethic groups. Write a dialogue passage for a: Hispanic, a black person, a Jewish person, a person of Irish descent. Compare them. If you leave off the ethic label, can someone else identify the particular ethnic group?

2. Write a dialogue passage using two people. Reveal the character of the two people, but do not use any tags or narration.

3. Write a dialogue passage, using narration and tags, that gives a good deal of information without being contrived.

4. Write a dialogue passage that uses contrapuntal dialogue.

5. Write a dialogue sketch using dialogue that punctuates action.

6. Write a dialogue sketch that uses dialogue to ironically counterpoint a situation or thought passage.

6

How to Develop a Good Style

Style is the unique expression of a writer—the *way* he or she says a thing. Can style be developed? Yes and no. In one sense, style is not developed from something that is not there in the first place; perhaps it is more correct to say that style can be *revealed*. For every writer has a definite personality, a definite manner of expression. What must happen is that the writer's style be cleared of impediments so the personality can shine through the writing in a natural, vital way.

Impediments That Prevent Good Style

The major things that weaken style are the use of language and punctuation. First of all, any writer who is serious about writing should be sure of his or her grammar skills. Editors have always been and will always be sophisticated and well educated. In today's competitive writing market, the writer must have *top skills*. You can't write well if you can't spell or punctuate. You need language skills to communicate. If they are less than adequate, admit it and take a remedial English class at your local high school or college; evening classes are generally available. Don't hide your head in a basket and think that editors will overlook your writing skills. They won't—and they won't have a copy editor go over your entire manuscript and correct it, either. In today's market, your work will have to be as perfect as possible to even get an editor to *look* at it.

What Exactly Do We Mean by "The Use of Language"?

Simply, the writer must be able to use words effectively to evoke in the reader the events and mood he or she wants to convey. Naturally, spelling and punctuation errors mar the effect the author wants to achieve. But many elements enter into the use of language.

The Generalization Trap

One of the main mistakes a new writer often makes is *generalizing* too much. A new writer is often inclined to describe the heroine as a "beautiful" woman. But what is a beautiful woman? If I ask you to close your eyes right now and then tell me what you see, you will find that you don't *see* anything—or, if you do, you are probably visualizing a woman whom you know or have seen; but *that* woman is not what the writer had in mind. Then, if you turn that new writer's page, you discover that he or she has added some further description, and the woman is indeed different from what you had imagined. This discrepancy usually jogs the reader out of the book and leaves him or her annoyed.

The great trick in writing is to keep the reader wholly involved in the book, for once the reader puts the book down he or she is unlikely to pick it up again. What every writer should strive for is to excite the reader so that the book is so good it can't be put down.

To keep the reader involved, the writer must use specific language that gives visual pictures and involves the reader's emotions. The writer must create a word picture so that the reader can *see* what the writer means, feel what the writer feels.

Rather than using a catch-all phrase like "beautiful," the writer should actively describe the woman so that the reader understands the woman is beautiful: "She had leaf-green eyes, black, black hair, and that peculiar translucent skin known only to the Irish. A faint blush reddened her high cheekbones, and her lips were full and soft."

Paint a picture in words of what you see.

If you get nothing more out of this book than the idea that "a picture is worth a million words," you will have learned a great deal about being a good writer.

A good exercise is to take a descriptive paragraph you've just written and analyze it for specific detail. Several years ago, a student asked for advice on his writing. The first part of his descriptive sketch read:

> A steady stream of water fell over the beautiful rocks to the bottom of the falls where it traveled on till soaked up by the ocean or the ground.

When I asked him what he meant by "beautiful" rocks, he quickly answered in specifics: red volcanic rock. Upon being prodded as to the shape of the rock, he replied: a ridge of red volcanic rock. When prodded further about the "color" of the water, he thought a moment and then said that it "frosts white," and he added that it fell to a shadowed streambed below. Now if you put what he actually *saw* in words, it would read:

> The water frosts white over the ridge of red volcanic rock, falling to the shadowed streambed below.

If you compare the two paragraphs, it is obvious which is the stronger. The point is that every writer sees detail quite clearly; yet in the case of many new writers, that information stays *in their heads* and never makes it to the written page. But the reader is not in your head and does not have your experience; all the reader can do is get impressions from the words you have written—and if your words are not "true," then the picture will not be true. Obviously, the greatest of challenges for a writer is to get what he or she has experienced out of the head and onto the page.

In a beginning writing class, if you asked the students to go down to the ocean and watch the ferry come in, many of the sketches would read: "Some gulls were flying over the dock as the ferry came in."

But here's how John Dos Passos wrote such a description in *Manhattan Transfer:*

> Three gulls wheel above the broken boxes, orange rinds, spoiled cabbage heads that heave between the splintered plank walls, the green waves spume under the round bow as the ferry, skidding on the tide, crashes, gulps the broken water, slides, settles slowly into the slip. Handwinches whirl with jingle of chains. Gates fold upwards, feet step out across the crack, men and women press through the manure-smelling wooden tunnel of the ferryhouse, crushed and jostling like apples fed down a chute into a press.

Compare the "generalized" description to Dos Passos' "specific" description. Again, which is stronger? In the first instance the new writer tells us about "some gulls"; but it's hard to visualize "some" gulls. Notice that Dos Passos writes, "three gulls," and the number engages the mind and enables the mind to create an image. He also shows the three gulls "wheeling" in flight. He creates a word picture. He shows, too, the water: green, littered with broken boxes and orange rinds. His image conveys "garbage," and the "spoiled cabbage heads" and the "orange rinds" engages not only appeals to the sense of seeing but also that of smelling: you can *smell* the garbage.

"Splintered plank walls" engages the sense of touch. "Handwinches whirl with jingle of chains" engages the sense of hearing. Dos Passos uses words like *spume, crashes*, and *gulps*, to give a sense of motion. He uses alliteration—the ferry "slides, settles slowly into the slip"—to make the reader *feel* the motion of the ferry. Moreover, all of the images together create a tone, a mood of *pessimism*. This is not going to be a happy book—not with all the garbage and people crushed like apples, their blood being drained from them.

Notice, too, how every word in this passage contributes not only to a specific visual picture but also to a central mood. The point is that no writer can afford to describe randomly or to use generalizations that cause flat writing.

Generalizations are always caused by not really looking at what you see. "Freshness" in writing is always achieved by writing *exactly* what you see, by using the precise words that capture the experience. In Galway Kinnell's poem "The Avenue Bearing the Initial of Christ into the New World," note the precise imagery in this stanza:

> In the pushcart market on Sunday
> A crate of lemons discharges light like a battery.
> Icicle-shaped carrots that through black soil
> Wove away lie like flames in the sun.
> Onions with their shirts ripped seek sunlight . . . .

Images like these make most writers bang their heads in desᵢ r and say, "Why didn't I think of that?" It looks so easy, so obvious. What else is a carrot but an icicle, and of course it looks like a "flame in the sun." Onions *do* look as if they have their "shirts ripped." Unfortunately, the gift of concrete observation is usually a stamp of genius. Too many writers either never see what is "true" or they overuse words and destroy the truth of what they saw.

The Trap of Excess Adjectives

Many new writers pepper their sentences with adjectives, trying to capture what they saw, but excess adjectives weaken a sentence and take its force away. Rather than adjectives, Hemingway advocated the use of nouns and verbs; and he said that verbs were the "guts" of the English language. Note how he artfully combines nouns, actions verbs, and a few well-chosen adjectives in this paragraph from *A Farewell to Arms*:

> In the late summer of that year we lived in a house in a village that looked across the river and the plain to the mountains. In the bed of the river there

were pebbles and boulders, dry and white in the sun, and the water was clear and swiftly moving and blue in the channels. Troops went by the house and down the road and the dust they raised powdered the leaves of the trees. The trunks of the trees too were dusty and the leaves fell early that year and we saw the troops; marching along the road and the dust rising, and leaves, stirred by the breeze, falling and the soldiers marching and afterward the road bare and white except for the leaves.

In this passage, too, the very rhythm of the sentences achieves the flow of water in the riverbed and the "marching" of the troops. The repetition of the word *dust* gives the reader a hot, dusty feeling, and the repetition of the word *white* in conjunction with *dry and white* and *bare and white* conveys the hidden image of dry, white bones—and death.

The problem with overusing adjectives is that the reader is inundated with modifying words and ends up getting lost in the adjectives so that the real meaning of the sentence is either not grasped or felt. If Hemingway had used adjectives wholesale, his famous passage might have read:

In the late hot summer of that terrible year we lived in a two-story Normandy cottage with green shutters and a tile roof in a small village that looked across the mighty Seine and the great vast plain to the towering purple mountains. Small, round white pebbles and great boulders glistened dry and white in the lemon-yellow sun, and the water was clear, cool, turbulent, falling in little rills here and there, and it was sparkling blue in the channels.

Obviously if Hemingway's novel had been written this way, it would never have been published. The writing is too cluttered, and the mind can't assimilate all of the description so that the paragraph has one central emotion. While a writer must be precise with description, he or she must also learn the right *balance*—how much description is needed to achieve the desired emotional effect.

The Trap of Excess Adverbs

Not only do adjectives weaken prose, but so do adverbs—modifiers which usually end in *-ly*. One adverb per paragraph is plenty. Consider the following passage:

He looked at her smilingly as she joyfully rose and walked to him liltingly. He kissed her passionately, and she sighed wonderingly. They were happily and marvelously in love—and arm in arm they walked ecstatically (and sickeningly) on the sand.

The point is, don't overuse adjectives and adverbs to pad sentences in which nouns and verbs haven't been precisely chosen. Rather, look for the *right* noun and verb and let them carry the weight of the sentence.

The Cliché Trap

Clichés—trite, overused phrases—also rob the paragraph of its power. The phrase "her cheeks were red as roses" is such a phrase. The very first time it was used (probably 3000 B.C.), it perhaps evoked a powerful image—skin textured like a soft, velvety flower petal, delicately veined—but the image has been used so often that the reader's mind is no longer stimulated to make that comparison. A common cliché that most new writers use is "chills ran up and down my spine," and when told it is a cliché they usually reply: "But that's what happens, isn't it?" The answer in most cases is no. The writer has just read that phrase somewhere. The best way to avoid clichés is to: (1) be aware of what they are, (2) avoid *any* phrase that comes to mind too easily, (3) and try to write exactly how *you* feel in that given situation. Rather than use a catch-all phrase, note exactly how you react when you're extremely frightened. It might be something like: "He trembled, listening to the pounding of his heart." What *you* see, what *you* feel, will always be more original than what another writer "saw" or "felt" years ago.

Today we are inundated by clichés on the radio, on TV, and in movies and in the newspaper. The only way to free yourself from clichés is to tune into yourself and to honestly write what *you* experience—in much the same way as an artist sets up an easel near the ocean and paints what *he or she* sees.

Children have a remarkable ability to see truly. Two-year-olds drop marvelous phrases—for example, saying that twigs look like "witches' fingers." Of course, twigs look like that. But why can't *we* see so clearly? Well, we probably once did; but the media and the writing of other people put a veneer over our own thinking. Yet the writer, if he or she means to construct powerful prose, must strip that veneer away.

It is true, however, that sometimes one can play off a cliché by revising it or adding to it. For example, "He looked gentle as a lamb, only he was really a pit bull." A cliché can also be used ironically, "Who does she think she is, the Queen of Sheba?"

The Trap of Archaic Words

Archaic words also weaken prose. Generally, people who enjoy reading period literature often fall into this trap. They read writers like Longfellow, Wordsworth, and James Fenimore Cooper and pick up words that are now out of date: *ere, oft, forsooth, whilst, whence.* However, one of the main tasks of writing is to try to capture the time in which you live, and so you should use the language of your time. Even in historical writing archaic words will strangle your writing. Remember that it's very hard for a twentieth-century reader to identify with archaic language; in fact, he or she may very well have never even heard of those words—which in effect will probably make your sentences meaningless.

It's good advice to write the way you talk—what words do *you* use? When was the last time you heard someone actually say "whence" or "albeit"? If you argue that in historical novels such words are regularly used, you will find that the better writers seldom use archaic words. Rather, they are more likely to sprinkle a few well-chosen expressions of the time (unusual ones) to give a flavor of the period. They also try, through cadence, to catch that flavor. Note in this paragraph from Fabian Davenport's Regency novel *The Rose of Devon* how the language catches the stilted flavor of the Regency period:

> "Aye, that I do," Lang'l agreed. "That missus of mine could talk the horns off a tin bull. But she's a fine lady."

Note, too, that the name *Lang'l* helps to establish the time of the novel.

Another archaic word to avoid is "thus," even in term papers. Try to find a fresher connective term.

The Trap of Inflated Language

Some writers are proud of their vocabularies and like to show them off. But inflated language—the use of words that are beyond the average reader's comprehension—does not impress the reader. Instead, such language turns the reader off, and he or she stops reading. The sentence "As he cogitated, he saw her shining countenance image in a phantasmal diorama in his mind" might be better understood by the reader if it were put more simply: "As he reflected, her shining face imaged in his mind."

Remember that if a reader doesn't understand a word, you might as well write *bltfzkkk* for all the meaning it will convey. One of the most important tasks of writing is to select the *exact* word that will convey the desired emotion. No writer can afford to use words that only a very few people understand. As Mark Twain and Hemingway both said: "Why use a quarter word when you can use a nickel one instead?"

The Slang Trap

It's a good idea to avoid slang, too. Slang not only dates a work, but often its meaning is lost over the years. Mark Twain tried to faithfully reproduce the actual slang the miners used during the gold rush; however, the modern reader is not able to understand the slang, and so some of Twain's short stories and novels are incomprehensible. Yet his *Huckleberry Finn* and *Tom Sawyer*, which were written in simple, unadorned English, remain classics.

The Flat-Phrase Trap

Flat phrases are ready-made phrases which do not evoke any new ideas or sensations. The flat phrase is made up of clichés:

> Amy Harrison is back from her trip, tired but happy and glad to be back. She visited many lovely spots of interest and historical sites in our great land—majestic mountains, the great rivers of the United States, and the great battlefields where history was made.

The writer, by using catch-all phrases, has not told the reader anything. "Tired but happy," "glad to be back," "many lovely spots of interest" are all clichéd phrases. Where *exactly* did Amy go? Did she visit Mount Shasta, Gettysburg? Mountains are always majestic, and many rivers are great—but what else can you say about them? Be specific!

The Surface-Glaze Trap

Less obvious than the flat phrase is the surface glaze. At first reading, the surface glaze seems professional—until you realize that the writer hasn't really said anything.

> John walked through the fields. Birds flew overhead, and clouds drifted by in the sunshine. Around him was the smell of hay. Beyond the wood he saw the outlines of the village, and he began to think of Ann, of their past life, of all the things they had done.

In the surface glaze, the style is more flowing, and the words fit with one another; but the words form a veneer that hides the lack of meaning. The words do not evoke any reaction from us. There aren't any new perceptions regarding the landscape or the character's mood. The words are not specific enough to create any new insights or to evoke any feelings in us. How *many* birds flew overhead; what kind of birds were they? Clouds have shapes; also, what kind of clouds were they—dark rain clouds, high cumulous clouds, clouds that sailed by like battleships? What does hay smell like? What kind of village is the hero going toward—a New England village, a small western village of weathered-board stores, a Mexican village with red tile roofs, an Indian village of dusty adobe houses? Each of these villages has a different kind of architecture. If you examine this passage closely, you'll see how devoid of meaning it is.

The Purple-Patch Trap

Of all the traps, the one most writers jump joyously into is the purple patch. This paragraph or page is the one the writer loves most. He's spent hours, days, weeks, rewriting it. He adores every word. The problem is—it's overwritten.

Stephen went to the canvas. He examined it carefully. It was a portrait of a harlequin—elongated, beautifully done, broadly stroked. The background was black. The head was a ghostly greenish-white scarred by thick red lips that twisted ominously, frighteningly. The satin costume of diamonds had a diabolic snake-like quality, sinuous and gleaming. But Stephen's eyes kept returning to the face—the black, beady eyes sunk in the decaying flesh … hypnotic eyes … serpent eyes. Yet the hellish thing was the human quality imbued in the features—the incongruity of the ruffled neckpiece. And down in the right-hand corner—blood. All the more awful because it was not flaming crimson that oozed from the clenched hand, but three drops of gray—blood from the soul.

The purple patch needs to be ruthlessly pruned of excess description. Hemingway once said that if you've spent an inordinate amount of time writing what you believe to be a superlative passage, the best thing you can do is to write a big X over it. If you don't, your editor most certainly will.

The purple patch is guilty of *sentimentality*. "Purple" does not necessarily mean "sickeningly sweet" but rather that the writing is weakly emotional and overstresses the feeling that the author meant to convey. Often editors and teachers will scrawl "Too much" over the offending paragraph.

The Punctuation Trap

Too many writers try to depend on punctuation for effect, rather than let the sentence itself convey the meaning; also, some writers do not understand punctuation devices such as the ellipsis, the dash, the exclamation point, and comma structure.

Ellipses The ellipsis has three dots (…), and when it is used at the end of a sentence it has three dots plus the period that would have ended the sentence (. . . .). In dialogue, ellipses indicates the voice falling off. "Oh, Joel … don't go." (**Note, too, the white spaces around the ellipsis.** The ellipsis is like a word and needs spacing between it and the preceding and following words.) Don't get into the habit of filling up your dialogue with ellipses. Many fine writers never use them at all.

The dash Another overused punctuation device is the dash. Some writers have "dash-itis." The dash is very showy punctuation, and here a little goes a long way. In dialogue, the dash indicates that the voice is broken off sharply: "Joel, don't—" Here, it indicates emotional intensity. It can also indicate that the speaker is interrupted. The dash is also used to connect phrases. "Joel, please—put down the gun!" In exposition, a sentence might read: "The flames licked up—a flaming spear fell at his feet." Note that **the dash connects the word before it to the word after it.** Leave no white spaces around the dash. One dash per paragraph is plenty, and some writers feel that one per page is too much. In a typed manuscript use two dashes to indicate a dash. The dashes will be set as a solid line when material is typeset. One dash is a hyphen. Example: Twenty-four.

The exclamation point   The exclamation point is used to signify strong emotion, but it becomes boring when overused: " 'Oh, James!' Lizzy cried. 'I'm so happy to see you!' She gestured to the sofa. 'Oh, darling! Do sit down; I want so to talk with you! I can't tell you how much I've missed you!' " This kind of writing wears the reader out. Lizzy sounds like a jumping jack. Actually, the sentences would convey her joy at seeing James if the exclamation points were removed. The exclamation point should be saved to show extreme emotion and should be only rarely used.

The comma   In the main, commas are used to connect a phrase to a sentence, to separate items in a series, and to set off elements (such as names) that interrupt the structure of the sentence. Commas should not be used arbitrarily to signify pauses in the sentence that the writer wants to indicate. Some writers put ten to twelve commas in a sentence, wherever they feel pauses are needed. If you have a comma problem, study a grammar handbook for advice on the various uses of the comma. But perhaps an old journalistic trick can be of some immediate help. Note the sentence: "The sea, blue, green, is quiet." The adjectives *blue* and *green* modify *sea* and are "nonrestrictive" in that they occur between the first and last comma in the sentence. If the sentence is constructed correctly, this nonrestrictive material can be deleted, and the remaining words should make a complete sentence: "The sea [, blue, green,] is quiet" = "The sea is quiet." You can test your sentences by making sure that the phrase before the first comma and the phrase after the last comma makes a complete sentence. For example, consider this sentence: "She went to the door, her heart fluttering, her mouth dry, her hands trembling, and her fingers closed on the doorknob." The sentence tests out. If you like to write long sentences, this simple technique may help.

The semicolon   Another punctuation device often misused is the semicolon. Its primary use is to connect two complete sentences to each other: "He went into the department store; it was musty inside." Do not use the semicolon to connect a phrase to a complete sentence: "He was hungry; very hungry" (incorrect). In this instance a comma, a dash, or ellipses could have been used to connect the phrase "very hungry"—depending on whether the writer felt a normal pace, an intense pace, or a slower pace should be emphasized.

The semicolon can also be used to separate items in a long series, for example:

My favorite novels are Dostoyevski's *Crime and Punishment,* a novel that emphasizes moral responsibility; Fowles' *The Magus,* which discusses the alchemic transformation of man; and Conrad's *Lord Jim,* which explores the nature and consequences of evil.

The semicolons act as "breakers" between the itemized novels and also the internal commas which might confuse the reader.

This brief discussion of punctuation is not meant to take the place of an English handbook, but it may help to clean up any glaring punctuation problems.

The Sentence Monotony Trap

A writer should also be aware of sentence lengths in a paragraph. If the sentences are too long, the paragraph will put the reader to sleep; if they are too short, the reader will feel a stacatto affect, although you definitely want short, pithy sentences for action scenes, especially fight scenes. To avoid monotony, *balance* your paragraphs by combining a long sentence with a medium sentence and then a short sentence.

Also, don't construct all of your sentences in the same way. Vary the placement of your subjects and verbs so that the monotony is broken up.

The *Was* and *Were* Trap

One of the best ways to strengthen prose is to eliminate the words *was* and *were.* They are paragraph killers and cause the events to be told. The author is talking *about* something or someone. By substituting an action verb, the writer is *showing* what is happening in action. It is better to say "I walked" than "I was walking." On the other hand, if you want to slow the pace of a paragraph you might wish to deliberately use *was.*

For example, if you were writing a short story about a very old man with a cane, you might say: "He was walking very slowly, he was leaning on his cane, and his chest was pumping up and down." Here the *wases* emphasize the slowness associated with age.

Be conscious of *was* and *were.* Prune them out. It's a good exercise to take a page or two of your writing and circle all the verbs *was* and *were;* then substitute action verbs and see how much stronger your writing reads. As a writing teacher and former agent, I have observed that this single polishing technique remarkably improves the work of most writers trying to publish.

Unfortunately, many new writers and professional writers in fields such as technical writing have learned to use the passive voice instead of the active voice. The active voice is strong and has a vitality. For example: "He shot the terrorist." Here, the subject (*he*) acted. The object (*terrorist*) received the action. The verb (*shot*) expresses that action. But in the passive voice, the subject *receives* the action: "The terrorist was shot by him." Analyze which statement is stronger.

If you use the passive voice, you should have a definite reason for doing so. Sometimes a writer may not want to reveal *who* the subject is. For example, if the X Oil Company made a $5 million profit last year, a writer who isn't interested in the name of the company might write: "A profit of millions of dollars was made last year by a comparatively small oil company."

In essence, the use of passive voice is often a definite evasion of responsibility, for in passive voice, one often doesn't know *who* did something. Consider these examples:

> The cost of the production was miscalculated.
> A letter to the school will be written.
> The suggestion was made that the department was top heavy and the work force needed to be cut.
> It was ruled that higher taxes need to be assessed.
> It was reported that water and electric bills will go up.

Of course, the reader of the evasive passive wants to shout *who* is the one causing or doing these things? The evasive passive gets committee members off the hook, and that very reason encourages its use in various reports and announcements.

Consistent use of the passive voice will definitely weaken your style. Readers do not want to muddle through a story and not know who is doing what to whom. They also prefer a character who is involved in direct action rather than an intrusive author who is *telling* them events in flat prose that uses passive verbs.

Other Devices to Improve Prose

Sentence Rhythm

A good writer uses language to give action to his or her writing and uses specific words to create the actual *movement* of what is happening. For example, note how the words in the following sentence simulate the movement of the action: "He dove under the giant waves and came to the surface gulping." Remember that the use of short stacatto sentences creates tension. Use short, pithy sentences for fight scenes:

> He jumped me from behind, I turned, smashing my fist into his stomach. I saw the raised knife and jerked back. A chain-link fence with barbed wire loomed ahead. He lumbered toward me. I kicked. He folded in two, clutched his groin. I ran past him.

Note, too, the absence of the passive verbs *was* and *were*, which would have slowed the action scene.

Dorothy Faeder, in her novel *The Queen of San Francisco,* matches sentence rhythms to the lightning storm being described:

> A second later, lightning struck the fir tree. The ground rumbled. The huge tree split in half. Searing flames ran down the forked trunk. The tree blazed, the earth trembling. Matt grabbed Fritz and they both ran, bent over, half crawling, away from the burning tree. The next blast of thunder knocked them down again. A bolt of lightning hit the big pine rooted in the pond. The trunk cracked, bursting into flames. Tongues of fire leaped and skimmed over the top of the pond, red devils writhing, careening, then sank with hissing steam into the sizzling water. The storm blazed on, the lightning going south. Thunder tagged it like a baying hound. The lightning struck further and further away now, great pillars of smoke and flame furling up into the sky, and the torrents of rain eased to a sprinkle.

Here, the words create the *passage* of the lightning storm as it blazes its way across the countryside. The first sentences are stacatto, capturing the shock of a lightning storm, and the sentences at the end of the paragraph lengthen out to show the intensity of the storm lessening.

It is also effective to combine action with dialogue, emotion, and as much characterization as possible:

> I heard the wind whipping the canvas. My God, I thought, the tent is going to go! Outside, the wind sounded like the rumble of a train engine. Then I saw the kerosene lamp tip, the flame licking out and up into the canvas. I tried to put it out, but it flared into a wall of flame. I dove under the canvas and outside. The wind caught the fire tongues and the next tent exploded into flames. I stood in the middle of an inferno. Nothing could stop it. I ran to the small clearing where other carnies gathered, and watching the tents burn I felt the angry tears in the corners of my eyes. I saw everything I'd worked for, my whole life, burning to ashes.

Note how the thoughts act as dialogue, reinforcing the action and giving the character's emotional responses to what is happening. Note too, that even in this long paragraph, no *was* is necessary.

Simile and Metaphor

You can also give additional dimension to your work by using simile and metaphor, methods of comparison. A simile uses the terms *like, as, as if,* and *seemed.* For example, "She was tall, long-legged, *like* a Las Vegas showgirl." Simile introduces an additional image that gives more depth to what is being said. In the previous description, the woman is not only tall, but it is implied that she is as striking as a Las Vegas showgirl. Simile is fairly direct, but metaphor is more subtle.

Metaphor links two dissimilar things together to form a new insight, a new feeling. Aristotle once said that it took a genius to be a master of metaphor. A metaphor does not say that something is *like* something else; it says, rather, that the thing you're discussing *is* something else:

> My thirteen-year-old daughter is a garbage disposal. Hamburgers, hot dogs, potato chips, pretzels, ice cream, candy bars, all slide in an endless stream down that yawning maw. Even now I can hear her grinding jaws.

Metaphor, because of its picture-evoking quality, is able to convey a deeper emotional feeling than words that are used in a less dramatic fashion.

Summary

When you're writing, strive for clarity of perception. Don't try to "impress" the reader with your large vocabulary and intricate sentence structure. If you do, you may be writing for yourself. Aim for simplicity of expression, but don't be childish. *Write what* **you** *see, what* **you** *feel*. Originality results from an honest, individual, thoughtful interpretation of life. Analyze what you see and be careful of the "too obvious" interpretation. The genius-writer looks at life, head cocked a little to one side, and he or she sees life differently from the way anyone else does. Develop that quality.

If you are content to look at life superficially, to use flat phrases, surface glazes, archaic expressions, inflated language, clichés, purple patches, and poor language skills, you will probably never be published. So work at your style until it is clean and powerful—until you are able to use it as an effective tool to truly **write what you see**. As Hemingway said: **"Find the authentic language of your own unique experience."**

Exercises

1. Look at a tree.
2. Look at a cloud.
3. Look at a flower.
4. Look at an animal.
5. Look at any object that interests you (a popcorn kernel, a beer bubble, a piece of chalk).
6. Write eight or ten specific descriptive sentences about the object you have chosen. Then, using your sentences, create a paragraph that carries out the mood you wish to evoke.
   Use this material and create a simile, a metaphor.

A particularly good grammar handbook is: *Handbook for Writers* (Prentice Hall), authors Leggett, Mead, and Charvat.

Cliché List

CLICHÉS OF COMPARISON

as the day is long
ate like a pig
behaved like a lamb
bigger than life
black as night
blind as a bat
blue as the sky
busy as a bee
clear as crystal
clear as mud
cold as ice
cool as a cucumber
cute as a bug's ear
dead as a doornail
deep as the ocean
drop like a hot potato
drunk as a lord
easy as pie
eager beaver
feeling your oats
filled to the brim
fought like a tiger
free as a bird
free as a breeze
fresh as a daisy
gentle as a lamb
gentle breeze
green as grass
green with envy
happy as a clam
happy as a lark
heart of gold
hot as a firecracker
hot as hell
hungry as a bear
jack of all trades
lay low

light as a feather
like a flash
like a graveyard
like walking on eggs
like water off a duck's back
naked as a jaybird
naked as the day he/she was born
out like a light
pleased as punch
pretty as a picture
pure as a lily
pure as the driven snow
purple with anger
quick as a flash
quick as a mouse
quick as a wink
quicker than you can say, "Jack Robinson"
ran like a deer
red with rage
rich as all get-out
rich as Croesus
rich as Rockefeller
silent as a tomb
slept like a log
sly as a fox
smooth as glass
smooth as silk
snug as a bug in a rug
sober as a judge
soft as silk
straight as an arrow
strong as a bull
strong as an ox
stubborn as a mule
sweet as honey
sweet as sugar
swift as a bird

DESCRIPTION CLICHÉS

absent-minded professor	matter of life or death
brilliant student	Mona Lisa smile
brink of disaster	new horizons
briny deep	remarkable technique
burning question	rich reward
burst of applause	ripe old age
busy executive	road to success
calm before the storm	sea of faces
cheeks like roses	ship of state
collapse of civilization	special occasion
dawn of hope	splendid achievement
debt of gratitude	startling phenomenon
depths of despair	straight and narrow
forests of masts	sumptuous repast
fund of knowledge	supreme sacrifice
harried housewife	tall, dark, and handsome
heart of gold	tide of events
impossible dream	trials and tribulations
laurels of victory	ultimate goal
lips like cherries	unexpected turn of events
liquid brown eyes	unknown factor
long arm of the law	unpleasant surprise
looked like a Greek god	veritable gold mine
madonna-like face	victor's crown, spoils
majestic mountains	viselike grip
man of integrity	word to the wise

7

How to Create Settings

In opening any fictional work, it's important to create the *locale* of the events: *Where* is this story taking place? Setting is the frame within which the story occurs; it can also be considered the scenic backdrop of the story. Note how Wirt Williams opens his novel *The Trojans:*

> Though the stars hold, the moon is gone. The black of sky already thins. Across the iron-dark sea the horizon is sharpening its edge. Southward from Greece the north wind blows, across the Aegean to these hills outside the walls of Troy. On the hills an army sleeps, the white points of its tents rising in row on furrow-even row from the shadowed slopes.

When Does the Setting Occur?

The setting of the story usually is shown very early, often on the first page. Remember that when you are watching a play or movie, the first thing you become aware of visually is a geographic setting—a street scene, a room in a house, a ranch in the desert, the ocean or the mountains. Also, the *time* of the story, contemporary or historical, is usually established by various clues: cars, wagons, clothes, architecture. Setting enables the reader to understand the environment in which the character is living, and it psychologically aids the reader in entering the character's mind and life. When you know where someone lives, his or her lifestyle, and his or her historical place in time, you know a great deal about that person.

Elements of Setting

To develop setting, four basic elements are essential:

1. atmosphere
2. tone
3. specific description of place
4. time

Atmosphere

Atmosphere is the *feeling* of a particular place; and the writer should try to catch in the initial images those sensations that this particular place evokes. Atmosphere helps to create authenticity of experience. Edgar Allan Poe in his "Fall of the House of Usher" creates a powerful, atmospheric image:

> During the whole of a dull, dark, and soundless day in the autumn of the year, when the clouds hung oppressively low in the heavens, I had been passing alone, on horseback, through a singularly dreary tract of country; and at length found myself, as the shades of the evening drew on, within view of the melancholy House of Usher . . . . I looked upon the scene before me—upon the mere house, and the simple landscape features of the domain, upon the bleak walls, upon the vacant eye-like windows, upon a few rank sedges, and upon a few white trunks of decayed trees—with an utter depression of soul which I can compare to no earthly sensation more properly than to the after-dream of the reveller upon opium: the bitter lapse into everyday life, the hideous dropping off of the veil. There was an iciness, a sinking, a sickening of the heart, an unredeemed dreariness of thought which no goading of the imagination could torture into aught of the sublime. What was it—I paused to think—what was it that so unnerved me in the contemplation of the House of Usher?

Examining the passage, one sees that Poe's use of words—*oppressively, melancholy, decayed, utter depression, hideous, iciness, sinking of heart, dreariness,* and *torture*—all contribute to the narrator's feelings about the House of Usher. Through these emotive words the reader is able to evoke the frightening image of the old house, and the words also accomplish a foreshadowing of terrible things to come. It is legitimate to point out here, however, that by modern standards the passage is overwritten.

Tone

Tone, the central mood of the story, reveals the author's attitude that shapes the material: humor, pessimism, optimism, irony. Note how tone, and adding a few appropriate words, can change the meaning of Poe's words:

Humor: I looked upon the scene before me ... bleak walls, upon the vacant eye-like windows—it *had* to be Dracula's pad (and me without my garlic).

Optimism: I looked upon the scene before me ... the bleak walls, upon the vacant eye-like windows—it needed a bit of work, but I knew that with painting and some brick work it would be a lovely place again.

Irony: I looked upon the scene before me ... the bleak walls, upon the vacant eye-like windows—its façade was suspiciously like that of an old lover.

It's unnecessary to give an example of pessimism, as Poe has already done that very well. But the point is that tone shapes a story and also its meaning.

As a rule, the strongest stories are those in which the tone is **consistent** throughout the work. Shifting tone is dangerous in short stories because a short story usually tries to capture one moment in time. Tone shifts are more easily accomplished in longer works, novellas, and novels. For example, Charles Dickens' *A Christmas Carol* begins pessimistically, but Scrooge does change, and the story ends optimistically. However, character changes and tonal shifts *take time* so that the change is believable. While old pros sometimes achieve an effective tonal shift in the short story—a case in point is Hemingway's "The Gambler, The Nun, The Radio"—the new writer is rarely that skillful. Most writers prefer to maintain a consistent tone, for sudden tonal shifts can shock the reader out of the story, can create a feeling of being "robbed" of a potentially good story, or can produce the feeling that the story is not credible. For example, adding a tone shift in Poe's story would destroy the unity of the tale and its whole central effect:

Yes, the House of Usher was depressing indeed; but just then the sun came out from behind the clouds, and I rode off with a song on my lips. It was going to be a wonderful day!

Specific Description of Place

Think of your setting as a stage set. What things are *absolutely essential* in order for the viewer/reader to imagine your locale? Remember that the only way a reader will be able to *see* the environment is through use of precise imagery. Note how John Steinbeck catches Cannery Row:

Early morning is a time of magic in Cannery Row. In the gray time after the light has come out and before the sun has risen, the Row seems to hang suspended out of time in a silvery light. The street lights go out, and the weeds are a brilliant green. The corrugated iron of the canneries glows with the pearly lucence of platinum or old pewter. No automobiles are running then. The street is silent of progress and business. And the rush and drag of the waves can be heard as they splash in among the piles of the canneries. It is a time of great peace, a deserted time, a little era of rest. Cats drip over the fences and slither like syrup over the ground to look for fish heads. Silent early morning dogs parade majestically picking and choosing judiciously whereon to pee. The sea gulls come flapping in to sit on the cannery roof peaks shoulder to shoulder. From the rocks near the Hopkins Marine Station comes the barking of sea lions like the baying of hounds. The air is cool and fresh. In the back gardens the gophers push up the morning mounds of fresh damp earth and they creep out and drag flowers into their holes. Very few people are about, just enough to make it seem more deserted than it is. One of Dora's girls comes home from a call on a patron too wealthy or too sick to visit the Bear Flag. Her makeup is a little sticky and her feet are tired. Lee Chong brings the garbage cans out and stands them on the curb. The old Chinaman comes out of the sea and flap-flaps across the street and up past the Palace. The cannery watch-men look out and blink at the morning light. The bouncer at the Bear Flag steps out on porch in his shirtsleeves and stretches and yawns and scratches his stomach. The snores of Mr. Malloy's tenants in the pipes have a deep tunnelly quality. It is the hour of the pearl—the interval between day and night when time stops and examines itself.

The purpose of the setting is to allow the reader to slip into an imaginary environment, to *feel* the milieu. When you are creating a setting, you should be able to see it in detail as clearly as the room in which you're writing. You need to be aware of the shapes and colors of the outdoor/indoor landscape: land mass, buildings, plants, furniture.

The reader should be able to sense:

1. the historical period
2. the season of the year
3. time of day: morning, afternoon, evening

The Historical Period

The historical period can be shown through clothing (costumes), types of transportation (horses, carriages, cars, planes), inventions (the radio, the wireless, television), and appliances (the ice box, the refrigerator, the typewriter, the computer).

The Season

The season can be indicated through clothing—sweaters, snow suits, bikinis—and through descriptions of the weather: rainy, sunny, hot, humid, snowing.

Time of Day

The time can be indicated by a clock, a wristwatch, adjectives that describe the time such as "inky dark," "soft silver grey of dawn," by stating the time: noon, twilight, or the exact hour and minute. A character can be shown eating breakfast, lunch, or dinner in a restaurant.

The Central Mood

Yet the four basic setting elements of atmosphere, tone, specific description of place, and time are always suffused with a certain mood, and the writer uses vivid, precise imagery to convey that mood.

In the Steinbeck example, note how variations of the color gray act as a unifying device to carry out the time of early morning: "the gray time," "silvery light," "pearly lucence of platinum or old pewter," "the hour of the pearl." These phrases contribute to the lonely feeling of early morning, and Steinbeck says this is a "deserted time," "the street is silent of progress and business," "it is a time of great peace." Other images—"silent early morning dogs," "cats drip over the fences," "the cannery watchmen look out and blink at the morning light," "snores of Mr. Malloy's tenants"—contribute to the interval time before daily life begins.

Try to use *unusual imagery* that stimulates the reader's mind.

Anton Chekhov contended that prosaic imagery such as "golden sunsets" evokes no response in the reader; people are too used to observing golden sunsets. Compare this flat image with Steinbeck's cats that "drip" over fences.

Setting adds reality to your story. It is not enough to merely open your story with a character in action. Compare which opening seems more "real" to you and try to analyze why:

> It was dark in the spaceship, and Landor, looking through the limscope, saw a movement below.

or

> It was dark in the spaceship, and Landor walked between the sleeping shelves of white plastic where men and women in orange space suits lay, like strange larvae in cocoons. The even hum of the land motors made the ship reverberate ever so slightly. He was a tall man, with light green skin and the violet bulbous eyes of his race, the Megatrons, and he glided a few inches over the sheening chrysolite floor. Uneasily he looked through the limscope, at the ice floes below, and saw a rippling gray shadow.

In the first example, there are not enough details to create the feeling of the spaceship or the character, and so the reader is not much interested in what happens to the character. In the second example, the detail of the orange space suits, white plastic sleeping shelves, the hum of the land motors establishes place. Also, the description of Landor gives the reader a sense of a distinct personality; he is more than a name.

Uses of Setting

Setting can be used in many ways:

1. as a means of establishing character
2. as a character
3. as a means of establishing a historical period
4. as destiny
5. as a narrative element
6. as a social protest
7. as a symbol of theme

Setting to Establish Character

An environment shapes the people who live within it. Small-town people reflect suburbia as city people reflect the metropolis. Wilbur Daniel Steele in his short story "How Beautiful with Shoes" presents his character Amarantha through setting:

> By the time the milking was finished, the sow, which had farrowed the past week, was making such a row that the girl spilled a pint of the warm milk down the trough-lead to quiet the animal before taking the pail to the well-house. Then in the quiet she heard a sound of hoofs on the bridge where the road crossed the creek a hundred yards below the house, and she set the pail down on the ground beside her bare, barn-soiled feet. She picked it up again. She set it down. It was as if she calculated its weight.

We see Amarantha through this pastoral setting. We know the routine of her life, and so we know much about her.

Setting as a Character

In the work of writers such as Giovanni Verga, Ole Rolvaag, and Hamlin Garland, setting can become a character. The land is the antagonist against which humans pit themselves. Wind, drought, and rain destroy the crops. The land bleeds people of their strength, money, and will to live. In Hemingway's *The Old Man and the Sea*, the sea is the old man's adversary. Throughout the entire novel, the sea is a great brooding female presence, and the fish are part of her essence. The old man describes the sea as:

... la mar, which is what people call her in Spanish when they love her. Sometimes those who love her say bad things of her but they are always said as though she were a woman. Some of the younger fishermen, those who used buoys as floats for their lines and had motorboats, bought when shark livers had brought much money, spoke of her as *el mar,* which is masculine. They spoke of her as a contestant or a place or even an enemy. But the old man always thought of her as feminine and as something that gave or withheld great favors, and if she did wild or wicked things it was because she could not help them. The moon affects her as it does a woman, he thought.

Setting to Establish a Historical Period

Mark Twain's "The Californian's Tale" catches the flavor of the post–Gold Rush days:

Thirty-five years ago I was out prospecting on the Stanislaus, tramping all day long with pick and pan and horn, and washing a hatful of dirt here and there, always expecting to make a rich strike, and never doing it. It was a lovely region, woodsy, balmy, delicious, and had once been populous long years before, but now the people had vanished and the charming paradise was a solitude. They went away when the surface diggings gave out. In one place, where a busy little city with banks and newspapers and fire companies and a mayor and aldermen had been, was nothing at all but a wide expanse of emerald turf, with not even the faintest sign that human life had ever been present there. This was down toward Tuttletown. In the country neighborhood thereabouts, along the dusty roads, one found at intervals the prettiest little cottage homes, snug and cozy and so cobwebbed with vines snowed thick with roses that the doors and windows were wholly hidden from sight—sign that these were deserted homes, forsaken years ago by defeated and disappointed families who could neither sell them nor give them away.

Setting as Destiny

Setting can act as the inevitable destiny that traps the character and from which there is no escape. In Giovanni Verga's short story "Consolation," the setting reveals a life that dooms the characters:

"You'll be happy but first you'll have troubles," the fortune teller had told Arlia.

Who would have imagined it when she married Manica, who had his fine barbershop on Fabbri Street, and she was a hairdresser, too—both of them young and healthy? Only Father Calogero, her uncle, hadn't wanted to bless that marriage—had washed his hands of it like Pilate, as he said. He knew they were all consumptive in his own family, from father to son, and he had been able to put a little fat on himself by choosing the quiet life of a parish rector.

"The world is full of troubles," Father Calogero preached. "It's best to keep away from it."

The trouble had come, in fact, little by little. Arlia was always pregnant, year after year, so that her clients deserted her shop, because it was sad to see her come all out of breath and cursed with that big belly. Besides, she didn't have time to keep up to date with fashions. Her husband had dreamed of a big barbershop on the Avenue, with perfumes in the window, but in vain he could go on and on shaving beards at three *soldi* each. The children became consumptive one after the other, and before going to the cemetery gobbled up the small profit of the year.

The barbershop is Arlia's world, and poverty and exhaustion destroy her and her family. The barbershop is an irrevocable destiny from which there is no escape.

Setting as a Narrative Element

When the setting is used as a narrative element, the writer gives us only as much as necessary to get into the action of the story. Saul Bellow's short story "A Father-to-Be" is a good example:

The strangest notions had a way of forcing themselves into Rogin's mind. Just thirty-one and passable looking, with short black hair, small eyes, but a high, open forehead, he was a research chemist, and his mind was generally serious and dependable. But on a snowy Sunday evening while this stocky man, buttoned to the chin in a Burberry coat and walking in his preposterous gait—feet turned outward—was going toward the subway, he fell into a peculiar state.

Bellow briefly sketches in a contemporary setting—that of a walk to the subway in the snow. It's all that is necessary for this man who is trying to decide whether he should marry his fiancée or not.

Setting as a Social Protest

Settings should be an integral part of your theme, your message, and can foreshadow the action of the story. Steinbeck's *Grapes of Wrath* described the filthy Okie work camps to show the exploitation of the workers. Dos Passos' opening passage to *Manhattan Transfer*—that of a ferry coming in to its mooring amid floating garbage, the jingle of chains, people pushing down the gangplank like apples going down a chute into a press—signals exploitation and destruction of the workers by a government that does not care about them.

In the following example, the setting provides a backdrop for the writer's social comments:

The derelicts, the shopping bag ladies, shuffle in flopping shoes as they wait in the line outside the mission. Some of them gum their lips uncomfortably as they watch the young families, the girls with crying babies in their arms, the tight lipped fathers, whose white faces lined with despair, hold the hands of strangely quiet children. A light snow dusts their faces. The line moves ahead, then stops. Inside is Christmas turkey, mashed potatoes, dressing, and pumpkin pie. A wino touches his half empty pint bottle in his back pocket. "What the hell's the country comin' to," he whispers to the man ahead of him. "They shouldn't be here. I mean, it's pretty bad when a man can't support his family no more and the kids got to stand in breadlines—why the hell we sending all our money to San Salvador?"

Setting That Symbolizes Theme

The setting of a story can be a symbol of theme. In Joseph Conrad's novella *Heart of Darkness*, the locale of Africa, usually thought of as the heart of the black nation, symbolizes the darkness of the civilized white man's heart.

Kurtz in part suggests the white man—the epitome of white civilization—who becomes exploiter and slaver, crueler and more savage than the most primitive of men. As the reader voyages into the inner recesses of Africa, he becomes aware that he is voyaging into hell to meet Kurtz, who in one aspect has become the devil.

In Bellow's "A Father-to-Be," his character Rogin goes into a delicatessen:

> Smells of pickle, sausage, mustard, and smoked fish overjoyed him. He pitied the people who would buy the chicken salad and chopped herring; they could do it only because their sight was too dim to see what they were getting—the fat flakes of pepper on the chicken, the soppy herring, mostly vinegar-soaked stale bread. Who would buy them? Late risers, people living alone, waking up in the darkness of the afternoon, finding their refrigerators empty, or people whose gaze was turned inward. The roast beef looked not bad, and Rogin ordered a pound.

Bellow's delicatessen symbolizes life: The unaware get the stale, tasteless food; but those who "see" try to get the best. Still, roast beef is hardly exotic, and Bellow indicates that contemporary life is a prosaic choice between soppy herring and roast beef.

Summary

The setting—the locale—forms the frame of your story: the "where" and "when" of the events. The initial setting of the story generally occurs very early in the story, often on the first page, in order to give a sense of place. Four basic elements are essential to setting:

1. atmosphere
2. tone
3. specific description of place
4. time

When creating setting, be aware of:

1. shapes and colors of the landscape
2. the season
3. the time of day
4. the weather
5. the historical period
6. the central mood of the story
7. striking imagery which conveys that mood

Setting can be used:

1. to establish character
2. as a character itself
3. as a device to establish a historical period
4. as destiny
5. as a narrative element
6. as a social protest
7. as a symbol

Setting is one of your most valuable ways to create "the illusion of life," and you should give much thought to exactly which elements are necessary to your story.

Exercises

1. Develop an opening paragraph that creates an atmospheric setting for a love story or a horror story.
2. Lightly sketch in setting elements in a fast-moving suspense story. Intersperse between dialogue.
3. Create a setting using an ironic tone.
4. Take two paragraphs to develop a setting, using your favorite place—a garden, the ocean, the mountains, a bar or restaurant. Try to use a few carefully chosen images that catch the feeling of the locale (reread Steinbeck's sketch of Cannery Row).
5. Develop a setting that reveals character or historical period.
6. Use setting to voice social protest.
7. Keeping a theme in mind, create a setting which symbolizes that theme.
8. Develop a scene for a humorous story.

8

How to Create the Story: Scene, Summary, and Transition

Every story has its own form and develops in its own way. The danger in the new writer's story is that he or she has a tendency to *tell* the reader too much and not "show" the events in action. That is, new writers often summarize rather than dramatize events in a *scene.* Readers, however, do not like to be *told* things; readers want to experience the story as if they were participants in the actual events.

How to Develop the Story

A story is generally told through an alternation of **scene** and **summary.** The first problem a writer faces in constructing the story is which events should be dramatized and which can be sketched in a few sentences. Think of a story as a diamond necklace: The important events are the diamonds, which are presented in **scenes,** each sparkling, each different, yet each fitting in and complementing the other diamonds. The **summary** is like the string that holds the diamonds together; it quickly relates less important, but necessary, events that link the scenes.

Scene

As you think of your story, notice that certain words begin to take shape in your mind, and then suddenly you see a vivid scene—for example, a husband and wife shouting at each other:

> Carol slammed down her coffee cup. "I want a divorce! I've had it. I never know where you are, who you're with—"
> "That's a rotten thing to say." He pushed back his chair and stood. "You're spoiled, selfish, and—" He sent his plate spinning across the table, smashing into splinters on the floor. He stopped, looking down at the broken egg yolks pooling on the linoleum floor. "If that's what you want, you've got it." Then he strode from the room.

A scene usually focuses on characters who confront one another and speak dialogue. Sometimes, though, a scene can involve only one person who is confronting a dilemma. Hemingway's old man, who pits himself against the sea and the great fish, provides a good example:

> It was on the third turn that he saw the fish first.
> He saw him first as a dark shadow that took so long to pass under the boat that he could not believe its length.
> "No," he said. "He can't be that big."
> But he was that big and at the end of this circle he came to the surface only thirty yards away and the man saw his tail out of the water . . . .
> The old man was sweating now but from something else besides the sun. On each calm placid turn the fish made he was gaining line and he was sure that in two turns more he would have a chance to get the harpoon in.
> But I must get him close, close, close, he thought.
> I mustn't try for the head. I must get the heart. "Be calm and strong, old man," he said.

Readers should feel as if they are witnessing an actual event, hearing the words, feeling the emotion behind the words, seeing the locale where the scene is set—as if *they were there.*

The scene should *build up to some kind of insight or revelation.* Avoid scenes that go no place.

A scene should be complete within itself. It has a shape: a beginning that builds to a definite result that justifies the purpose of the scene. A scene can:

1. reveal character
2. reveal important information
3. reveal the problems the character is facing

A good scene makes readers aware of the character and his or her goals, antagonists, and obstacles. A scene must have:

1. Well-delineated characters.
2. A clearly defined conflict—an encounter in which questions are asked and answered.
3. A described locale (where are we?).
4. A sense of time (contemporary, historical, the future).
5. A specific emotion expressed—anger, love, joy, resignation.
6. A definite purpose that moves the story forward or reveals character.
7. A climax, either major or minor, in which the main character either wins or loses but generally learns something. In this encounter, questions are asked and answered. Goals are asserted. In some cases, the reader may be more aware of what is revealed than is the character.

The end of the scene should point to another scene. For example, if a husband and wife are shown in a family row, the husband might shout: "I'm leaving, dammit." The next scene might show him packing his suitcase and leaving the house.

Scene reveals character and moves the plot forward. It creates the tension in a work.

When you are thinking of a story, it's a good idea to see it in a series of pictures, in segments of scenes. Visualize those scenes in detail and act them out. Become emotionally involved. Be aware of the actual emotions your character is feeling.

Make a list of those scenes and write a paragraph for each one. Sum up the main events of the scene in the paragraph. When you write the story, you will develop those scenes into much longer sequences. But in this "scenario" form, you will be able to see the design of your story. If a scene is not leading anywhere, you can delete it.

The Key Scene One of the scenes should be a key scene—it should influence the outcome of the story. The key scene does not necessarily resolve the story, but it always provides important information that leads to the resolution. New writers often make the mistake of not *playing* the key scene. For example, the fighting couple might reconcile in a love scene:

> She opened the bedroom door, saw him packing. "Tom?" He turned. "I'm sorry," she said.
> "So am I." He threw some shirts into his suitcase.
> "It's just—you're gone so much, and I get afraid sometimes."
> "Well, I'm a salesman," he said, "and that's my life." He raised his eyes, and she saw the mixture of guilt and anger. "Other women learn to put up with it. Dammit, it's all I know. It's all I'm good for. Look, you live next to your mother—you're safe enough."
> "It's not that." She shook her head. "It's what's happening between you and me. I—I just think we're going off in two different directions. And I don't want that."
> He stood there, a folded shirt in his hands. Then he dropped it on the bed.

"Neither do I," he said. They looked at each other a long while, and then he pulled her to him. "I can't quit," he said.

She felt his heart beating against hers, felt the warmth of his body. And suddenly she knew that it really didn't matter. She could put up with anything—the weekly trips to New York, Seattle. What he'd said had made it all right. She could go through it all, like every other salesman's wife.

In this story, the reconciliation of the couple is a key event; you can't just say: "They made up." You have to *show* it.

How to Show and Not Tell

Showing is dramatizing an event. Compare these two key scenes and analyze why the dramatized events are stronger in the passage marked "Showing."

Telling

It will be the first time for a successful attempt on this face of El Capitan. It doesn't really seem like a month but then the days have merged into a single moment, that moment of triumph. The food is low but then that's the way it's been for the last two weeks. What seems to hurt the most is the cold at night. Maybe I should have gone with the rescue party but then all the agony of the last weeks would have been in vain. I want to hurry now with only 200 feet left to go but know enough to go slow as the next overhang will be the roughest. Why does it have to be so damn icy when we're so close?

Dean seems to be going slower than usual. I hope he isn't having trouble. If I could only see what the hell is happening up there. Why all the slack in the rope and that shower of ice and rock falling? The sound of his breathing seems deafening and now that muffled cry.

The problem with this scene is that the writer is telling us in a very flat, uninspired way about the events going on. There aren't enough *details* to stimulate the reader's imagination so that the reader can participate in the scene. Note the effect of the rewritten scene.

Showing

He finished hammering the piton in the crevice directly above his head. Looking up past the ledge he saw the chalk-white, slate rock disappear into the clinging mist surrounding the cliff above. El Capitan. He took a deep breath, his lungs red with pain. No one had ever been this close. He felt the rope tighten in his frozen gloves as he fumbled, trying to slide the toe of his boot into the ice below. It hadn't seemed long, but all the days had combined into this moment—the final push up. As he gained his toehold he thought of the past two weeks. He had planned on only two weeks and now the food was low. He thought of steaks covered with slippery mushrooms, and lobsters with melted butter. He'd get these soon enough. What hurts most was the cold. Maybe, he thought, I should have gone with the rescue party but then all the agony of the past two weeks would have been in vain. He had to hurry now with only two hundred feet to go, but he knew enough to go slow. The next overhang would be the roughest. Why does it have to be so damn icy, he thought, when I'm so close.

The ice chips cascading around his face made him look up again. The top was out of sight, just beyond the mist. He seemed to be going slower than usual. Abruptly, he heard the sliding sound. If only he could see what the hell was happening— Just then the rope tightened with a quick jerk and another shower of ice and rock splintered against his face. The sound of his breathing seemed deafening and then he heard the slow rumble that made him hang frozenly motionless, like a fly about to be crushed.

Examining both passages, one sees that some of the elements which make the last passage stronger are:

1. a more clearly defined character
2. a more clearly defined viewpoint
3. a more clearly defined setting
4. more clearly defined actions
5. specific detail: "chalk-white slate," "steaks covered with slippery mushrooms," "lobsters with melted butter," "ice chips cascading"

When you write a scene, ask yourself, What emotion is the character experiencing? *Exactly what* is the character thinking about? What kind of actions is he or she engaged in? Always specifically describe food. Never just say: "They ate dinner." Readers read to experience life vicariously. They enjoy reading about "plates heaped with mashed potatoes," "butter melting in little streams down the sides," and "great platters of golden fried chicken." Charles Dickens was famed for his banquet imagery; it was an element in his writing that certainly contributed to his popularity.

Like food, sex is a national pastime and should not be dismissed summarily. *Play* your love scenes and avoid catch-all phrases like "the next morning" to indicate that sex has taken place. Sex is important to the reader. It can be presented romantically, mystically, or explicitly—depending upon you and your genre. It's your choice as to how you handle your sex scenes. But don't completely dismiss the subject unless you're writing teenage-romance novels in which the emphasis is on "falling in love." On the other hand, overemphasis on sex can be a bore.

Summary (Narration)

Besides scene, you will need summary to show less important action and to bridge the scenes. Summary can cover long periods of time in a sentence or two. But summary should be more than just a recounting of events. It should not be flat and dull. *Concrete detail produces good summary.* Note how

Faulkner uses summary in "The Bear" to tell how the protagonist, the boy Isaac McCaslin, goes searching for the bear:

> He ranged the summer woods now, green with gloom, if anything actually dimmer than they had been in November's gray dissolution, where even at noon the sun fell only in windless dappling upon the earth which never completely dried and which crawled with snakes—moccasins and water-snakes and rattlers, themselves the color of the dappled gloom so that he would not always see them until they moved; returning to camp later and later and later, first day, second day, passing in the twilight of the third evening the little log pen enclosing the log barn where Sam was putting up the stock for the night.

The narration now leads into a scene as Sam Fathers says to the boy:

> "You ain't looked right yet," Sam said.
> He stopped. For a moment he didn't answer. Then he said peacefully, in a peaceful rushing burst, as when a boy's miniature dam in a little brook gives way: "All right. Yes. But how? I went to the bayou. I even found that log again. I—"
> "I reckon that was all right. Likely he's been watching you. You never saw his foot?"
> "I ..." the boy said. "I didn't ... I never thought . . . ."
> "It's the gun," Sam said. He stood beside the fence, motionless, the old man, son of a Negro slave and a Chickasaw chief, in the battered and faded overalls and the frayed five-cent straw hat which had been the badge of the Negro's slavery and was not the regalia of his freedom . . . . *The gun*, the boy thought. *The gun.* "You will have to choose," Sam said.

Sam makes the boy realize that if he wants to see the bear he will have to put aside his gun, for the bear is a wily old beast.

The narration as Faulkner uses it here sets scene, describes the character Sam, gives the reader the feeling of the boy, and establishes that three days have passed. It also poses a dilemma for the boy—he will have to go into the woods without a gun for protection if he means to see the bear.

Summary, then, can give the reader:

1. description of a locale
2. the background of a situation
3. new information
4. motivation of characters and motivation of the events to follow

Summary can also act as a transition device, and it controls the pace (the movement) of a work, and time. Summary can condense five years by the mere statement "Five years went by."

Remember that too much narration (summary) is dull. If you need to give several pages of narration for background, **enliven the narration with:**

1. a line of dialogue
2. some thoughts
3. a scenette (a mini-scene with only a line or two of dialogue)

Never have a page of straight narration without some thoughts or dialogue, and stay in viewpoint when giving information. Faulkner doesn't come in as author and tell you about the boy; rather, we see the boy in action and perceive details through the boy's eyes.

Design of the Work

No one can tell you which scenes you must write and how much narration to use to bridge scenes. But remember that everything *important* should be shown in scenes. Try to balance your narrative and scenes harmoniously, but this balancing cannot be done methodically—that is, one paragraph narration, one paragraph scene throughout—for the structure will be monotonous.

Too much narration is dull, and too many scenes will destroy the dramatic structure. It's a good idea to examine your work to see if you have summarized important material that should be dramatically presented in a scene. On the other hand, are all your scenes necessary, or could some of them have been summarized?

Examine your scenes, too, to see if all of the narrative parts *need* to be there. The fact that your protagonist unlocked the front door, blew his nose, took ten steps across the room, and turned on the light in the living room might as easily have been summarized in a few words: "He went inside and turned on the light."

Transitions

Many writers have a problem moving their characters from scene to scene. If transitions are not made smoothly, the movement of the story—the pace—will seem jerky. New writers make either overly long transitions or ones that are too abrupt. You should try to telegraph that a transition is coming so the reader is not surprised. Note how jerky the following passage is:

> Adam kissed her goodbye at Disneyland. At work the next morning he saw her at the water cooler.

The problem is that the transition—the time passage—is too quick. One minute the reader is at Disneyland, the next at work. Try to make the reader *anticipate* transitions:

> Adam kissed her goodbye at Disneyland. "I'll see you tomorrow at work," he said. She nodded, then ran off. The next morning, when he walked into the office, he saw her standing at the water cooler.

Some ways of making transitions are through:

1. the hiatus (leave four blank lines between paragraphs)
2. the one-sentence transition
3. the standard phrase
4. the longer-passage transition
5. dialogue
6. thoughts
7. emotion
8. an object
9. time
10. weather
11. narration
12. name

The Hiatus (Four White Spaces)

The hiatus always indicates a change of place, time, or viewpoint. To use it, simply leave four white spaces between paragraphs. It's the easiest way of making a transition. An example is:

> Cal took out his shaving cream. "You're going to be late for rehearsal, Sully." The black man sent him a wry look and Cal grinned. Only time Sully'd ever miss a rehearsal was if they laid him out in a box six feet underground.

> When he and Sully got to the club, at three, the other guys were already there, putting their instruments together.

The hiatus is often used in suspense fiction in which there are many changes of viewpoint and scenes. But if you overuse the hiatus it will create a "jerky" effect in your work.

The One-Sentence Transition

If not too much time has elapsed, a transition can often be done in one sentence: "Martin saddled his horse and rode into Salinas."

The Standard Phrase

Using standard phrases, such as "the next morning," "that afternoon," "in spring," "by winter," is a simple way to bridge time. "At sunrise he was ready." But don't overuse standard phrases. Having too many of them in your work indicates lazy writing, or even worse—a lack of imagination. Try to *vary* the types of transitions you use.

The Longer-Passage Transition

Sometimes you may want to use a longer passage to achieve a transition:

> He knew Al Hirt was in town and he gave the cabby the address of the after hours joint where Hirt usually played. He liked to watch Hirt blow when he was really on. He leaned back against the seat. The passing streetlights haloed a fuzzy white in the dark night sky, the neon signs rosy patches of flickering light. Then the cab stopped and Cal leaned over the seat, slipping the driver a couple of bills. Hearing the music blasting from the open door he got out of the cab, stood there a moment, listened to the honey horn. All right, he thought, all right! And he went inside.

The longer-passage, or longer-paragraph, transition gives the writer an opportunity to create atmosphere and sometimes to reveal character while getting from one place to another in the story. But be careful using it, for it can also stop the action of a story.

Transition Through Dialogue

Sometimes you can use dialogue to achieve a transition:

> "Willie," she said, "let's go to the fair!"
> "Why not?" he said. She looked so gay, so young—she could talk him into anything.
> At the fair, they walked down the midway, their arms interlinked like two kids.

Transition Through Thought

Like dialogue, a central character's thought can anticipate a transition:

> He kept wondering when he would see her again, when she would call. He knew she would not make it easy for him. Did she love him? Or was it just a game with her? It was something he had to find out ... tonight.
> It was dark in the club, people jamming against the bandstand, and then he saw her long blonde hair, the sleek red sheath.

Transition Through Emotion

Perhaps the emotion of your character can signal a transition:

Had it really snowed! Looking outside, Sue felt her heart pounding as she saw the thick white snow crusted on the hill. The sky was black overhead, little ice blue stars twinkling. Then she was running outside, all bundled up, her nose freezing, her arms spread as if she were flying. Everything so icy and wonderful— And she flung herself down on her sled—flying, flying down the hill.

The girl's exhilaration as she thinks about the snow emotively leads to the scene in which she goes sledding.

Transition Through Objects

Occasionally, an object can be a transitional device:

Dazed, Jillian glanced at the blue vase Barrie had bought her. It was cracked ... like their marriage. How had it cracked? she wondered. She was still staring at it when she heard the footsteps in the hall, the door opening.

In this passage, the cracked vase is **symbolic** of the relationship between Jillian and her husband.

Drinks and cigarettes also serve as transitions:

Three martinis [or cigarettes] later, Bill left.

Transition Through Time

Probably one of the most often-used transitions is that of time:

John looked at his watch—three o'clock! An hour later, he walked into Jerry's Bar.

Transition Through Weather

Sometimes weather can serve as a transition:

He heard the hail popping against the tin roof and he stared at the dead man in the corner, propped up against the corrugated aluminum wall. It was still hailing when the sheriff arrived.

Transition Through Narration

Much transition is done through straight narration:

They had nearly frozen in Wisconsin, Elliot out of a job, and the baby only two weeks old, so it was nothing less than a miracle when Elliot was offered a position in Phoenix, Arizona. They packed the baby and what few possessions they had in the rusted Volkswagen and headed for what they believed was paradise.

Transition Through Name

The name of a character often offers an easy transition:

What had happened to Cathy? he thought wildly. If she didn't show up, he'd lose his job. He'd promised she'd do the murals.
   At every bar he asked, "Have you seen Cathy Riley?"
   Till one bartender yelled over his shoulder. "Yeah. Hey, Cathy—some guy is looking for you."

Here, the character needs to find Cathy to save his job. In his search, he asks for her. The repetition of the name acts as a transition to the scene in which he finds her.

If you intend to switch viewpoint in a story, the **name transition** works well:

Margaret Wilson felt the despair. Her brother did not know about the rains, the high tides wiping out the homes in Malibu—his home, the dream home it had taken twenty years to build. All of those wonderful treasures Harry'd collected from India, Africa, China, Japan—gone. Everything gone.

Harry Wilson had partied too much. He lay in his New York hotel room, a pillow over his face. If only he were out of this damned icy hole and back in Malibu, toasting his hide under the warm California sun.

In this sequence, a hiatus (four blank lines) occurs to signal the change of scene. But the name *Wilson* connects the characters and acts as a transitional device to bridge the scene in California and the scene in New York.

   Don't waste a lot of words on transitions. Scenes are the **heart and life** of your story. Get to the scenes as quickly as possible with appropriate transitions instead of wasting hundreds of words in moving your characters back and forth.

   A scene can be only a few lines long, as is the case with a scenette, or it can take up several pages. Occasionally, it can be a whole chapter. Whenever you have two or more people in a specific environment talking to each other, you have created a scene. A scene also occurs when a single character is in a particular environment and is talking or thinking to himself or herself. In other words, dialogue and thought are important elements of scene.

When the main action of the scene is concluded, the author then uses summary, which includes some type of transitional device to move to the next scene.

Summary

Every story has its own form, but **it is generally told through the alternation of scene and summary.** Put your most important material in scenes. Don't *tell* the reader about events and people. Rather, let the reader experience the characters and what happens to them through the characters' thoughts, actions, and dialogue. Scenes involve characters in conflict. When the key events have been *actively shown or revealed* in the scene, then use summary to make a transition to the next scene.

Always remember that readers hate to read long passages of dull, factual material. The writer must be creative and inventive in getting necessary background information across. One of the best ways is through dialogue. Then, too, sometimes a writer can use a paragraph of summary and spice it up with a line of dialogue.

A scene may be quiet or dramatic, but it must have a purpose that advances the plot. Scenes may reveal character and/or conflict, describe a locale, give a sense of time, express a specific emotion, and culminate in a win-or-lose situation; but a character should learn something from the encounter.

Summary should use concrete detail to be interesting. It can give the reader background, new information, an understanding of character motivation, and the motivation of events. It can bridge scenes and prepare readers for an upcoming scene. It should be enlivened with a line or two of dialogue, thoughts, or mini-scenes. Study the writers you like best; see how they vary their narration, how they use it to lead into scenes. Notice how the best narration has a distinct flavor of personality and is never a flat telling of events. Study the variety of transitions listed in this chapter and practice them as devices to link your scenes.

Exercises

1. Write a love scene, a fight scene, or a scene showing your character's disillusionment.
2. Write a scene in which your character is alone and confronted by a dangerous situation.
3. Write a key scene in which your character realizes something of great importance.

4. Write a scene in which a specific setting is important to the action of your story.
5. Write a paragraph of summary that prepares for a scene to follow.
6. Write a few lines of summary that act as a transition between two scenes.
7. Write a summary that reveals the character's background and integrates the way he or she thinks.
8. Write a scene and use a transition of your choice to link it to another scene that occurs several years later.
9. Write a scene and use a transition of your choice to link it to a scene that is very close in time to the first one.

9

How to Get Back and Forth in Time

Choosing the time sequence of the events in your story is often a difficult choice, for the wrong selection may well affect the very success of your story. You may choose to tell the story in:

1. chronological time
2. a series of flashbacks
3. time shifts
4. frame structure

Chronological Time

Few writers choose to write a story in chronological time—that is, from the very beginning, in the exact order the events happened. Generally, this early background is dull, and it takes too long to get to the peak points of action that involve the reader. However, if you choose to present your events chronologically, be sure that those events are interesting and not mere background or the reader will go to sleep. An example of chronological time might be:

Peter opened the package, stared at it: a small plastic grave marker with his name on it. Who had sent it? Why? What did it mean? He would have to find out.

An advantage of chronological time is that the reader is caught up in the present action and is motivated to move forward in time with the character. The forward action of the story does not have to be stopped in order to supply background information.

Series of Flashbacks

Often a story cannot be told in chronological time because a certain amount of background must be given to the reader. In this case, the flashback is a good technique. The writer interrupts the forward action of the plot to "flash back" (move back in time) to a scene in a previous time which relates essential happenings that illuminate the present events.

Flashback Technique

There are three elements to the flashback:

1. reflecting in present time
2. remembering
3. the actual experience

Each of these elements has a particular fictional purpose, and all three are usually used by the writer to delineate the experience to be shown.

Reflecting Reflecting is the process of interior thought. The character "thinks" about present events. For example:

He thought how lovely the weather was, the trees so green, the poppies orange and nodding.

When a character is reflecting, *the time is now.*

Remembering The character's mind *begins to focus on a previous experience*, a memory:

Annie had loved poppies. Yes, she had once told him that poppies were God's gold coins.

Note that the character is still *thinking* about the memory. *The time is back then.*

The actual experience   When the actual scene, the memory, begins to appear in the character's mind, the flashback is occurring:

> He remembered how Annie had knelt in the grass, her hands full of golden poppies. "Oh, Dave, aren't they lovely!" The mountains loomed purple behind her and puffy white clouds floated lazily across a deep blue sky. Suddenly, she buried her face in the poppies and began to weep. Not in sadness, but in joy.

In the flashback the time is in the past, but it is presented as if what is taking place were in the present. Notice that only one *had* signals that we are in the past. From that point on, we have the feeling of the present. We do not need to use a series of *had*s to indicate past time.

The scene should achieve a cameo picture and should have an "I am here" quality for the reader.

Note, too, that the flashback is meant to capture a remembered experience and so will not show *all* of the events that happened. Rather, it will show only the important details which the character remembers.

Part of the flashback device is an initial **hinge sentence** that swings the character from present time to past time:

1. "She thought back"
2. "He remembered"
3. "How long had it been ..."

When the scene has been presented, another hinge sentence swings the character up to the present:

1. "Now, twenty years later, he was alone."
2. "He could not believe twenty years had passed."

Words and phrases such as *now* and *twenty years later* delineate movement in time. **If you do not use hinge statements, the reader may be confused as to whether a flashback is occurring or whether the flashback has ended.**

When using the flashback, be careful to keep it short so that the reader does not get caught up in the past action and lose interest in the present events. Generally, the reader likes to participate with the character in moving from a series of exciting events to a resolution. Stopping the story causes loss of suspense.

Also, avoid *"had*-itis" in the flashback. For example, note the excess *had*s in this paragraph:

> Philip thought back to that first time he **had** seen Angela. She **had** worn a black sheath and white pearls and she **had** looked at him piercingly. Her voice **had** been husky, honied with wine, and she **had** touched his arm, her deep,

dusky eyes glowing with tiny glints of merriment, and he **had** blushed. Later, when he left, she **had** come after him and they **had** just looked at each other in the hallway.

One or two *had*s is enough to signal a flashback.

Philip thought back to that first time he **had** seen Angela. She'd worn a black sheath with white pearls, he remembered, and she looked at him piercingly, her husky voice honied with wine, and when she touched his arm, her deep, dusky eyes glowed with merriment. He blushed. When he left, she came after him and they just looked at each other in the hallway.

If you've already used a *had*, consider using a contraction for variety, as in "*She'd* wanted to see him."

When using the flashback, don't spend too much time on it, for you may lose the whole design of the story. Some editors dislike the flashback because if it is not handled properly, it can be boring. It also can take the reader into the past so completely that the reader may not want to return to present events. Always ask yourself if a flashback is really necessary. Ask, Can this information be conveyed in dialogue, or perhaps in a letter the character reads? Sometimes, too, it might be better to start earlier in the story to prevent a flashback—providing, of course, that you begin your story at an interesting place.

Other Ways of Flashing Back

1. Flashback through narrative technique   Use a direct statement of past events. Tell the reader what happened; be specific in detail and keep your writing vivid:

Governor Cary was a brilliant man, and even a gifted artist. Thirty years ago, he'd won an art scholarship. But polio had reduced his drawing hand to a claw. He withdrew into himself then, threw away his easel, his paints. When he emerged from his "sulking," as he called it, he went to law school. He never painted again and he avoided art shows.

2. Flashback through reverie   A character can "think" about the past:

At thirty, she reflected, she had dreamed of love, had pictured her wedding, the house she would have, had walked through every room in that house: a Georgian manor with mahogany furniture. Now, of course, she would never have either the wedding or the house.

3. Flashback through dialogue   The past can be conveyed in dialogue; however, be careful to avoid contrived dialogue—that is, dialogue which conveys too much information. When using dialogue to convey past events, strive for naturalness.

"Why did you marry Dick, anyway?" Mary asked.

Sally grimaced. "Boredom. I was twenty-eight, with no place to go and nothing to look forward to. So I married him. It was a mistake."

4. *Flashback through self-analysis* The character can analyze what he or she did or thought in the past:

He'd been a fool not to have gone to school. There he was, nineteen, living at home, his parents willing to send him to any college he wanted. Instead he ran away, bummed around the country. He wanted to be free, without any pressures. How could he have known that what he wanted was impossible?

5. *Flashback by comparing the past with the present* The character can compare what she'd done before with what she is doing now.

She had cleaned offices, toilets even, and now she owned the company.

6. *Flashback by reminiscing* A character can reminisce in dialogue:

"When I was ten I knew I'd be a doctor. I read all the books on anatomy I could get my hands on. I knew I was going to be a surgeon."

7. *Flashback by using objects to evoke the past* A character can observe or touch an object which evokes memories.

He stared at the small china ballerina, remembered his mother and how she'd danced before him. Her face pale, like the figurine, her eyes vivid blue chips. She had been no more than twenty-three, and he four.

8. *Flashback by using letters and diaries to reveal the past* A character can write to a friend or keep a diary that gives important information about the character's past life.

She reread the letter as she had over the years: My dearest Laura, I cannot marry you. I have tried to tell you so many times, but I could not. I am already married. Forgive me. I cannot leave her. But I will never forget you.   *Ben*

The Time Shift

While the flashback is clearly marked by hinge statements—"he remembered," "she never forgot that time when …"—the time shift is more sophisticated. There is a more gradual merging into the past:

Elliot knew Ann wanted a divorce. They both realized they had little in common, and she had met Peter. He knew he must let her go; he wanted to let her go, but still he felt ... miffed. It was like losing an important strand in his life. He sensed she was eager to go her own way, to try something different as she had when she first met him.

"You are Elliot Townsend," she'd smiled, her navy blue eyes assessing him, "and I am Ann Randall. I am free, adventurous, and I detest strings. Do you understand?" He had smiled then; yes, he thought he understood. But he learned he did not. So there you are. Yes, he would give her a divorce—but not without some regrets which he suspected would trouble him.

The trick of the time shift is to lead the reader into the character's thoughts or emotions and then bridge into a scene in the past or, as illustrated above, a mini-scene (scenette).

The Frame

The frame structure begins in the present, moves back into the past *for the entire story,* and then at the very end moves back to the present.

A fine example of the frame is Wirt Williams's novel *Ada Dallas*. It begins in the present with the hero, Steve Jackson, who is driving to Baton Rouge to attend the funeral of Governor Ada Malone Dallas, his former lover. The book moves back to the time when Jackson first met Ada and recounts their love affair, her rise to power, and her murder. The book ends with his return to New Orleans after the funeral.

A diagram of the frame looks like:

Montage

Occasionally, the story demands that a passage of time occur, and a simple transition statement such as "a year passed" won't work. In this case, montage may be necessary. In motion pictures and television, a rapid sequence of images is used to simulate the passing of time: calendar pages flipping; a series of walking legs to show leaving a destination and arriving at another; pictures of spring fading into summer, into fall, into winter.

Note the montage sequence in Casey Scott's *One More Time:*

> Time for Cal moved in twenty-four-hour blocks of fifteen minutes each. One thing, though, he felt his solidity. Every time he looked at his watch, he marveled at how slowly time could pass. He counted the hours by the sets, by

watching Sully mechanically open the folded paper napkins and squint at the scrawled requests. He played the standards, the way he did when he was tired. No improvisations. Safe, without thinking. Then, right before midnight, he saw her . . . .

The montage continues at a slower pace: "The following Sunday, Cal stood up under spots." Additional phrases—"a week later," "exactly one month later," and "each Sunday and all the following ones"—take the reader through the next year and quickly sketch the events that make a TV star out of Cal.

Summary

The handling of time in a story is important. Time in a fictional work cannot flow in a measured sequence as it does in real life. The author shapes time according to the events that need to be explored. He or she may condense years in a few lines of summary. On the other hand, a novelist may take a whole book to explore one instant in time.

How one views the time pattern of events in the story determines the way the story is structured—as to whether the story will be told chronologically, through a series of flashbacks or time shifts, or in a frame. However, it's important not to lose the reader in the time shifts. Equally important is that the flashbacks not stop the forward progression of plot. Each story has its own time clock, and, while the reader should feel satisfied with the movement of events, the writer should feel that he or she has made the most effective use of time sequences to present the story.

Time is the vehicle the writer uses to show those events he or she means to stress, those events which ultimately carry out theme and which reveal the writer's values.

Exercises

1. Write a scene in which the hero (or heroine) is facing a problem and flash back into the events that caused the problem. Be sure to use a hinge statement that swings you back into the past and a hinge statement that swings you up into the present.
2. Write a scene, shifting back and forth in time by using emotions or thoughts to trigger the shifts. Try to avoid obvious hinge statements.
3. Write a frame short story—a short story that begins in the present and focuses in the past, then returns to the present.
4. Write a paragraph using montage, showing several months passing.

10

Theme: What's It All About?

One of the most common mistakes a new writer makes is writing a story that has no significance. A story cannot be a mere recitation of events that happened. It must have a theme, a message, and the writer must ask, "What is the *meaning* of this story?"

The Intention of a Fictional Work

Every story has its own meaning, its own *intention*, but that intention is not necessarily the author's intention for writing the story. It may be that an author quarrels with his wife and writes a story about marriage. Yet his own anger, one intention, is only the fuel that sparks the creative fire; and the story itself, with its individual problem as expressed by the created characters, may have a meaning that far surpasses a marital quarrel over breakfast.

A famous literary case in point is that of Thomas Mann, whose wife spent some time in a sanitarium. He wrote one of the greatest philosophic novels of twentieth-century literature, *The Magic Mountain*. It deals with a young man, Hans Castorp, who also is confined to a sanitarium. Yet the novel, which does not even concern Mann's wife, goes far beyond her personal experience.

Every Element in the Story Must Reflect Theme

Every element in the story's form—plot, character, tone, atmosphere, style, setting—is an integral part of theme. Theme is the *writer's vision* that holds all of these things together. It is an idea, but an idea expressed emotively: an idea that can be felt, *experienced* by the reader. It is a message conveyed by the writer to the reader, and it may be very simple or it may be complex. It may be as simple as "Crime does not pay," a theme often expressed on TV private-eye shows but also expressed with infinite more complexity in Dostoyevski's *Crime and Punishment*. It may be complex as in *The Old Man and the Sea: Each man is a Christ if he meets his own crucifixion, and the ordeal is an eternal one which we meet again and again.* It may be an idea with which many people disagree; perhaps it is even untrue. The important thing is that it has truth for the writer, and that the reader can realize and *feel* how these particular characters look at things.

How Do You Go About Finding the Theme of Your Story or Novel?

Generally, the writer does not begin a story or novel with a theme in mind; rather, characters with a problem usually spring to life in the writer's psyche, and it is pretty much a truism that these characters will ultimately reveal the theme. In fact, beginning with a definite theme in mind may hamstring the writer before he or she gets started. Often, even if a writer mentally knows where the work is going, the writer still may not complete it exactly as originally envisioned. Characters grow, exciting new characters appear, and new and better situations arise. All of these things lead to different scenes, different outcomes, and different perceptions. Even if a writer is aware of a particular theme before beginning a work, by the time he or she finishes writing it, the theme will be much richer and will have many more levels of meaning than when it was first conceived.

Joy of discovery is part of the creative task. On the other hand, it is certainly true that great writers such as Dante and Goethe had a definite design and theme in mind before they started writing. Again, pros are more aware of design than novices and over many years of writing have developed the discipline to carry out complex tasks that would stagger the new writer.

Clues to Discovering Your Theme

When reading your story, ask yourself:

1. Why did I write this?
2. What emotions do I feel?
3. What did I want to show?
4. Why did I choose this particular person for my main character? What does this character represent?
5. What is the meaning behind the character's main speeches?

Once You Know Your Theme, What Then?

When you have found your theme, you may have to go back and restructure your story. You may have to eliminate irrelevant characters and irrelevant scenes, no matter how much you like them. You will have to reshape your story so that it moves irrevocably toward that single meaning—a major theme. In a more complex work it is true that you may have a minor theme or even minor themes, but one major idea should control your work. If friends read your story and each gets a different meaning, you have not written a successful story. On the other hand, if your friends get variations, shadings, of the central meaning, then you have been successful, for each person will color that meaning with his or her own personality, likes and dislikes, and attitudes.

Verbalize Your Theme

It's a good idea to try to say your theme in a *complete* sentence. A fragmented idea—"the despair of life"—is too general. What *about* the despair of life? A more precise theme might be: "Suffering is universal, but learning its meaning is man's task."

What if Your Theme Sounds Too Simple?

Don't worry about your theme. If you let your characters act out your story, they will show your theme in a way that no one has quite perceived it, for this story is *your own variation* of that particular truth. Remember that no one looks at life exactly the way you do. You, like the snowflake, cannot be duplicated. Your mind is uniquely yours, and you have experienced life's events in your own particular way. If you write truly of your experience, your writing will always be fresh and will seem "different."

For example, take ten people who have fallen in love. Although the event of falling in love is the same, not one of the ten people experienced that event in exactly the same manner.

Lovers meet at ski resorts, buying antiques, in Algeria, in a doctor's office, in a classroom, while riding horses. Where did you meet your lover? What did love teach you? That life is cruel; life is unbearably lovely; life is a trap; life is a school of learning; life is meaningless without love; life is a process of growing? So varied are all of these experiences and the "truths" derived that love stories remain the most popular of fiction. The point is, don't worry about the *significance* of your theme—just show it as truly as you can through characters who live and breathe on the page.

Is Your Theme Salable?

Editors are always interested in works that have something to say about contemporary problems. While some themes are universal—"Good will ultimately prevail," for example—some are simply outdated. A theme of the 1930s—that a woman must remain a virgin to get married, perhaps—will hardly get much reader identification in today's market.

Some themes are taboo or socially unacceptable. For example, few editors would consider a novel whose theme is that child molesters are really warm, lovable people and that children have sexual needs too. Similarly, convicts write books about their crimes and indicate crime is fun and there's nothing wrong with a little mayhem and rape. Theme is the heart of your book, and it should be one with which the average reader can identify.

In category fiction, themes are often very general, but they fit the genre. Some romance themes are: a strong, good woman deserves a strong, good man; love is all; love conquers all; romantic love fulfills a woman's life; a smart, inventive woman can get her man. In mystery writing some common themes are: no matter how hard a criminal tries to hide something, the truth will always be revealed; the good guy (the private eye) will win; bravery and courage mark a real person; crime doesn't pay; greed and cruelty destroy.

In category writing, characters and situation are more important than theme. If we like the romantic heroine or the private eye, we are more interested in what happens to them and how they solve their respective problems than in what the theme or message is.

On the other hand, in a mainstream novel we may watch a ruthless politician in his fight for wealth and power as he destroys the people around him and betrays his public trust; and the theme that unbridled power destroys both people and nations is of great significance in the book.

How Can You Develop Theme in Your Work?

Theme can be revealed through:

1. direct statement in dialogue or thought
2. character
3. action
4. motif
5. atmosphere
6. symbol

Theme Through Dialogue

One way of handling theme is to let a main character say it in a direct statement. A young wife might tell her husband:

> "You don't appreciate anything—don't you see how important life is? Every one of us ... we're only here for such a short time. Everything anyone does is life energy that runs out. So appreciate—appreciate, please!"

She, of course, might "think" these same words. While thematic material is often emphasized several places in the story—through thought, dialogue, and action—the final statement of theme generally occurs at a key point in the story, usually near the end.

Theme Through Character

The description and actions of a character can illustrate theme. Note how Faulkner describes Flem Snopes in *The Hamlet:*

> ... a thick squat man of no establishable age between twenty and thirty, with a broad still face containing a tight seam of a mouth stained slightly at the corners with tobacco, and eyes the color of stagnant water, and projecting from among the other features in startling and sudden paradox, a tiny predatory nose like the beak of a small hawk. It was as though the original nose had been left off by the original designer or craftsman and the unfinished job taken over by someone of a radically different school or perhaps by some viciously maniacal humorist or perhaps by one who had had only time to clap into the center of the face a frantic and desperate warning.

Faulkner's description of Flem's nose as being like the beak of a hawk keys in Flem's predatory nature. Later in the novel we see how he preys on others. Some people are victims and others are the Flem Snopeses of the world.

Another famous novel character who illustrates theme is Flaubert's Emma Bovary. Emma represents the romantic individual who pursues the goal of idealistic love in a realistic world and who is destroyed by her sensibilities.

Theme Through Action

Theme does not always have to be directly stated but can be implied through action. In Hemingway's "The Short, Happy Life of Francis Macomber," the sequence of events reveals theme. Francis Macomber, a wife-dominated husband, incurs his wife's contempt when he bolts from a charging lion while on a safari. His guide, Wilson, saves his life by shooting the lion. Macomber's wife enjoys his defeat and compounds that defeat by sleeping with the guide. Later, Macomber faces a cape buffalo and regains his manhood. Wilson and Macomber see the bull

> ... coming out of the bush sideways, fast as a crab, and the bull coming, nose out, mouth tight closed, blood dripping, massive head straight out, coming in a charge, his little pig eyes bloodshot as he looked at them. Wilson, who was ahead, was kneeling shooting, and Macomber, as he fired, unhearing his shot in the roaring of Wilson's gun, saw fragments like slate burst from the huge boss of the horns, and the head jerked, he shot again at the wide nostrils and saw the horns jolt again and fragments fly, and he did not see Wilson now and, aiming carefully, shot again with the buffalo's huge bulk almost on him and his rifle almost level with the on-coming head, nose out, and he could see the little wicked eyes and the head started to lower . . . .

For Macomber, the confrontation is an exaltation. But Macomber's wife shoots at the bull too and "accidentally" kills her husband. The guide realizes it wasn't an accident, that she couldn't bear Macomber's becoming a man again. Macomber, however, died at his moment of triumph. While Hemingway does not state the theme, it is understood to be: It is worth any price for a man to achieve his own identity—to step free from fear and domination.

Theme Through Motif

An interesting way to develop theme is through a motif—an image that, like the refrain of a song, is repeated. In Leo Tolstoy's *Anna Karenina*, train stations are a recurring motif.

Anna and her lover, Vronsky, first see each other at a railway station. As their affair progresses, they meet again at a railway station. Anna commits suicide at another station, and Vronsky leaves for war from a railroad station. When Anna had first met Vronsky, she'd witnessed an accident—a man had been crushed to death—and she'd seen a small peasant with a sack, who muttered something in French, and she heard the sounds of a hammer on iron. Later, both Vronsky and Anna have terrible dreams of a peasant bending over to do something and speaking French.

The train station seems to indicate an irrevocable fate from which one cannot escape. The "crushed man" reveals that the image of the train station is fused with death. Ultimately, Anna throws herself under the wheels of a train—the incident foreshadowed by the recurring motif of the train station. It is a remarkable coincidence that the author, Leo Tolstoy, died in a train station. In this case, a literary motif actually foreshadowed Tolstoy's own life.

Theme Through Atmosphere

Atmosphere is the *feeling* of the particular locale where the events of the story take place, and atmosphere can reveal theme:

> The room was cloying, sweet, the smell of decaying flowers thick around me. Dust covered the tables, the faded upholstered rose chairs. The mummified dog lay before the fireplace, his jaws open as if death had caught him yawning. The tea service, once gleaming silver, was now darkly tarnished. Dust coated the fireplace hearth. Above the chair turned to the fireplace, I saw the matted hair, and, looking down, saw the bony claw resting on the arm. Death had come suddenly and stayed for tea.

As the passage indicates, death comes suddenly, and no one knows when that hour may be. The room, with its tomb-like atmosphere, emphasizes the theme.

Theme Through Symbol

A symbol stands for something else. Gold = wealth; the flag = country, patriotism; the cross = morality. In Katherine Anne Porter's story "Flowering Judas," the character Laura is fused with the "Judas tree," the redbud tree from which Judas is said to have hanged himself. As Judas was the betrayer of Christ, so Laura becomes a betrayer figure. At the end of the story, when Laura has a vision of eating blossoms from the Judas tree, the meaning is that she is partaking of the sacrament of betrayal, of death, and not of the life that Christ promises.

Richard Brautigan in his short story "The World War I Los Angeles Airplane" uses symbol ironically to develop theme. The narrator in the story tells of his wife's father, who has just died. The father had been a pilot in World War I and escaped death several times while flying. Once

> ... he was flying over France and a rainbow appeared behind the tail of his plane and every turn that the plane made, the rainbow also made the same turn and it followed after him through the skies of France for part of an afternoon in 1918.

The rainbow is a traditional symbol of God's promise to preserve man, a symbol of immortality. Yet, ironically, in Brautigan's story this favored pilot who "had been followed by a rainbow across the skies of France while flying a World War I airplane carrying bombs and machine guns" died a drunk. Death and decay catch everyone, Brautigan says, even those protected by rainbows.

The Last Paragraph

The last paragraph of any story is important to theme, for it is here that the theme is often punctuated or even directly stated. Theme is generally built up in a work in a gradual progression of events, and the hero or heroine's realization in the last paragraph is the expression of theme. Sometimes, too, an image that expresses the theme rounds off the story. In Porter's "Flowering Judas," the short story ends with the image of the betrayer Laura eating the blossoms of the Judas tree:

> Then eat these flowers, poor prisoner, said Eugenio in a voice of pity, take and eat: and from the Judas tree he stripped the warm bleeding flowers, and held them to her lips. She saw that his hand was fleshless, a cluster of small white petrified branches, and his eye sockets were without light, but she ate the flowers greedily for they satisfied both hunger and thirst. Murderer! said Eugenio, and Cannibal! This is my body and my blood. Laura cried No! and at the sound of her own voice, she awoke trembling, and was afraid to sleep again.

Summary

Theme is the meaning of a work, its *significance*. It is the intention of a story, an idea experienced emotively, and the design of a work. Theme fuses all of the story elements—plot, character, tone, atmosphere, style, and setting—together. If a story is well written, you should not only be able to state the theme but you should also be able to *feel* it. The entire short story should coalesce into a single idea.

DISCOVER THEME BY ASKING

1. Why did I write this story? What do I learn from it?
2. What do I mean to show through my main character?
3. What emotions do I feel? Are they a key to certain attitudes and ideas?
4. What ideas occur in my characters' main speeches? Is there a central idea?
5. After finishing my story do I feel a single emotion or several emotions? *Is there a central mood?*

WHEN YOU KNOW YOUR THEME

1. Reshape your work; eliminate irrelevant characters and scenes. Are symbols integral or just "stuck in"?
2. *Try to verbalize the theme in a complete sentence.*
3. Don't worry about the theme being too simple; just let your characters come to life on the page and act out their stories.
4. *Rework your last paragraph to emphasize the theme.*

SOME WAYS OF REVEALING THEME ARE THROUGH

1. direct statement in dialogue or thought
2. character
3. action
4. motif
5. atmosphere
6. symbol

No one can tell you which of these are best for your story. The *form* of your story, the development of action and character, will give you valuable keys as to the strongest way of presenting theme.

Exercises

1. Take one of your own short stories and examine it for theme. Through which device have you revealed theme?
2. Pick out a favorite short story, written by someone else, and examine it for theme. How did the writer develop it? How does the last paragraph tie in with the theme?

11

Do Titles Really Matter?

Publishers say that the title is responsible for one-third of the total sales of a book. Any magazine editor will tell you that a good article title can be responsible for selling an issue of a magazine. Yet while you may spend weeks, months, even years finding a good title, it's almost a certainty that the publisher will not use the title you've selected. Does this mean that you shouldn't search for a good title? Definitely not! You need a good title to attract an editor's eye. Remember, it's the first thing he or she sees of your work—and the editor who likes the title will begin reading your manuscript in an optimistic frame of mind.

The Dull Title

Put yourself in the editor's place. The editor may have thirty or forty manuscripts to read. Many of the titles are a bore—*A Day at the Farm, A Summer in the Woods, Happy Times in the Mountains, Beloved Mother*—all sounding like high school essays. The editor does what you would do: puts the dull titles on the bottom of the pile and begins reading the provacative ones, hoping to find a good story or article. The assumption is that anyone creative enough to think up a good title has a "fresh idea" and is a good writer. By the time the editor gets to the "dull" titles, usually at the end of the day, Grumpy and tired, not expecting much to come of this batch of stories, he or she doesn't give these manuscripts as much of a reading as the first ones read at the beginning of the day. In fact, let's be frank—if the manuscript has a really dull title, the editor may not even read it at all.

You do exactly the same thing when you pick up *Reader's Digest.* You turn first to the article that has the most exciting title, and you may never bother reading an article that has a dull title. **So your first concern is to hook the editor and the agent with a good title.**

How to Find a Good Title for Your Book

First of all, be aware of the trends in titles. Do you look at the bestseller list every week to get a feeling of the kinds of titles that are popular now? Titles that were good years ago are not good now. Times change, trends change, and what held the public's interest then may not do so now. Many things have influenced our present culture—drugs, the women's movement, the one-parent family, latchkey kids, child abuse, terrorism, the rise in violence, loosened sexual mores—and these things produce a different readership. Besides today's different readership, a higher reading level existed several years ago—and "intellectual" titles such as *The Agony and the Ecstasy, Of Human Bondage,* and *For Whom the Bell Tolls* may not be as immediately evocative to today's readers as *Sophie's Choice* or *Gorky Park.* The contemporary title is shorter and punchier. Consider the title *Heiress.* In fact, as one writer wryly quipped, you can find your title on the horse racing page in the sports section of your local newspaper—which may not be a bad idea.

The Best Place to Find Your Title
Is in Your Own Book

Look for your title in your own work—especially in your thematic or descriptive passages. It is at these times you are most likely to tap the deepest, most creative part of yourself, which often expresses itself lyrically. This is the time when "great lines" spring effortlessly from your mind. Read over your passages carefully and look for unusual lines. You may find several, or as many as fifty. It's a good idea to jot them down. Then a day or two later, when your enthusiasm has cooled, look again at your list and see if you can prune it down to five or so. Perhaps one line will stand out over all the rest; that, of course, is your title.

If a publisher buys your book, it's not a bad idea to send your editor the list of the other five titles; if the publishing house doesn't like your selected title, it may use one of the other ones.

Why Do Publishers Change the Titles of Books and Articles?

Most of the time, an author picks a title for an emotional reason that only he or she understands. The publisher is in business to make money. Publishers want books to sell. Obscure titles with no general significance do not attract the book buyer.

Years ago, before I understood the business of writing, I titled a book I had written *Kilometer 39*. I thought the title a good one because it referred to a little place in Mexico and summed up the mood I'd felt there. The publishing house changed the title to *Ocean's Edge*. While I was discussing the title change with an editor, he remarked that *Kilometer 39* indicated only a measure of distance and nothing else. Had the location been more well known, *Kilometer 39* might have made a good title. He defended the title *Ocean's Edge*, saying it implied more—the "edge" of something, a nervous breakdown, high tension. It also gave a locale (the story did take place in a beach location). *Ocean's Edge* implied that *something was going to happen*, whereas *Kilometer 39* was a static title.

You will probably prefer your own title, but publishers have marketing in mind—and let's face it, *they've* bought your book and have the advertising expertise to sell it. Similarly, a magazine editor will often change the title of a short story or article to one that will appeal to the readers of that magazine. Again, the editor has bought the manuscript and is entitled to aim for the highest readership.

If the Editor Is Attracted to the Title in the First Place, Why Does He or She Change It?

An editor has probably chosen to be an editor because he or she enjoys reading and is a literary person. Perhaps your title *did* intrigue the editor in a literary way, but the editor may recognize that your title does not have the commercial value needed to reach a mass market audience. Consequently, the editor will change the title to a more marketable one.

How Does the Publisher Arrive at the Title?

After your book has been bought by a publisher, the editorial staff discusses it and its marketing potential at an editorial meeting. All present, including the sales staff, suggest titles. They are aware of recent titles used by competing publishing houses, and they might point out that the same title has just come out or is about to come out, or that a similar title did not sell. Your book is generally renamed at one of these editorial meetings.

If you are an established writer with a wide reading audience, such as James Michener, Harold Robbins, or Sidney Sheldon, you have a much stronger chance of keeping the title you have selected.

What if You Can't Come Up With a Catchy Title?

Often a sure-fire way is to "ask" your unconscious for a title. At night, just before you go to sleep, while you're slipping into that drowsy state just between being awake and being asleep, ask that a title be given you for your book. Then, when you finally fall asleep, your unconscious mind will work on it all night. Of course, you won't get much real sleep, and you'll certainly toss and turn a lot. But, often, your title will come to you by morning. Many students have tried this method and found that it worked for them. However, one of them remarked that the title had indeed come in the wee hours, but he had been so tired he didn't want to get up to write it down and so when he arose the next morning he had forgotten it! Yes, you will have to write it down—so keep a pen and paper handy.

If you don't get a title the first night, don't give up. Give your unconscious a fair try—at least for a week. If it still doesn't give you a title, then you may have to try other sources.

The Bible, Greek Tragedies, and Shakespeare's Works Are Rich Sources of Titles

The Bible has always produced good titles: *The Grapes of Wrath, The Strange Woman, The Day of the Locusts, Exodus*. The Greek tragedies have many wonderful lines that would make excellent titles, as do Shakespeare's plays. Be sure, though, that when you take a line from the tragedies or the Bible you don't pick a flat line that has no zip: for example, In His Mantle, or His deeds, *First and Last*.

Can Your Title Be Tied to Some Great Event or Person?

If your novel can be tied to a famous event or person, you may have a great deal of built-in advertising. Readers like to read about historic situations and great people. Titles like *Raise the Titanic, Augustus, The Last Temptation of Christ, Mary Queen of Scots, The Rise and Fall of the Third Reich* and *I, Claudius* and *I, Judas* attract a large reading audience.

Should the Title Be Related to Theme?

A title should not blatantly sum up the theme: for example, *Do Unto Others* ... Rather, it should subtly refer to theme. The title *Scruples* certainly hinted at theme, as did *The Grapes of Wrath* and *The Little Foxes*. *The Grapes of Wrath* concerns the anger of people who are being dehumanized by the economy, and *The Little Foxes* symbolizes predatory people who devour their fellow man. Very often, the title *is* a line taken from a thematic passage in the book.

Try a Popular Expression

Sometimes a well-known expression makes a good title: *One More Time, Once in a Lifetime, The Green Years, Staying Alive, The Cat's Pajamas, Sauce for the Goose, Into Your Tent I'll Creep, The Living End, Chinaman's Chance, Good as Gold*.

The Twist

Try twisting a clichéd expression for a title: *Let Me Kill You Sweetheart, A Stab in the Dark, I Hear America Swinging, Without a Stitch in Time, You Only Live Twice, Three at Wolfe's Door, If Life Is a Bowl of Cherries What Am I Doing in the Pits?, The Grass Is Greener over the Septic Tank*.

A twist turned the mythical subject of the golden fleece into the title of a mystery novel: *Goulden Fleece*. "Southern Comfort," a brand name, became *Southern Discomfort*. John le Carré's novel title "the little drummer boy" was changed to *The Little Drummer Girl*.

The Emotive Word

Words like or related to *death, terror,* and *murder* promise exciting reading: *The Dead Zone, Fools Die, Prelude to Terror, Dead Heat, Dead Bolt, Dial M for Murder*. In romances, words such as *passion, love, affair, seduction, ecstasy,* and *dream* promise romantic encounters: *No Love Lady, Desert Dream, Corporate Affair, Follow Your Dream*. In this genre, the word *rose* symbolizes passion and is often used: *Tears and Red Roses, Champagne and Roses, The Dark Rose*.

Bestseller Titles

One-word titles have been a large part of the bestseller list: *Misery, Empire, Jade, Scruples, Jaws, Palomino, Centennial, Roots, Illusions, Airport, Bloodlines, Hotel, Exodus, Godfather, Coma, Nile, Choices, Game, Jailbird, Lace, Shōgun, Pathfinder, Firestarter, Cujo, Creation, Masquerade, Space, Max*.

In fact, most of the titles on the bestseller list are either one- or two-word titles—*Presumed Innocent, Princess Daisy, Love Story, The Island, Fools Die, Loon Lake, The Covenant, Noble House, Mistral's Daughter, Different Seasons, Foundation's Edge*—and some three-word titles: *The Haunted Mesa, A Perfect Spy, The Bourne Supremacy, The Thorn Birds, Eye of the Needle, Jonathan*

Livingston Seagull, An Indecent Obsession, The Parsifal Mosaic, The Dead Zone, Breakfast of Champions, Winds of War, War and Remembrance, Rage of Angels. Very few titles on the bestseller list have more than three words.

Pronunciation Is Important

Note how easy it is to pronounce all of these titles—a quality important to publishers, for book buyers often have to ask for a book. A difficult title intimidates book buyers and makes them feel foolish if they can't pronounce it.

Don't Try to Tease Readers with a Hard-to-Understand Title

If readers can't understand the title of your book, they probably won't buy it. Books are expensive these days, and who wants to waste money on an unknown quantity? If you try to tease readers with a difficult title, you may pay for it in low sales.

A title should mean something to the reader. It should excite the imagination and promise that something is going to happen. The ideal title should have some relationship to the book. A title that has no meaning confuses readers; they don't know what the book is about and so may not read it. For example, several students commented that they didn't want to buy the book *Lace* because they thought it was similar to *Arsenic and Old Lace*, and, having already read that, they didn't want to read the novel.

Jaws is a better title. Short, easy to pronounce, its one word promises adventure, terror, and excitement, and it directly relates to the shark plot in the novel. *Jade*, too, is a good title. A book about China, it promises a tale of the exotic east. The title *Nile* evokes Egypt, and the book is about the Arab–Israeli conflict. *Hawaii* promises a novel rich in the lore of the Hawaiian people and hints at the history of Hawaii. The classic title *Orient Express* carries a whole mystique of intrigue and adventure.

You may argue that some people like enigmatic titles, but publishers don't care about a few people; they want *everyone* to be attracted by the title.

Strive to Make Your Title Easy to Remember

Word-of-mouth promotes bestsellers, and if a title is too long or hard to pronounce, it's hard to talk about the book at a party or when friends get together. It's also hard to order a book if you can't remember its title.

A Good Title Should Not Give Away the Story

A good title is like frosting on the cake—but it's not the cake. It attracts you to the cake. The title is there to make you read the book. If you give away too much of your story, readers may decide that they don't want to read it; they already have an idea of what's going to happen. While you may pick a title from the novel itself, never, *never* pick a title that sums up how the story was resolved. For example, *Mary's War* is better than *Mary Won the War with Her Sixgun*.

Titles Should Fit the Genre

Readers do not like to be misled. When they buy a romance, they want it to be a romance. If they buy a mystery, they want to read a mystery. A romance entitled *The Big Mine Crash* would be a wrong choice. *The Big Mine Crash* promises adventure and terror. A better choice for the romance might be *Passion Island*. Misleading titles cause angry customers who return books or who get angry at the bookstore where they bought the book.

Can You Use a Title That's Been Used Before?

Titles cannot be copyrighted and so can be used again. My own book *One More Time* came out just before the musical production *One More Time*. Barbara Conklin's teenage romance *P.S. I Love You* came out shortly before Peter Sellers's biography *P.S. I Love You*. The disadvantage is obvious. A customer might be confused when ordering a book or when buying it. Publishers try to avoid this coincidental titling, but sometimes they can't help it.

Summary

Think carefully about your title. It's the first thing the editor sees, and attracting the editor's eye is one of your first priorities. Remember that the title is one of your greatest sales tools, especially in fiction. Work to find just the right title for your book. If you're lucky, you may even get to see it in print. But resign yourself to the fact that the editor and the advertising department will probably pick their own title for your book. Again, you may like it—and the high sales it brings.

Title Checklist

Use this checklist as a guide to create your title.

1. Is the proposed title interesting?
2. If you're having trouble finding a title, did you look for a title in your own work, in thematic or descriptive passages?

3. Have you looked for a title in the Bible, in the Greek tragedies, in Shakespeare's plays?
4. Can you tie the title to a great event or famous person?
5. Have you tried to make a title out of a popular expression?
6. Have you tried twisting a cliché or a clichéd expression to make a title?
7. Is the title short, consisting of between one and four words?
8. Is the title easy to pronounce?
9. Is the title easy to remember?
10. Does the title *mean* something, convey something intelligible?
11. Is the title related in some way to the book?
12. Does the title promise that *something* is going to happen? Does it promise mystery, suspense, adventure, love, exotic intrigue? Is it thought-provoking?
13. Does the title give away the resolution of the book?
14. Does the title fit the genre?
15. Does another well-known book have the same title?

Exercises

1. Keep a small notebook entitled "titles." Look through the Bible and Shakespeare's plays and write down any phrases which you think would make good titles.
2. Each week, read the book section in your local newspaper. Note the types of titles on the bestseller list. Are the majority of them one word, two words, three words?
3. Try asking your subconscious for a good title before you go to sleep. Tell it that you want a good title in the morning.
4. Take a cliché or a popular expression and see if you can create an interesting title from it.
5. Take an emotive word like "dead" or "ecstasy" and try to create an evocative title.

12

Research Made Easy

Whether you are going to write an article, a nonfiction book, or a novel, you need facts to substantiate your material. If you just start writing without any research, you will usually find that you sound vague, and your writing will lack authenticity.

You Must Establish Credibility

In articles and longer nonfiction manuscripts, your narrative must be balanced with examples, anecdotes, and statistics to prove your position. If you are writing a novel—especially a historical novel—you need a great deal of research to establish background. You should know what type of clothes people wore, the furniture of the period, and similar details. What major events happened during this time? Who were the world leaders? What were the expressions of the time, the songs, the political issues, the cultural mores, the inventions? What kind of cars were driven? Were electricity, gas, the telephone, the telegraph, the radio in use? Is the actual history of the period clear in your mind? Knowing all these things will give life to your article or book.

If you are inaccurate in your research, and your article or book is published, specialists will write to your publisher, pointing out your discrepancies. If you write inaccurate articles, you will not help your career: Truthfulness is a major part of being a journalist. In a nonfiction book, inaccuracy destroys your credibility as an authority figure. In the novel, other than science fiction and fantasy, inaccuracy will jolt the reader from the illusion of life you are trying to create; and, moreover, the reader will probably not believe your book.

Where to Begin

Research can be done through:

1. talking to relatives, friends, and specialists in a field
2. the media: newspapers, magazines, radio, TV programs
3. the library and its many resources

Each has its own advantage.

Relatives, Friends, and Specialists

You can't beat talking to someone who's lived through an exciting experience or a certain period of time in a particular country. Grandmother or Uncle Bill often remembers exciting tidbits that you never thought of. If you need to know how something was developed, a specialist can give you all the background quickly and concisely. The specialist, a personal "I" witness, usually supplies colorful insights and dialogue along with the enthusiasm of having undergone the experience. This emotional tone will give life and reality to your work.

On one occasion, I wrote a murder scene in which the police arrived. Later, I checked it with the police department. A wonderful police captain spent an hour telling me police procedure. I had written the scene all wrong; in real life, my detective would not have done the things he did, nor would he have said the things I wrote. The police captain filled me in on the type of questions the police ask. If I'd checked first, I would have written the scene differently—and *correctly*. I learned quickly that talking to a specialist *before* writing saves hours of time rewriting.

Don't be afraid to talk to experts. Tell them you're writing a novel or an article—most of them will be delighted to help you. In fact, the police captain was especially pleased to set me straight. As he said, "I get so sick of reading incorrect police novels."

It's best to take a tape recorder along to get the whole experience. Use your interview techniques, but in the case of gathering material for a historical novel, it's often wise to just let the person talk freely. Many incidents generally surface which will produce a fine sequence in your book or article.

You'll probably have to check actual dates of things happening because people tend to forget the exact time period. Don't count on people's being totally accurate; they won't be. But what you're looking for here are the "feelings" and "insights" of the person who has actually experienced the events.

The Media

A great deal of factual material can be gleaned from old newspapers and magazines. Newspapers give you the daily happenings, the major concerns of the times, the political framework. Trade magazines give you many articles about a particular subject, and magazines such as *Vogue* and *Harper's Bazaar* are good sources for women's fashions.

Don't overlook radio and TV talk shows. Experts often discuss new inventions, sociological problems, "the way it was" twenty or thirty years ago.

The Library

The number of reference sources the library has is mind-boggling, and to provide a comprehensive list of all of them here would only be confusing. The best advice is to seek out the reference desk.

The reference librarian   Reference librarians are truly the writer's guardian angels and can save you hours, if not weeks, of research. They know *all* the research sources. There are literally hundreds of books in the library that can tell you where to find something, and reference librarians can direct you to those books in minutes.

The simplest way to begin researching in the library is to *look up subjects and authors in the card catalogue.* Many of the books listed will contain bibliographies that will lead you to other books and magazines on that same subject. Read everything possible. When you are researching one subject in depth, you will probably gather enough material for several articles or books.

Newspaper indexes   Most major newspapers have an index which lists the articles, by subject, that have appeared in them, along with the dates of publication. The reference librarian can direct you to these indexes. The *Newspaper Index*, published by Bell and Howell, indexes the *Los Angeles Times*, the *San Francisco Chronicle*, the *Houston Post*, the *Washington Post*, the *Chicago Tribune*, the *Detroit News*, and the *New Orleans Times-Picayune*.

Current and very recent issues of the various papers are generally on the shelves; older issues are on microfilm.

Magazine indexes   If you need to look up magazine articles, check the *Reader's Guide to Periodicals*, which has a subject index that will give you the name of the magazine in which the article appears, as well as the week, month, and year of the magazine's publication.

Some lesser-known periodical indexes are:

Agriculture Index (1919 to date): agriculture, forestry, botany, horticulture

Applied Science and Technology Index (1913 to date): aeronautics and space science, computer technology, engineering, the food and textile industries

Art Index (1929 to date): archaeology, architecture, ceramics, graphic arts, painting, sculpture

Business Periodicals Index (1958 to date): advertising, business, finance, labor, taxation, marketing (this index was preceded by *Industrial Arts Index* [1913–57])

Educational Index (1929 to date): educational psychology, bulletins and reports

Social Sciences and Humanities Index (1907–1974): scholarly journals in the humanities and social sciences

In June 1974, this index divided into two parts:

1. *Social Sciences Index* (1974 to date): economics, geography, law, criminology, medical sciences
2. *Humanities Index* (1974 to date): language, literature, performing arts, religion, theology, philosophy

Don't be frightened by microfilm   Most libraries have microfilmed indexes to magazines and newspapers. You look up your subject in the index and then ask the librarian for the microfilm file, which is in a sense a videotape cartridge without sound. You then put the "cartridge" into a special microfilm viewing machine and read the contents on a monitor that looks like a TV screen. By turning a knob or pressing buttons, you can move the material on the screen up, down, or sideways. You can even make copies of articles to take home.

Special collections   If you need highly specialized information, you're best off at the nearest university library, where you can generally research without a library card, or at the main reference library (your local librarian can direct you to this location). The university library and the main reference library have many more research resources available than your corner library.

The university library often has "special collection" rooms or shelves of rare historical material, such as journals kept by early settlers or rare first editions. Often this material is kept in cases or under lock and key, and you will have to receive permission to view it.

SOME HELPFUL RESEARCH GUIDES

1. Encyclopedias will give you an overall condensed version of your subject. Each individual "article" has a bibliography that will direct you to further information.

    The Encyclopaedia Britannica has a research service available to buyers of its encyclopedia. This service either provides you with printed research that is already in existence or it will research the subject for you and send you a printout. This will probably not supply everything you need, but the condensed form is certainly helpful, and you will gain many additional leads.

2. Need facts for a particular year? Almanacs, which come out every year, are a wonderful source of events that happened during that particular year. They're full of all manner of facts and statistics. If you're writing a historical novel, looking things up in the almanac for that year is a must. Try the following:

    The World Almanac & Book of Facts

    Reader's Digest Almanac

    Information Please Almanac

3. Need biographical information?

    Biographical Dictionaries Master Index (1975 to date) lists the names of more than 750,000 people who appear in biographical directories and refers you to particular directories such as the Marquis Who's Who publications—*Who's Who in America, Who's Who in the West, Who's Who in Jazz.* These directories give names and addresses of well-known people and in the case of celebrities often lists their agents. *Webster's Biographical Dictionary* lists more than 40,000 condensed biographies.

4. Need statistics and facts galore?

    Facts on File (1940 to date) is a world news digest issued weekly, and it cumulatively indexes world and national affairs, obituaries, and news of science, sports, religion, and finance. If you need statistics, try this fine publication.

    Statistical Abstract of the United States (1878 to date) gives statistics of marriage, divorce, death and birth rate, even temperatures of various American cities.

    Statistical Yearbook (United Nations Statistical Office, an annual publication) lists statistics for U.N. countries: population, agriculture, mining, manufacturing, trade.

    Europa Year Book (annual publication in two volumes) gives comprehensive statistical and political information on the international scene. It consists of two volumes: Volume 1 covers Europe; Volume 2 covers the rest of the world. It also lists publishers, newspapers, and radio and TV stations of every country.

    Statesman's Yearbook (one volume) lists who governs each country, current welfare benefits, crime statistics, national resources, and energy.

5. Need illustrations or want to see what period furniture looked like? *Illustration Index* (1966, supplements through 1971) indexes illustrations of practically everything you want, guiding you to periodicals in which these illustrations appear. Illustrations are listed by subject.

6. Need to locate someone?

    Polk's Directory publishes city directories for all major cities and some suburban areas. It is a "reverse" directory—you can locate someone by address or phone number.

Standard and Poor's Register of Corporations, Directors, and Executives (annual) lists names of officers of corporations, names, addresses, and phone numbers. It also lists the yearly sales figures of some 40,000 American corporations.

7. Want to read about the latest psychological discoveries?

    Psychological Abstracts (1927 to date—monthly bibliography) indexes, by author and subject, new books, journal articles, and technical reports and has a brief discussion after each item.

8. Do you want to read all the current books on a particular subject? *Subject Guides to Books in Print*, an annual guide, lists all books in print by subject.

9. Want to look up a particular author to see how many of his or her books are currently in print? *Books in Print* lists books by subject, author, and title.

10. Want to look up a paperback author to see how many of his or her books are currently in print? *Paperback Books in Print* lists paperback books by subject, author, and title.

11. Need to look up foreign phrases? *Dictionary of Foreign Phrases and Abbreviations* by Kevin Guinagh will give you common phrases in Hebrew, French, German, Greek, Italian, Irish, Spanish, Latin, and Portuguese, translated into English.

12. Need travel information?

    Hotel and Travel Index (quarterly publication) gives worldwide information on hotels and room rates.

    Travel Research Bibliography by the Travel Reference Center lists books on travel in five sections:

    periodicals and reports

    bibliographies

    travel in the United States (national publications)

    travel in the United States (state publications)

    international publications

13. Need quotations?

    Familiar Quotations. John Bartlett. Paperback (Citadel Press). A collection of passages, phrases, and proverbs traced to their sources in ancient and modern literature. *The Home Book of Quotations* (Dodd) has quotations, alphabeticall; arranged.

    Peter's Quotations: Ideas for Our Time, Lawrence Peter, paperback (Bantam), gives ancient and modern quotations and is indexed by subject and author.

14. Need to find geographical locations? Try *Goode's Atlas* (Rand McNally).

15. Need to find a particular reference book? Try *Guide to Reference Books* and *American Reference Books Annual* (1970 to date).

Summary

Each writer has his or her own research method. Some writers like looseleaf pager in a ring binder with file tabs indicating particular subjects; others like notecards. I prefer to use large (5" × 8") notecards. Title each card by subject, then add the title of the article or book, the author, publisher, and place and date of publication.

An easy way to do your notecards is to photocopy the material you want (photographically reducing it, if possible), then cut it to size to fit the notecard and tape it on. "Hilighter" pens can accent the information you need. This method is a blessing if you hate writing in longhand and particularly if your handwriting is bad, for it's not uncommon to do a lot of writing on your notecards and then discover you can't read what you've written! Having the remarks in context helps, too, when using the material in an article or nonfiction book.

Don't forget to number your cards—1, 2, 3, and so on—for each part of the article so that you will have the material in order.

If you are doing a novel, you may wish to title the cards with various research information: clothes; specific years and the particular events that happened in them; furniture; music; automobiles; plants, city or hometown information; name, description, and background of various characters; theme and related thematic ideas; technical information (for example, how to detonate bombs); police procedure; information relating to a particular occupation.

Properly prepared, you'll discover that researching is great fun—and many writers like it as much as writing itself! Research gives you a chance to investigate all those subjects you've always wanted to know about, and it gives the breath of life and authenticity to your work.

Exercises

1. If you are writing a historical novel, make a scrapbook and create sections for it. Entitle the sections: clothing, houses, vehicles, furniture, world events (which happened at this time), famous people of the time, World leaders, songs, political issues, inventions, kinds of utilities available (gas, electricity, telephone, telegraph). Cut out pictures of various people and things from assorted magazines and put them in your scrap book. (You may also use notecards.)

2. If you are able, interview people who lived during this period. See the interview section in this book. If this is an early period in history, set up an interview with a specialist in the period, such as a college or university professor. If you are writing material in the present time interview appropriate people such as: policemen, reporters, anthropologists, business people, doctors, lawyers, etc.

3. Go to your local library and make up a bibliography of books, both nonfiction and fiction, which deal with the period of time you are researching.

4. Go to the library and look up your subject in the *Reader's Guide to Periodicals*. Prepare a bibliography of appropriate articles.

Fiction Writer's Bonus

Article/Nonfiction Section

Includes Sample Query Letters/Proposals
and Synopses

*For Fiction Writers Who also Want to Write
Articles and Nonfiction*

Many fiction-writing techniques such as characterization, setting, and dialogue are used in writing fiction and nonfiction.

13

Article Writing:
How to Begin

What Does It Take to Be an Article Writer?

Do you prefer to write about things that are actually happening around you? Do you get angry about things in the news, so angry that you want to sit down and write a letter to the editor? Are you incensed by injustice, to the point of often collecting facts to gain more knowledge on the subject? Do you have an incurable bent for arguing and proving your point? Do you have an insatiable curiosity about local history, sports, unusual pastimes, celebrities, how a business was started, or what launched a particular person into a particular career? Are you an armchair authority on a particular field? Do you like to travel to seek out things that fascinate you? Do you enjoy talking to people, or, more important, *listening* to what they have to say? If you answered yes to most of these questions, and you love to write, you have all the earmarks of an article writer.

How to Begin

There is no easy way to become a writer. Nor is there a fairy godmother to wave a wand over you and *make* you a writer. You have to do that job yourself. But there is one foolproof way to become an article writer, though it requires more work on your part than just reading a book on writing.

1. Pick out a magazine you wish to write for and read one full year's worth of issues. If you have time, read two full years' worth of issues.
2. Select the articles you believe to be the best.
3. Then, one by one, copy the articles either on your typewriter or in your own handwriting. As you type or write, you will *see* how the best journalists put their articles together. In this way, you can absorb techniques that it has taken great journalists years to learn.

Two things make a good article writer: creativity and craft. You either have creativity or you don't. But you can learn craft, and you will learn it faster by analytically studying good articles than by just reading a book.

A selling article writer not only knows the craft of writing but is also adept at marketing. He or she *knows* the magazine and slants articles toward that magazine. After you have studied the magazine you want to write for, notice the kind of material it publishes. Make a marketing survey.

How to Make a Marketing Survey

1. Make a list of the subjects covered for the last two years in the magazine of your choice.
2. How is this material approached?
   a. In a folksy manner?
   b. In a sophisticated manner?
   c. Intellectually?
   d. Emotionally?
   e. Anecdotally?
   f. With facts and figures?
   g. Is the emphasis primarily on shock, or is the material presented in a low-key way?
   h. For what age group? If you wrote a profile of the average reader of this magazine, what would you write?
   i. Do you detect any biases the editor has?
3. What is the circulation of the magazine? Does it reach a wide audience or a limited one? For example, is it designed for the traditional family group or just young mothers with new babies?
4. What *kinds* of articles does this magazine feature?
   a. how-to?
   b. societal problems?
   c. family problems?
   d. profiles?
   e. professional advice?
5. Are all the articles written by staff members, or does there seem to be a chance for freelance writers? Check *Writer's Market* to find this information.

6. What stylistic devices do you notice?
    a. long/short sentences?
    b. ordinary language usage or professional jargon?

Make a Market Research Card

After you have made your marketing survey of a magazine, take a 5" × 8" notecard and record your insights on the back.

On the front of the card, in the left-hand corner, write the magazine's name, address, and telephone number, and the editor's name. Then type in the article requirements as listed in *Writer's Market* (or photocopy the listing and tape it onto the card to save typing).

It's a good idea to begin with a file of at least fifteen cards. Be sure to pick the magazines you really want to write for. If you regularly submit to these fifteen magazines, the editors will soon recognize your name.

What Exactly Is *Writer's Market*?

Writer's Market is an updated, very complete guide to magazines that buy freelance writing. You can order *Writer's Market* by writing to F&W Publishing Corporation, 1507 Dana Avenue, Cincinnati, OH 45207–1005, or you might find it at your local library or bookstore. Most college libraries have the most recent issues of *Writer's Market*. It covers advertising copywriting, book publishers, subsidy book publishers (places where you pay to have your book published) company publications, consumer publications, gag writing, greeting card publishers, scriptwriting/playwriting/syndicates/trade/technical/professional magazines, and agents. It also has "nuts and bolts" articles, such as how to submit manuscripts to publishers and magazines.

Writer's Market generally gives the name of the editor (though you should always compare that name with the name of the editor on the masthead of a recent issue of the magazine to be sure the editor is still working there). Note how much is paid for articles, the information as to photographs and rights purchased, and whether multiple submissions are accepted.

Sample listings are:

THE SATURDAY EVENING POST. The Saturday Evening Post Society, 1100 Waterway Blvd., Indianapolis, IN 46202. (317)636-8881. Editor: Cory SerVaas, M.D. Executive Editor: Ted Kreiter, 40% freelance written. A family-oriented magazine published 9 times/year covering preventive medicine and health care. Circ. 700,000. Pays on publication. Byline given. Buys all rights. Submit seasonal/holiday material at least 3 months in advance. Simultaneous, photocopied and previously published submissions OK. Computer printout submissions acceptable. Reports in 1 month on queries; 6 weeks on mss. Writer's guidelines for business size SAE and 1 first class stamp.

Nonfiction: Barbara Potter, articles editor. General interest, health, interview/profile, religious. "No political articles, or articles containing sexual innuendo or hypersophistication." Buys 40–60 mss/year. Query with published clips. Length: 750–2,500 words. Pays $100 minimum. Sometimes pays the expenses of writers on assignment.

Photos: State availability of photos with submission. Reviews negatives and transparencies. Model releases and identification of subjects required. Buys one-time rights or all rights. Payment and rights negotiable.

Columns/Departments: Money Talk and Gardening/Home Improvement. Travel (tourism-oriented). "See recent issues for topics and slant." Query with published clips. Length: 750–1,000 words. Pays $150 minimum.

Fiction: Rebecca Whitney, fiction editor. Adventure, historical, humorous, and mainstream. "Anything except humor has only a *remote* chance." Buys approximately 2 mss/year. Send complete ms. Length: 2,500 words. Pays $150 minimum.

Fillers: Jack Gramling, Post Scripts editor. Anecdotes, short humor and light verse. Buys 200+/year. Length: 300 words maximum. Pays $15.

Tips: The areas most open to freelancers are "Post Scripts—no cute kiddy sayings; keep submissions up to date—no put downs of hippies, etc. when submitting, let the editor make up his own mind whether your material is humorous—and Travel—no first person—it's egocentric, thus boring; select mainstream locales; and have lots of pictures or know where to find them."

SELECTED READING. The National Research Bureau, Inc., 424 N. 3rd St., Burlington IA 52601. Editor Rhonda Wilson. Editorial Supervisor: Doris J. Ruschill. 75% freelance written. Eager to work with new unpublished writers, works with a small number of new/unpublished writers each year. For industrial workers of all ages. Quarterly magazine. Pays on publication. Publishes ms an average of 1 year after acceptance. Buys all rights. Previously published submissions OK. Computer printout submissions acceptable; prefers letter-quality to dot-matrix. Submit seasonal/holiday material 6–7 months in advance of issue date. Reports in 3 weeks. Writer's guidelines for SASE.

Nonfiction: General interest (economics, health, safety, working relationships); how-to; and travel (out of the way places). No material on car repair. Buys 10–12 mss/year. Query. A short outline or synopsis is best. Lists of titles are no help. Length: 400–600 words. Pays 4¢/word.

Tips: "Writers have a better chance of breaking in at our publication with short articles and fillers because all of our articles are short."

Researching the market guide to publishing is a must. The point is that a seasoned writer never sits down and just bats out an article without a designated market. He or she studies the market carefully and aims at a particular magazine. If you examine the *Saturday Evening Post*'s want list, you will see that the articles it wants have very specific characteristics:

1. Articles must be written for a conservative, middle-aged, college-educated audience.
2. The *Saturday Evening Post* prefers a positive, upbeat approach for both fiction and articles.
3. Fiction and articles are of general interest.

After you have made a marketing research card, have absorbed all your recorded information, and have read as many back issues as possible, you are ready to use this material to **slant** the article you write toward that magazine. You will write with a *specific* market in mind.

How to Find Salable Topics

First of all, your market survey of each magazine should have given you some tips. Certain types of articles recur in certain magazines, and this preference indicates that the editors have a special interest in those subjects.

It's a good idea, too, to note the "Letters to the Editor" section. You will be able to determine what kinds of articles have appeared in past issues, and this will give you a clue as to whether the magazine is open to controversial ideas that draw reader reaction.

Salable ideas are all around. Years ago, the publisher of *Collier's* magazine, Tom Beck, bet two of his staff writers that he could find a hot lead for *Collier's* at any point a taxicab would stop. The three men got into a cab and when one of the two writers yelled, "Stop," Beck would climb out of the cab, look around, and point out a lead that the other two writers had to admit was good and highly publishable.

If there's a successful or unusual business in your neighborhood, that business might make a fine article. For example, a small neighborhood theatre might manage to stay in business while many other theatres are folding—what is the theatre owner doing to attract so many customers? If you have a hobby, it might be the source of several articles. Your job, your house of worship, your club, your friends and relatives may offer fine article material. Don't forget small news items in the daily papers that offer article leads.

Pick Topics You Enjoy

While good articles are everywhere, you also should consider: Do you really *want* to write this particular article? In the main, it's good advice to write about subjects that really interest you. *Pick out topics you like, topics you enjoy researching!* Your enthusiasm will show. You'll have what Ray Bradbury calls *zest*. Also, you'll be far more productive if you genuinely like what you're doing. Also, try to submit your work to magazines you enjoy reading; you won't hate rereading back issues to keep up with slant and special requirements.

Specialize in a Specific Area

It's also good advice to become an authority on certain subjects. For one thing, you'll establish a reputation in those fields, and editors will automatically think of you when they are considering articles in those areas. Then, too, knowing a particular subject well will probably save you from having more researching, analyzing and revision, and endless sweat than you'd have when writing unfamiliar material.

A case in point is Dick Trubo, who enjoys writing on health. His articles have appeared in *Cosmopolitan, McCall's,* and many other women's magazines. When editors think of health articles or books, they seek him to do them.

Parlay Your Research

Trubo recommends "parlaying" research. The research he used to write a nonfiction book on health provided him with material for numerous articles. For example, the subject of dental care might be parlayed into dental care for the young mother, dental care for the infant, dental care for the senior citizen, and perhaps even an article for a trade journal: "Do Dentists Neglect Their Own Teeth?" Each of these articles appeals to a different market, yet only one major research job is necessary.

Keep Files on Subjects That Appeal to You

Make a habit of clipping news items and filing them in appropriately labeled folders. For example, if you're interested in writing family-oriented articles, you might have a file folder entitled "Divorce" or "Child Abuse." Such a collection of articles is invaluable for instant research, such as much-needed statistics and surveys; also, the articles may suggest spin-offs—a "pro" or "con" article, or additional ideas that have not been covered. By rereading your files, you will often come up with a new idea. You'll have all your research material available, but with a different slant.

Sometimes you'll spot trends in writing. Perhaps an article entitled "Five Rules for a Successful Marriage" may stimulate you to write an article questioning these rules.

Remember that you are not stealing. An idea cannot be copyrighted. You are, rather, compiling material for an article.

Take Time to Read Other Articles Written on Your Subject

If you want to check on what has been published on a particular topic you want to write about, begin with *Reader's Guide to Periodicals.* It is catalogued alphabetically both by author and topic. If only a few articles have been written on your topic, you may have a definite advantage. If many articles have been written on your subject, you may have to think of a new slant for this material.

Summary

The main reason many new writers do not sell is that they do not understand the importance of marketing. Writing is a business, and it must be approached in a businesslike way. DO YOUR HOMEWORK. Study every magazine as a text. Copy an article to see how it is written. Always read the back issues of the magazines you want to write for. Make a marketing survey. Note what kind of approaches each magazine prefers. Note what kinds of articles are featured, and make a profile of the reader who reads each particular magazine. Make a marketing information card for each magazine. Study *Writer's Market* carefully. Keep alert for salable ideas around you, in your neighborhood (ideas may spring from friends, relatives, and working associates). Don't forget to *milk* your topics so that you get several articles from your idea.

If you approach writing in this businesslike way, you'll be a success. Don't sit down and write an article off the top of your head, an article that may not have a market. Know what sells—*then* write it!

Exercises

1. Read the *Writer's Market Guide* and look up magazines that you would like to publish in. Note the various slants. Considering the style and slant of the magazine you like best, write a lead and tailor it to that magazine.

2. Take an article you really admire and type it out on your own typewriter or word processor. When finished, study the article to see how it was constructed.

3. Research at least two years of issues of the magazine you want to publish in. Make a list of the subjects covered in those last two years. Does the editor seem to favor certain subjects? Are there some subjects that have never been covered, subjects which you believe the editor might be interested in?

4. Research the leads of the articles in the magazine you wish to publish in. Is there a particular type of lead that the editor seems to favor?

5. Start a research file for a particular subject you want to write on. Write an article from the material you've gathered in your research file.

14

How to Write
the Query Letter
for the Article

Once you have made your market survey, know the magazines you want to write for, and have several topics in mind that are suitable for these magazines, you are ready to write the query letter. Also, if you have finished a novel and are looking for a literary agent or an editor, the query letter is your "foot in the door."

What Is a Query Letter?

A query letter is primarily a sales letter, designed to sell your article to an editor. It is a *showcase* of your writing, revealing your knowledge of article technique, and for this reason you should proofread it to be sure it has no spelling or punctuation errors. Your grammar must be impeccable, and typographical errors should be neatly corrected.

Why Is a Query Necessary?

Successful writers do not have time to write articles on "spec" (speculation —"without pay"). So they query first to see if an editor is interested in an article on this particular subject. If the editor says yes, only *then* does the writer begin work on the actual article.

If you send in an article "cold," without having had an editor express an interest in it, it could be rejected for many reasons: The editor may not like the subject, it may be a subject not related to the interests of the magazine readership, it may be too long or too short, it may be written in a style different from that ordinarily used in the magazine, or the editor may not like the way the material is presented. Remember, the editor is very busy. He or she has already okayed queries on articles that seem right for the magazine and now has to read those articles. Plus, those articles need to be proofed and sent to the layout department. On a small magazine, the editor may have to worry about financial considerations—such as readership—besides editorial responsibilities. Consequently, the editor may take anywhere from two to six months to read your article. If the article is rejected, which may well happen, you will have lost a great deal of time.

On the other hand, a one-page query would have received the editor's attention right away, and you would have known within two to six *weeks* whether the editor was interested in your material.

If you are a new novelist and seeking an agent, note that one of the best ways to get an agent is through a query letter. The agent is primarily a salesperson and does not have time to read unsolicited manuscripts. A professionally written query letter, accompanied by a synopsis and three chapters (a "package"), may attract his or her attention.

Similarly, if you wish to submit your novel to a publishing house, it's best to send *a package*—the query letter, a synopsis, and three chapters—to the fiction editor. Editors are deluged by unsolicited manuscripts and rarely read them. These "over the transom" manuscripts are often given to the telephone operators, the clerical staff, the maintenance crew, and anyone else handy at the publishing house to read. In fact, many editors send back the manuscripts unopened as soon as they arrive. Very few of them are ever bought. But both fiction and nonfiction editors will read a query letter and respond to it. If the editor likes the first three chapters of the work you've submitted, he or she will write and ask to see the rest of the book. Now, you have a very interested editor.

Why Does an Editor Prefer a Query to a Complete Manuscript?

Role play being an editor. Manuscripts to read crowd your desk, and new ones are stacking up in a great mound on the incoming-mail shelf. You have two phones buzzing with important calls, layouts to be approved, captions to be changed, proofs to be read. Naturally, you will do the easiest things first. Several professional-looking one-page queries catch your eye. It takes only a few minutes to read them to see if the ideas interest you; and you can scribble a short note, yes or no, stick the answer into the self-addressed envelope, and get the reply right back to the writer.

Besides the advantage of eliciting a quick answer, the query also gives the editor a chance to *participate* in the writing of the article—a definite psychological advantage. He or she may add a few suggestions that improve the structure, meaning, or slant. The idea of the article may also spark the concept of a whole monthly focus on that particular subject. Editors have to think three or four months ahead. An article bought in July may appear in November or December.

May You Query More Than One Editor at a Time?

Definitely yes! If you're specializing in articles, it's a very good idea to send out as many as fifteen queries at a time, one to each magazine you have selected. Out of the fifteen you may receive three responses. Out of those three, pick the magazine you most favor (because of prestige or amount of money offered) and send your completed article to it. **Do not send the completed article to all three magazines, or you will be in serious trouble.** If one of them buys it, you will then have to write the other two magazines and tell them they can't publish the article. Remember that once the editor has made up his mind on an article, he has probably made plans as to magazine layout, and if you back out on him you will probably anger him to the point of his never wanting to accept an article from you again. Wait till the first article has been rejected before sending it on to your second choice.

If the article is purchased by the first editor, you might consider writing another version of the article, from another slant, and submitting it to the second editor. If you sell three versions of the same article—congratulations!

On the other hand, if you're a novelist, you may have to judge whether sending out a multiple submission is worth it. It's true, you can send fifteen packages to fifteen agents and pick the agent who seems most interested in your work. But you may wish to concentrate on one particular agent. In this case, you may wish to send your material to him or her alone.

Many publishing houses openly state that they are not averse to reading multiple submissions. Check your marketing guide to be sure which houses those are. Some houses dislike reading multiple submissions because an editor may spend a great deal of time on a manuscript only to find that you've already sold it to another publisher.

Should You Query if You Have Not Yet Written the Manuscript?

Article writers rarely submit a complete article to a magazine. For the non-fiction writer, the query is asking a magazine whether it is interested in this particular idea. However, you should provide enough information/statistics in your query to sound authoritative. You do not have to do a thorough research job *until* you write the article. If you have a good clipping file, you may already have the statistics you need. Also, if you have access to a good researcher, you may be able to get needed information quickly and easily. If you decide you need a research assistant, a good place to find one is at your local university. Often, students will do research for a fee. Contact the student employment office.

New novelists should generally have a complete manuscript ready, for the agent or editor might ask to see the rest of the book. Recognized novelists are in the enviable position of either calling their agents or editors and telling them about the idea in mind, or typing a query letter. Established novelists are usually able to sell books on synopses and three chapters. Meanwhile, such writers as Harold Robbins and James Michener merely have to mention that they have an idea, and their respective agents are able to negotiate megabuck contracts on the unwritten idea.

Theme

Although the article writer need not have done all of the research before querying, the writer should know the "theme" of the article—the way the article will be shaped thematically. Avoid generalizations in queries. Don't say, "I want to write about the ocean." Rather, say, "The Atlantic Ocean is becoming dangerously polluted with radioactive substances, and sea life is threatened." Try to state the theme, the message, of your article in one specific sentence.

In the fiction query, theme is also important. The events that occur in plot are relatively common. What is there about *your* book that is different? Why will it sell? Is this a book that will have meaning to today's reader? Does it say something? Is this a book of significance?

How Long Should a Query Letter Be?

A query letter is generally one page long, single spaced, typed, with double spaces between paragraphs. Use 8 ½" × 11" good white typing or computer paper. Don't use peculiar sizes and shapes. Avoid erasable bond paper, as not only may it smudge, but occasionally the print may wipe off. You may also want to use letterhead paper with a distinctive logo or imprint to help the editor remember your name. Be sure to leave 1 ½" margins on all sides of the paper—editors like to write things in the margins. Indent paragraphs five to six spaces, and be sure you have a good, dark, black typewriter ribbon, and that your typewriter is clean. Few things infuriate an editor more than having to figure out what you're saying because your ribbon was worn out or you didn't clean your typewriter keys.

To Whom Do You Send Your Query?

Magazine writers should always address a query letter to a particular editor, whose name either appears on the magazine masthead or is listed in *Writer's Market* or *LMP* (*Literary Market Place*). Use the salutation Mr. or Ms. If you don't know whether the editor is a man or a woman, use the whole name: "Dear Dale Cromby." Don't make the mistake of addressing your query to "Dear Editor"; it will receive the same attention *you* give to junk mail.

Novelists should address their package to a specific agent or editor. Be sure the name is spelled correctly. If you're not sure, make a telephone call to the agency or publishing house. A really well-known agent or editor can be turned off when his or her name is misspelled. Consider that most agents and editors have spent years establishing their literary reputations. They're proud of their reputations. Besides, the idea of submitting your work to this particular agent or editor should indicate that you think very highly of this person and *want* him or her to handle your work. If you don't even know how the name is spelled, you don't know much about the person—and the impression is that you obviously don't care, either.

What Is the Format of a Query Letter?

A query letter generally consists of four paragraphs.

The First Paragraph

In magazine writing, the opening paragraph should feature your idea, should present a theme (message), and should be written in a way that "grabs" the reader's attention. Work to create an exciting first sentence. The opener might be a:

1. **Statistic:** "Eighty-six percent of homicides are alcohol related."
2. **Anecdote:** "On black Friday, John Harris killed a three-year-old girl. He didn't use a gun. He used his car. John Harris was a drunk."
3. **Straight news lead expanded:** "Jody Campbell, noted rock musician, confessed that he lost his wife, his children and his professional career because of heroin."
4. **Quotation:** " 'You try to stay sane and live each day,' says this man on death

row. John Daily is tall and quiet. He looks like Clint Eastwood. Convicted of murdering a family camping out in Mojeska Canyon, he says angrily: 'I didn't kill anybody.' Newly discovered evidence may prove him right. Is John Daily a victim of our court system?"

5. **Question:** "Who pays for alcohol abuse? Despite our weak economy, U.S. citizens spend $77 billion a year to support alcoholism. But what about the lives destroyed? Who can put a dollar value on lives or families?"

The Second Paragraph

The second paragraph should expand your topic, giving further information and perhaps some of the choicest anecdotes you're going to use. An expansion of the topic five (question) lead might be:

> Alcoholism is a progressive disease. The end is insanity or death. There *is* something you can do to help; it's called "caring intervention." Lynn Jones, thirty-three-year-old teacher, and her family priest turned her husband's life around dramatically. It was not an easy experience. When they confronted her husband, James, he walked out of the house and slammed the door behind him. "I almost didn't come back," he said. But "caring intervention" saved this marriage, and it may save a person in your own family.

The Third Paragraph

The third paragraph should give your credentials as an authority to write this article. For example, if you're a counselor working with alcoholics, say so. If you have related academic degrees, mention them. Also, if you're writing from direct experience, this is important; it gives authenticity.

If you're not an authority in the field, disregard any mention of your credentials and instead give the title of the article you're proposing, the length of the article (number of words, not number of pages), and whether you can supply photographs. If you have any *major* magazine publications to your credit, have published books on the subject, or have lectured widely and have perhaps appeared on radio and TV shows, this is the paragraph in which to mention these facts.

For example, an appropriate paragraph might be:

> As a psychologist and a college counselor lecturing on alcoholism, I feel that the method of "caring intervention" is a constructive one that may possibly save families years of heartache, secret shame, and even perhaps the very life of the alcoholic.

The Fourth Paragraph

The last paragraph should be a persuasive close. If you have used paragraph three to give your credentials, then include in paragraph four the title and length of the article. Using topic five, a suitable close might be:

As 1 out of 3 Americans is a potential alcoholic, the dynamics of "caring intervention" are vital information which a large percentage of your [name of magazine] readership will value. The article "Can You Help an Alcoholic?" should run about 1800 words (no photos). I have enclosed SASE (a self-addressed stamped envelope) for your reply. I look forward to hearing from you.

Cordially,

(your name)

Try to be positive in your close. If you ask a question—"Is your magazine interested in this article?"—it's easy for the editor to say no. It's more affirmative to say: "I look forward to hearing from you."

Final Touches

After you have finished typing your query letter, *proofread* it to catch any technical errors, and correct your typos neatly. It's a good idea to photocopy copies of the queries, leaving the editor's name and address off (make sure the photocopies are good ones). Then you can type the name and address of each editor individually. If you are fortunate, you have a word processor, for in today's writing field, a word processor is practically a necessity. Editors value the uniform, neat manuscripts produced. **Be sure to keep a copy of your work for your file;** you can also duplicate this copy to make more copies.

After you have signed the query letter, you can mail it in a number 10 envelope, with a number 9 envelope (or a folded number 10) inside —postage affixed.

Keep a Record of Your Queries and Article Submissions

Take a 5" × 8" notecard and title it with the name of the article. Then, underneath the title, put the date the query was mailed and the names of the magazines to which it was sent. Leave a space for the date it was returned to you and also some room for editorial comments—if you have sent your queries to fifteen magazines and have not received any "bites," some of the comments received may help you to create a more dynamic query.

If an editor wants to see the article, enter on the card the date the article was sent; if it is returned, enter the date you received it back.

Submissions Card Format

You may want to use different colored cards for different types of magazines (ladies, mens, self-help, etc.) (5" × 8" index card)

Title: "Can You Help an Alcoholic?"

1. 8/20/88 <u>Ladies' Home Journal</u> (editor)   Returned 9/1/88

   Comments

2. 8/20/88 <u>Redbook</u> (editor)   Returned 9/8/88

   Comments

3. 8/20/88 <u>McCall's</u> (editor)   Returned 9/4/88

   Comments

4. 8/20/88 <u>Cosmopolitan</u> (editor)   Returned 9/3/88

   Comments

5. 8/20/88 <u>Family Circle</u> (editor)   Returned 9/4/88

   Comments

If you do not hear from a magazine within six weeks, it's a good idea to send the editor a self-addressed postage-paid postcard in an envelope. On the back of the postcard type:

Dear (Editor's name):
Name of Magazine
Address

The article [title] which was mailed on [date] has arrived _____ . has not arrived us _____ .

Thank you,

your name

The advantage of a postcard worded in this way is that the editor can make a quick check and send the card right back. He or she can also scribble a note on it. If you ask for your manuscript back, the editor might just send it back and you will have lost a sale. The postcard method politely jogs the memory and reminds the editor to do something about the article.

Queries: Some Dos and Don'ts

1. Don't try to make the editor "promise" to buy your article or offer you a fixed price before he or she has even seen it.
2. If you can't provide photos, say so.
3. Don't include too much information—just enough to *tease* the editor into reading more. Save some of your choice material so the editor will want to read the complete article. Your task in the query is not to do a *Reader's Digest*-type of condensation, but rather to pique the editor's curiosity.
4. Don't threaten or insult the editor: "If you don't publish this, you're stupid!"
5. Be *specific* with facts and statistics. If you're talking about accidents, don't say "some" accidents if you can say, "Fifty-one percent of accidents."
6. Don't try to impress the editor with your oversized vocabulary, and don't try to swamp him or her with technical jargon. Simple, pithy explanations are best. If you can't communicate with the editor, how can you communicate with the magazine's readers, who probably have lower reading skills?
7. Don't tell the editor this article is really "hot" or "a big one" and ask for expense money. The editor is pretty jaundiced about "big" stories. After all, the article might not be that "hot" in three or four months, when it's to be published. Besides, maybe it's libelous, obscene, and not publishable at all.
8. Don't tell the editor how much your relatives/boss/friends enjoy your writing or that you are "noted" for your letters back home.
9. Don't tell the editor you need money right away and to send a check immediately. Keep your family problems out of your queries. Besides, asking for an immediate check is unprofessional.
10. Don't send gifts with your queries. If you have a good concept, you don't need to offer a bribe. Besides, the editor might not like your gift.
11. Don't tell the editor you're in a writing class and you'd "really appreciate help." The editor is looking for professionals, not amateurs.

On the other hand, if an agent or editor sends you an incisive letter about your work, pointing out what needs to be corrected and encouraging you, do write a thank-you letter. Sometimes, a very valuable relationship is built in this way. Also, editors and agents like to be appreciated, too.

The Waiting Game (Its Name Is Optimism)

Don't be discouraged by brusque letters or printed rejections slips. The adage (in reverse) is: "What is gall for one is honey for another." The article one editor doesn't consider suitable may be the exact thing another editor is looking for.

Selling your writing by mail is not unlike the job of a door-to-door salesman. Fuller Brush says its average sale is one in eight. Queries have a similar ratio. Many writers send off fifteen queries per idea and have three ideas (forty-five queries) in the mail at all times. Expect to wait four to six weeks to hear from a magazine. But in time you'll be writing the articles as the affirmative queries come in, and you'll be generating new query letters and mailing them out.

Also, as editors come to know and depend upon you, your batting average will improve; and editors will be calling *you* to do articles they have in mind. To be a success, you can't afford to be depressed. Keep writing!

Summary

Query the editor before writing your article. Don't be afraid to send multiple copies. Research just enough to give authenticity to your concept and do a complete research job only when you have an okay to do the article. Keep your query letter to one page, four paragraphs:

1. Use an exciting opening sentence that leads into your idea. Intrigue the editor, who is your first reader!
2. Your second paragraph should expand upon the idea. Use statistics and quotations by authorities to bolster your presentation.
3. The third paragraph should give your credentials.
4. Your fourth paragraph is a persuasive close, also giving catchy title of your article, word length, and information on the availability of photos.

Address your query to a *named editor* and make a submissions card that records where and when your article was sent. If the editor doesn't reply as soon as you'd like, send a reminder postcard.

If you approach article writing like a professional, you'll soon be making professional wages!

Sample Article Query

Your Name
Your Street Address
City, State, ZIP
Telephone Number

Date

Editor's Name
Magazine
Street Address
City, State, ZIP

Dear (Editor's name):

Who pays for alcohol abuse? Despite today's weak economy, U.S. citizens spend $77 billion a year to support alcoholism. But what about the lives destroyed? Who can put a dollar value on a life or a family?

Alcoholism is a progressive disease. The end is insanity or death. But there is something <u>you</u> can do to help; it's called "caring intervention." Lynn Jones, thirty-three-year-old teacher, and her family priest turned her husband's life around dramatically. It was not an easy experience. When they confronted her husband, James, he walked out of the house and slammed the door behind him. "I almost didn't come back," he said. But "caring intervention" saved this marriage, and it may save a person in your own family.

As a psychologist and a college counselor lecturing on alcoholism, I feel that the method of "caring intervention" is a constructive one that may possibly save families years of heartache, secret shame, and even, perhaps, the very life of the alcoholic.

As 1 out of 3 Americans is a potential alcoholic, the dynamics of "caring intervention" are vital information that a large percentage of [name of magazine]'s readership will value. The article "Can You Help an Alcoholic?" should run about 1800 words (no photos available). I have enclosed an SASE for your reply. I look forward to hearing from you.

Cordially,

(your name)

Sample Novel Query

Your Name
Your Street Address
City, State, ZIP
Telephone Number

Date

Agent's/Editor's Name
Agency/Publishing Company Name
Street Address
City, State, ZIP

Dear (Name):

Enclosed you will find a synopsis and three chapters of a novel, *The Loves of Mary Magdalene*. A historical novel that takes place in Magdala in 17 A.D., it is the tale of a woman who dreamed of love and power and found more than she dreamed.

The young Jewish girl Mary Magdalene is entranced by a "golden lover on a white horse"—the Roman centurion Quintus Gallus. Sensuous, with powerful emotions, and born with "second sight" (clairvoyance), Mary sees fragments of her future life. Seduced by Quintus, she is later captured by Arabs, then escapes to Caesarea only to be thrown into a life of prostitution. She becomes a courtesan in Caesarea and, for a time, the mistress of Pontius Pilate. But her painful love for Quintus leads her to hashish and finally to insanity; she is "possessed" by a devil, a dark voice in her mind. Mad on the streets and tormented by her "devil," she faces stoning but is rescued by a strange Galilean who has marvelous powers of healing: Jesus of Nazareth. It is Jesus who reveals the real mysteries of love to Mary and who teaches her to "walk the rainbow" to spiritual understanding.

This is a novel of people, adventure, and passion. But it is also a Jungian alchemic parable of transmutation, and it has much meaning for those interested in mystical Christianity, yoga, holistic health, ESP, and mythology of the Joseph Cambellian variety. Mary is a questing hero, but she is also the eternal questing hero of the mythic round; and if Jesus is the Biblical Christ, He is essentially the Magus figure who leads humanity to a higher state of consciousness.

I have a Ph.D. in comparative literature, specializing in myth, and have published two novels, *One More Time* and *Ocean's Edge*, both of which won literary awards. Thank you for your consideration. I look forward to hearing from you.

Cordially,

(your name)

Exercises

1. Type a query letter and proofread it. Check the dos and don'ts section of this chapter and the query format to be sure your query is professional. See pages 179 and 180 for sample queries.
2. Photocopy fifteen copies of the query, leaving the editor's name and address off. Then type in the respective names of the magazines to which you wish to submit your work.
3. Mail the queries. Good luck!!

15

Writing the Article

An article is not written like a news story. The news story is written in pyramid style: The major facts are condensed in the first paragraph, then the following paragraphs form a pyramid, each one referring to the lead paragraph and giving additional details. In a perfect news story, the paragraphs can be cut—from the bottom upward—until only the lead, with the essential facts, is left. News stories are written in this fashion so that the paper may print as much of the story as it has room for. However, an article cannot be cut in this fashion, for cutting the conclusion of the article would destroy the summary of the article—the *message* that the writer means to convey.

The article has three parts: the lead (the introduction), the body, and the conclusion. The lead is to the magazine writer what the "hook" is to the fiction writer. It evokes interest—it hooks the reader. The body is the main part of the article, and the conclusion wraps things up.

The Lead

The lead, the opening paragraph, does three things:

1. It gives the reader an idea of what the article is going to be about.
2. It indicates the tone, the mood, of the article.
3. It catches the reader's attention and makes him or her want to read on.

The reader is hooked by three things: the title, the subhead, and the lead. The title is always important because initially it hooks the editor, but often the editor changes the title to appeal to a wider audience. The editor will also invent a subhead to attract the reader and this subhead often appears on the cover of the magazine; so the one thing the writer must create is a strong lead.

To find the lead, look over your research—at the facts, the statistics you have gathered. It's a good idea to organize your research by topic. Some writers like to use:

1. notecards
2. a large notebook with divider pages labeled with topic names
3. loose sheets with topic headings and cut-and-pasted bits of photocopied research that were originally pinned up around the typewriter
4. large blackboards with involved diagrams

Do whatever feels comfortable to you—but do use some method of organizing your material.

After going through your research, use the most important fact you have for your lead. If you don't have one big fact, combine several smaller ones or use the most startling statistics, or pick out what seems to you the most "exciting" fact. For example, let's say you have a documented quotation which states that more than 79 million people over the age of twelve own a bike. Such a quotation could be used as a lead for a health article, a safety article, an article about how to buy a bike, an article on how to repair a bike, or an article on bike tours. By this time, of course, you have selected the "direction" of your article. However, your research can always be used for several other types of articles.

Once you have selected your fact or quotation and know the direction of the article, the next thing is to **tie your facts to your reader.** Using the quotation about bike owners, one might write: "Over 79,000,000 Americans over 12 own a bike—are you one of them? If so, do you know about the many exciting bicycle tours in the U.S.?"

Before Beginning the Lead

When you are constructing the lead, you should know:

1. how you're going to use the material you have—the direction you're going to go with it
2. the ending of the article (if you know the ending, you can write to it)
3. the controlling idea (the theme)

You should have a pattern in your mind of the article, and when you have that pattern, you are ready to begin your lead. Remember that the most important factor in the lead is **catching the reader's attention.** You must make your readers feel that this topic is vitally important to them, or it is something exceedingly interesting, or it will just plain amuse them—and most of all, you must make them want to keep reading!

While you must catch the reader's attention in the first paragraph, many writers will try to hook the reader in the first couple of sentences:

> This year over 160,000 children will suffer an eye injury—will your child be one of them? Yet 90% of these injuries are preventable, and a few simple precautions might save your child's sight.

Kinds of Leads

There are approximately ten kinds of leads and, of course, many variations.

The Summary Lead

In the summary lead the writer sums up the main points to be discussed or states the point he or she intends to prove in the article. The advantage of this lead is that it lets the reader know exactly what the article is about. For example:

> You can protect yourself against inflation through art, antiques, real estate, international sanctuaries, tax shelters, and estate planning. Each has advantages and disadvantages.

The Anecdote Lead

The basis of the anecdote lead is a "story" the writer tells about someone or something; this incident applies in a direct way to the article:

> It was June, 1937, in Berlin, and Fritz Leib had just crossed the street to get a newspaper. Suddenly a patrolman, a young blond man, walked toward him. "You're Jewish, aren't you?" Fritz felt his heart pounding, felt his mouth go dry. "Yes," he replied. "Come with me," the patrolman said. "You're under arrest." The next morning, after a sleepless night, Fritz found himself being loaded into a truck headed for Oranienburg—one of the most terrible concentration camps.

The anecdote lead is used often, and fiction techniques such as dialogue, description, tension, and emotion are part of it. It's a good idea not to use your best anecdote for the lead; rather, save the best one for your conclusion.

The Shock Lead

The shock lead is based on some startling statement. For example:

> When Fred Kimball tells you, "A funny thing happened to me at the zoo last night—this tiger says to me …" Don't raise the eyebrows, baby; Kimball's job—and he gets paid for it—is talking to animals. Now a lot of people talk to the pooch in the back yard, but the remarkable thing, according to Kimball, is that the animals *answer him back!*

Usually an exclamation mark punctuates the last sentence in a shock lead. Some writers habitually use this type of lead to open an article, and, unfortunately, not a few times the lead has little to do with the actual article. Yet the lead should always have an integral relationship to the article. One of the problems with this type of lead is that the information may be a half-truth, slanted writing, which reputable authorities may refute. Remember, when you use a "shocker" your article has to deliver what you've promised—and sometimes it can be difficult to live up to the intensity of the lead.

Be sure, too, that when dealing with any controversial material you use as much documentation as possible to support your case.

The Atmosphere Lead

The atmosphere lead depends upon the description of a place or thing. It catches the mood of a particular locale. It demands fiction techniques and a great deal of sensitivity.

> The carnival—yellow dust-flecked shafts glance from canvas tents in the tall, wet-green grass. The wind twists the red and green pennants into small glittering kites, and the ferris wheel glints silver in the bright blue sky. The carnival winds its way down the green heartland of Mississippi into Alabama. Who are the people that set up the tents? What are they like, and why do they prefer the open road to a cozy home in the city?

The Personality Lead

The personality lead is used when you are writing about a celebrity or a well-known person in a particular field. The object is to make the reader "see" the person and to catch the "essence" of his or her personality.

> The one word you think of when you hear George Probert's silver soprano sax sing out is: soul. Exciting to watch, and more exciting to listen to, George gets down in the dark music. He broods over the straight sax, the dark v of his hair a shadow over the triangular vein bulging across his high forehead. Standing, his big body slightly hunched, dark eyes intense, Probert immediately impresses you with the delicate, finely balanced complexity of the real jazz musician. He has a master's degree from Stanford and is a film editor in

addition to being a mainstay member of the Fire House Five Plus Two. In George, intellect, emotion, and fine musicianship fuse.

The Question Lead

With the question lead, the writer poses a question that hooks the reader:

> What do you tell a boy whose heart's dream is to be a pilot, who eats, sleeps, and lives airplanes, who collects every airplane picture he can get his hands on (even draws them superbly, with the most fantastic detail), what do you tell him ... when he's retarded?

The strength of the question lead is that the reader is tricked into involvement by the question asked. However, avoid using too many questions, for the reader may be confused as to the intent of the article:

> Where is America going? Why is crime rising? Why are farmers going bankrupt? Should America go back on the gold standard? Why is American youth turning to drugs? And what can be done about young unmarried mothers?

Note how diffused this lead is; it would be hard to write a unified article dealing with all these questions. Each of the questions demands complex answers, and an entire article could be written about each of them. To try to cover them all in one article would result in a hodgepodge.

The Controversy Lead

This lead catches the reader in a controversy, and he or she has to read along to see which side you take and whether he or she will agree with you. The lead uses a statement that appears difficult if not impossible to prove:

> A prominent researcher says that telling lies is essential to a happy marriage.

The reader will often read such an article to see if the writer presents some convincing evidence that will prove the controversial statement.

The "Brand New Bit of Information" Lead

The "brand new bit of information" lead promises the reader startling new information that will dazzle everyone. It should imply that very few people know this particular thing—and *everybody* should be aware of it.

> An amazing new medical breakthrough is the new heart bypass that takes only 10 minutes. Thousands of Americans will be able to lead healthy, productive lives without undergoing costly and painful surgery.

Words like *amazing, revolutionary,* and *miraculous* are often used to describe the discovery.

The Delayed Lead

With the delayed lead, one of the most difficult to do, the writer "backs" into the article:

> A million years ago (before Ph.D.s began defining jazz as polyphony, antiphony, augmented sixths, etc., to head-nodding freshmen), jazz in New Orleans lingo meant *filling up the holes in the music with a little horn or piano.*
> The recipe for jazz is basic. Main ingredient: one musician in love with what he's blowing and two good ears tapped into the music. But the first real thing about jazz is that it *is,* not that it *was.* The only way to look at jazz is the simplest. As the great jazz drummer Baby Dodds once remarked of his great-grandfather, who played African drums, *"He talked on them."* Jazzmen are still talking; and the language ranges from controlled chamber talk to frenetic orgy. But the point is: Where is jazz going?

Note that the last sentence is the thematic statement of the article. The writer's use of language carries the lead; but if the writer didn't handle prose so sensitively, the reader might have been turned off.

The Statement Lead

Ideally a lead should be controversial, but if controversy is lacking, the lead may sometimes be tied to the reader in a direct statement.

> You can have more energy than you've ever had in your life. The secret is good nutrition, exercise, and *meditation.*

This is a good lead for articles that present personal anecdotes. But don't get preachy, patronizing, or too personal. As writer, you still have to maintain a distance from the reader.

The Body of the Article

Once you have the lead, you are ready to begin the body. In the lead, you should have established the **tone**—serious, light, or frothy. The lead entices you to read the article; the body is the core or substance of the article. The lead **promises** the reader something worthwhile; the body carries out that promise and must hold the reader's attention.

Structural Elements in the Body

The structural elements of the body of the article are:

1.   point of view
2.   theme
3.   transitions
4.   paragraphs with anecdotes, statistics and facts, and quotations

Point of view   An article can be written in first person ("I" viewpoint), the objective viewpoint, or, in the case of the interview article, from the viewpoint of the interviewer. Whichever viewpoint is chosen, the point of view should remain consistent throughout the article.

First person is always more personal, while the objective viewpoint reflects a straightforward presentation of facts. The interviewer's viewpoint, while appearing objective, is personal in that the interviewer selects the questions asked and so slants the interview. Each of the viewpoints has its own strengths and weaknesses.

First person enables your reader to identify with you as a person, and you are able to give your insights and impressions. Suitable articles might be: any personal experience, travel, house hunting, job hunting, how to do it, baby care, animal care, fishing/hunting, computer discoveries, special recipes—how "you" did these things or reacted to them. An example of first person is:

> I've been a teacher for over twenty years and I'm really angry at the severe cuts in education. At my college, part of a three-college system, 21,000 students will not be allowed to take classes. Vital programs such as nursing, speech, psychology, marine biology, and history have been cut. Music and theatre arts have been severely curtailed. Our college, one of the finest community colleges in the United States, has been decimated. And what of the students who won't be able to take those classes? Studies of disadvantaged students show that if an education is interrupted, the disadvantaged student may never complete his or her education. When a student's ready to go to college and can take that valuable time of his life to do it, we should give that student every encouragement. A year later may just be too late.

The advantage of first person—its capacity to present a personal reaction to situations—is also its disadvantage. Some readers feel that they're getting only one side of a situation, an opinionated impression, and not a balanced viewpoint.

Third-person objective is more suitable for discussing politics, business developments, socioeconomic conditions. Yet it would be boring if used to describe a fishing trip in Montana. The same passage on education might read:

> _____ College has suffered a $9 million budget cut in two years. Vital programs such as nursing, psychology, marine biology, speech, and history have been cut. Music and theatre arts have been severely curtailed. _____ College, one of the finest community colleges in the United States, finds itself

in dangerous straits. Over 21,000 students will not be able to take classes in the _____ Community College system. An even more grim note is that recent studies of disadvantaged students show that when their education is interrupted, many may never find the time or the money to complete their education.

The interview viewpoint is an interesting one to give an insight into a particular personality, but it could not be used successfully to give a synthesized viewpoint of the political situation in the United States today. Using the example of education cuts, the interview viewpoint could be:

INTERVIEWER: Senator X, why have the community colleges been cut so severely in California?

SENATOR X: Frankly, there just isn't any money. Everything is being cut proportionately. We have a deficit and the governor is determined to pay off the deficit as quickly as possible.

INTERVIEWER: Senator, are you are aware that _____ College has received a more than $9 million budget cut in two years?

SENATOR X: Yes, other colleges have been severely cut too. But there just isn't any money.

INTERVIEWER: Did you know that vital programs such as nursing, history, marine biology, ecology, and speech have been cut? And music and theatre arts have been severely curtailed. In fact, the college is decimated—and you're aware that _____ College was once considered one of the finest community colleges in the United States.

SENATOR X: Yes, I do know about _____ College, and I must say that I'm sorry to hear these things, but again there just isn't any money. Perhaps in two or three years—

INTERVIEWER: That may be too late. Studies have shown that when a student's education is interrupted, that student may never go back to school again.

SENATOR X: All I can say is that I do care about these things; I am a friend of education. But there is no money. I also think that if a person wants an education he will find a way. Frankly, though, I don't think much of public schools. I sent my own children to private school.

The interview article enables the writer to get a personal viewpoint from an authority figure, and it may add some interesting sidelights to the problem discussed. In this case the senator betrayed his own personal feelings about public education and also his hypocritical claim of being "a friend of education."

Point of view is determined by the type of article you choose to write and your relationship to the material—whether you want to discuss it from your perspective or more objectively synthesize the material, or from the perspective of a specialist in that field. Remember that while people will enjoy your own recounting of personal events, they will not give as much credence to your "opinion" of a world happening or a scientific achievement as they will to that of a world leader or an authority in the field. Point of view can be very important in selling your article, so think deeply about which viewpoint you ultimately select.

Theme   Every article has a theme: a statement of purpose, the message—the point you want to make.

Theme determines *how* you will present your facts. It shapes your article. Every word, every example, every statistic must be related to theme. Before you even start writing, you should be able to state your theme in one sentence. But avoid being too general. For example, one might say: "Crime is costly." An article based on this generalization is too vague. Editors know that crime is costly; after all, they read the paper every day. But one can zero in on a focus: "It costs $660,000 to jail a man for forty years and $1.8 million to execute a criminal—yet our nation is cutting education, perhaps the only thing that might prevent a life of crime."

Having established the theme, in this case how education might save many people from becoming criminals, one might go on to give further statistics and examples of people who were saved from a life of crime by education or hardcore criminals who lack an education.

If you have collected research on a subject and do not have a theme, you will end up being very confused by the shapeless mass of material. Don't try to write anything at this point. Rather, look over the material and see what possibilities occur to you. Usually, a particular quote or a statistic will inspire an idea. Once you have your theme, then sift through your material and check every fact that relates to the theme. You probably will have several categories. For example, using the education theme, some of the categories might be: high court costs for criminals, rehabilitated criminals who went back to school and are now constructively contributing to society, and criminals in prison who did not have a good education. Each of these categories is a part of the article's structure. Your facts and statistics, then, can be separated into these three categories.

You will be always be ahead timewise if you know beforehand what your theme is. Try to think about the focus of your article *before* you gather your material or arrange an interview. Then you will gather only relevant facts. And in an interview, you will ask only pertinent questions.

Be consistent thematically. If an idea isn't relevant, delete it. If it's an interesting idea but isn't very relevant, try to find some way to relate it to theme.

Theme can be presented chronologically or through flashback.

CHRONOLOGICAL PROGRESSION OF THEME

If you are presenting theme chronologically, you **start at the beginning** and show things in the order in which they happened. An article on Abraham Lincoln, using chronological progression, might begin: "The Great Emancipator, Abraham Lincoln, was born on February 12, 1809, in a cabin near Hodgenville, Kentucky." The article would then trace the events of Lincoln's life in the order they occurred—his moving to Indiana; the death of his mother; his father's marrying again; the younger Lincoln's move to Illinois and occupation as a lawyer; his marriage; his entry into politics, which resulted in his becoming president of the United States; and finally his assassination.

However, note the word *emancipator*; it signals the thematic structure. In other words, regardless of all the events of Lincoln's life, if those events do not directly relate to the theme of emancipation they should not be included in the article. Remember, you can't show *everything* just because that's the way "it really happened." Similarly, if you planned to write on Lincoln's political career, his supposed romance with Ann Rutlege would probably not be a relevant part of the article. Also, some incidents are just plain boring and who cares.

FLASHBACK PROGRESSION OF THEME

If you present the article in a series of flashbacks, you usually begin at the most exciting point in time and flash back to various other points of action. For example, the Lincoln article might begin: "On April 14, 1865, Abraham Lincoln was assassinated in Ford's Theatre in Washington, D.C.—the Great Emancipator was dead." The article might flash back to Lincoln's boyhood, then move up in time to his political career and emphasize Lincoln's achievements, and finish with the details of the assassination.

Regardless of which type of theme progression you use, remember that you must always have a controlling idea that shapes the article and holds it in form, and anything irrelevant must be ruthlessly pruned out.

Transitions   Transitions are linking sentences that connect your paragraphs or ideas. Transitions make the article flow. Using the Lincoln article as an example, three ideas might be important: He was a compassionate man, a good politician, and an effective president. Each of these ideas might take several paragraphs to discuss, and you would need specific examples to prove to the reader that these points were true—a story of Lincoln's kindness to a little girl, his proposal of a bill for the emancipation of slaves in the District of Columbia, and his Emancipation Proclamation when he was president. But you can't just move from one topic to another without a transition. In the Lincoln article a suitable transition might read: "However, not only was Lincoln a compassionate man, but he was also a good politician." Then a further transition sentence might be: "While Lincoln was a good politician, he used his political acumen to become a highly effective president." Without good transitions, the text will be jerky, and the reader will be uncomfortably "jogged" out of the article.

Strong paragraphs   The body of the article is meant to prove what has been asserted in the lead. So each paragraph must support the theme with statistics, examples, or anecdotes—proof that convinces a reader. You can't just say a thing is so, for the reader may not believe you.

Every paragraph must be related to the theme. If a paragraph can be cut and it doesn't affect the meaning of the article in some way, then that paragraph shouldn't be there.

Sometimes you may have a paragraph that doesn't seem related to the theme, but it sticks in your mind. Often there *is* a relationship to theme, but you have to struggle to find it. In the Lincoln article, one of the suggested "proofs" was a story about Lincoln's being kind to a little girl. This story could be tied to the fact that Lincoln's compassion, shown in everyday affairs, was a key quality that led to his emancipating the slaves. **Always look at each anecdote, each statistic, as a way of bolstering theme.**

When you are faced with cutting a paragraph, ask yourself:

1. Why did I feel that this material was so important?
2. Why did I put this material in the particular *place* that I did? How does it relate to the paragraph above and below it?
3. Is there some sentence related to my theme that could be used to tie in this paragraph?
4. Why did this anecdote, this statistic, this quotation, this remark catch my attention?

If you test in this way each paragraph you plan to cut, you may find that you were right to include the material—that your mind had sensed a unity with the theme, a unity you did not consciously see.

ANECDOTES

Anecdotes are little dramatized stories that illustrate your points. Each point you discuss should be "shown." Anecdotes are little parables. If you tell a reader something, it sounds preachy; if you *show* the reader through a little vignette experience, he or she will enjoy it.

For example, if you write that Lincoln was a sympathetic, caring person, you haven't really made the reader *experience* his caring personality. On the other hand, you could tell a story about him which reveals that particular trait:

> Once a little girl approached Lincoln and looked up at his craggy face. She frowned a minute and then said, "I think you'd look much better with a beard." Lincoln smiled, and a few months later he rode by her house to see if she liked his new beard.

Anecdotes give the feeling of life to your work; they make your article more appealing and convincing. If your article is going along in a flat, lifeless way, you probably aren't using enough anecdotes to spice it up.

STATISTICS AND FACTS

Facts and statistics can make a good lead and are also important in giving credence to the point you're making in a particular paragraph. Rather than write, "A lot of people will have heart attacks this year" it's more powerful to write that "700,000 people will have heart attacks this year." Be sure, of course, that your information is accurate—otherwise every authority figure in the United States will take the time to refute you!

Keep your statistical data short and to the point. Don't overuse statistics, as too many of them can be boring. Try to make the statistics "real" to your reader. For example, rather than say that 1 million people will be killed next year, it is much stronger to point out that next year one out of ten people will be killed.

QUOTATIONS

Another way of proving a point in your paragraph is through quotations. If you as the writer say something to the effect that the heart bypass will save many lives, it will not be as strong as if you quoted an authority figure—for, after all, you are not a surgeon. On the other hand, you could point out that Dr. Michael DeBakey, world-famous cardiac surgeon at Baylor University in Houston, remarked:

> We now have more than 18 years' experience and have performed bypass surgery on more than 15,000 patients at our center. Not only did they live longer than the patients who did not have a bypass, but they were also able to resume and enjoy more normal activities.

Note that before an authority is quoted, you should give that person's background to qualify him or her as a genuine authority figure. So when you mention an authority, you should give the person's name, occupation, and reputation in his or her particular field. Also, when you refer to that person again in the article, use only the last name. Only if you are a personal friend are you entitled to call the person by the first name.

When you have completed the body of the article, you have given all your points in a logical cause-and-effect pattern. But you are not finished yet. The most important part of the article is yet to come—the conclusion!

The Conclusion (the Wrap-up)

To an article writer, the conclusion is the punchline. It is that part of the article which "nails" your points in the reader's mind. Remember that by the time the reader has read the article, he or she will have forgotten some of the points. You don't want to make the reader go back and read the article again. The conclusion is meant to gracefully refresh the reader's mind about what has been written.

The conclusion should be one succinct paragraph that winds up the article. In fact, it should be so powerful that the reader should be able to remember it long after the article has been forgotten. Each of your main points should be referred to in the conclusion. For example, the Lincoln article might end: "Lincoln's great compassion enabled him to be a great politician and an effective president, but more than any other quality it fitted him to become 'the Great Emancipator.' " After you have referred to your main points, it is often a good idea to end with either a direct quote or a very short anecdote that bears out your theme. A suitable quote might be: "As War Secretary Edwin M. Stanton said of Lincoln, 'And now he belongs to the ages.' "

If an article is humorous, then use your funniest anecdote to close. If your article is a persuasive piece, written to make people act, then the conclusion should sum up the reasons that a person should *do something now!* If you have startling statistics, use them: "Fifty-five percent of all car accidents are caused by alcoholics—please don't drive when you've been drinking."

Writing a graceful, pithy, succinct conclusion is an art. Don't get discouraged if you feel you've failed. Write what you feel is necessary, then let it sit overnight. The next morning when you reread it, you will have more objectivity and will probably be able to rewrite it in a more powerful way. Most writers overwrite the conclusion, and it has to be pruned of excess verbiage. By letting your writing sit overnight, it's much easier in the fresh light of the following day to see what needs to be cut. It's always hard to objectively view what you've written during the flush of creativity. What is important, however, is to get the words down in the first place—even if they seem awkward at the time. Later, when you rewrite, the right words will usually come as you reread what you've written.

How to Find a Good Title for Your Article

When writing for a particular magazine, examine carefully the titles of the articles for trends. How many words are in most of the titles? Note the blurbs that describe the articles—sometimes they're more interesting than the titles, and they often reveal the editor's real interests. It may be that the editor would really like to see an article that follows the idea of the blurb.

Your title must attract the reader, tell the reader what the article is about, and excite him or her to read further. For example, a suitable title for a health magazine might be: "You Can Lose Twenty Pounds—Now!"

The Importance of Rewriting

Any writer who has been writing for some time will tell you that the first draft of a story or article is only the beginning. In the first draft, the writer gets the material down on the page. Then, when he or she has captured the experience, the fire, the spontaneity, the writer polishes and polishes the material until it sparkles. If you are a real writer, you *know* that **rewriting is the name of the game.**

It is not uncommon for a new writer to have to rewrite an article six or seven times until the prose flows well. A seasoned writer is often able to do only a first draft, a rewrite, and then a final polish.

One of my students, who has published seven novels, remarked (after seven rewrites of her first novel): "I didn't know writers had to rewrite. I guess it was the most surprising thing I learned." Oddly enough, most people think that because they know how to write with a pen or a typewriter that's all there is to writing.

Exactly Why Is Rewriting Necessary?

When a writer is in the artistic flush of creating, the fever of excitement in re-creating an experience is so compelling that the writer often is unable to control the form of the work. It is only after the initial writing is over that the writer is able to properly shape the work so that the piece conveys the intended meaning.

In this first-draft stage, excess words will have to be ruthlessly pruned out. Sentences have to be recast. Sometimes the right word is lacking, and the writer must find it. In the flush of creativity, the experience may come so fast that the writer cannot capture the entire scope and design of the work. It is only later, when the writer has achieved some detachment from the work, that he or she can—with critical analysis—write additional scenes that should have been there or cut irrelevant material.

Summary

Don't use the news story as a model for the article. The form is different: Though the end of the news story can be removed without harm, the end of the article cannot be removed without damaging the article.

The article has three parts: the lead, the body, and the conclusion

1. The lead entices the reader to read the article.
2. The body is a series of paragraphs linked by transitions which state a message that is *proven* through anecdotes, statistics, or direct quotes.
3. The conclusion sums up the main points in the order in which they were presented, and it either impels the reader to think about what has been said or persuades the reader to act in a certain way.

While the structure of an article may seem mechanical, remember that the form is there only to enable you to present what you have to say in an organized way. It is the coat rack on which you hang your beautiful coat of words. Your theme, your unique way of expression, your anecdotes and choice of quotes and statistics are the things that breathe life into an article and make it distinctly your own.

A CHECKLIST

1. Is all your research legibly written or typed and organized in such a way that you can easily use it (card file, by topic, or pasted on catalogued sheets or diagrammed on a blackboard)?
2. Is your lead a genuine grabber or is it merely adequate? That is, does it have the necessary 5 W's and an H, but is lacking excitement?
3. Did you save your best anecdote for your conclusion? Your next-best one for the lead?
4. Can you state your theme in one sentence?
5. Are all your anecdotes in the article related to the theme?
6. Is each paragraph in your article bolstered by an anecdote, a statistic, or a direct quote?
7. Is every paragraph directly relevant to the theme?
8. Did you carefully research your article and select reputable authority figures?
9. Is your article logical—do the paragraphs have a cause-and-effect relationship?
10. If your article is primarily humorous, do you have genuinely funny anecdotes?

11. Is there any irrelevant material that could be cut? Is there additional material that should be included?

12. If you have written an article designed to make readers "act," have you given them names and places where they can write? For example, if your message is "Stop Vivisection," you will have to tell the readers how they can go about stopping it—such as by writing to specific legislators, for example.

13. Did you refer in the conclusion to your main points?

14. Did you *rewrite* the article so that it flows well?

15. Have you carefully proofread the article before sending it out?

Exercises

1. Study the magazines you hope to write for. What types of leads do they use?

2. Write a question lead, a "brand-new bit of information" lead, and a personality lead.

3. Organize the material for the article you want to write and write at least three different types of leads for it. Read each lead aloud to your friends or in your writing class and see which one your friends or the class feel is most effective.

16

The Art of Magazine Characterization

Whether you're doing a profile or an article in which particular people are important, you need to know how to characterize. Even though you're writing about real people you must be able bring them alive. Characterization is the art of creating living beings on paper. Characterization gives life, zest, sparkle to an article. It makes the reader aware that the article is not just a collection of opinions, but rather that living people are vitally concerned with the problems presented.

Characterization is often the heart of an article, the human element that makes the reader want to read further. Readers aren't interested in abstractions but in other people. What is your main character like? How does he or she feel about life? What are his or her ambitions, hopes, fears? How did he or she achieve success, suffer failure? What have other writers written about this person? What are your own observations? These questions cannot be answered easily. They must be thought about, assimilated, until the writer can understand and *feel* the person. Only then can the writer catch, like an elusive butterfly, the wriggling human spirit and fix it on the page.

If you're doing a profile, you will probably need to do an in-depth characterization of the personality figure you have chosen. If you are using a character only as an authority figure, you may need to use only one or two characterization techniques.

Introduction of Character

Whenever you mention a character, three things are important:

1. name
2. occupation
3. reputation: the reason for using this particular person as an authority figure

Authority is very important in an article. The more well known the person is in his or her field, the more validity will be given to the opinions expressed in the article. For example, if you were attending a world peace conference and the premier of Russia angrily said that war was imminent between Russia and the United States, you would certainly feel a great more trepidation than if a drunk at a local bar told you the same thing. In other words, the premier of Russia has a great deal more credibility; and a very important part of magazine writing is to establish as much credibility as possible so that your article will be taken seriously.

Comparison of Characterization in Fiction and Nonfiction

In fiction, the writer "creates" character. In nonfiction, the character is already created; he or she is alive and has a history. A fiction writer usually prepares a "dossier" of imaginative facts about the main characters, but a nonfiction writer has to research a live character and collect biographical facts. Like a fiction writer, however, the nonfiction writer has to be able to:

1. describe a character physically
2. describe a character psychologically, revealing central traits
3. show a character in action

Characterization in the article must be done quickly and economically, in contrast with characterization techniques in the novel and short story. While a novelist may spend several paragraphs on description, the article writer often has to catch the *feel* of personality in a few lines.

Elements of Character Presentation

One-Word Characterization

As in fiction, the article writer may zero in on one word that captures a trait of the person important in the article: *dynamic* Neil Diamond, *versatile*

Ben Kingsley, *witty* Henry Kissinger, the *distinguished* screenwriter Jean Aurenche, the *brilliant* director François Truffaut.

One-Sentence Description

Sometimes the writer will describe the character in a short, descriptive sentence:

> Stocky, intense, serious, Buckminister Fuller has been labeled both crackpot and genius.
>
> Alberto Ginastera, the enormously prolific composer, was a scholarly, fiercely nationalistic Argentine.
>
> Horn rims glinting from the light of the hanging light bulb, Ken tosses ideas at you in an incredible, fast-moving stream of dialogue.
>
> Collins, 53, bald, bearded, and spritely, interprets tennis and interviews players at Wimbledon for NBC television.
>
> Tanned, dark, and in pinstripes, Phil evokes the image of a conservative Sylvester Stallone.

Character Through Exposition

Sometimes you may want to briefly describe a minor character, sketching in just enough details to catch the individual's personality or character. In this mode, the camera eye of the writer does not record facial description or depth of character. Usually, when you use this technique of expository writing, either the idea of the article or another character will be more important:

> Dave was a great fisherman, always ready to find that big yellowtail south of the border, or explore some new cove along the Baja coast when the albacore were running. He inevitably had a story to tell about the "big one that got away"—though most of his tales were about the "monsters" he caught. He liked lake fishing too. He was the kind of fisherman who would crawl twenty miles through the brush with his flyrod between his teeth.

This kind of character delineation does pique interest, but you must also show the character in action so the reader will really believe it. Again, it is important not to just "tell" the reader about a character but to "show" that individual physically in action and to use dialogue.

Character: The Photograph

You may want to just physically describe the character and capture his or her features, as does a photograph, so that the reader *sees* the character but does not get the feeling of intimately knowing the person:

> Fragile, platinum blonde, and slender, Susie is twenty-three. She moves

gracefully in the sky-blue dress that softly drapes over the boyish chest, over the curving female hips. Her vivid blue eyes sparkle with an unconscious blend of childish joy and sadness.

The "photograph" depiction of character can be enhanced by zeroing in on a specific trait, a series of traits, a mannerism, a physical feature, or an action:

1. *Trait:* "Dressed in a trim blue suit with matching pumps and leather bag, Claire's *incisive* blue eyes and *no-nonsense demeanor* of her heart-shaped face tell you she is a shrewd businesswoman."
2. *Series of traits:* "Al is stocky, his cerulean blue eyes accenting a tanned, broad face, his well-shaped lips set in an ironic cast. His forehead is a wide dome, and he looks like a Roman senator. *Witty, erudite, decadent,* he is also an extraordinarily fine novelist."
3. *Mannerism:* "Sy *balances on his toes* as he talks, a wiry man of sixty in a gray three-piece suit. Gray eyes glint humorously in the narrow, angular face with high cheekbones. He has been an auctioneer for over thirty years."
4. *Physical features:* "He is tall and dark, and his *hawk nose* overshadows his scarred face. Dominick's dark, unsmiling eyes flank that great nose and warn of reprisal. He is only thirty-three, but Las Vegas insiders say he is a man to be feared."
5. *Description through action:* "Alton Purnell is: dark felt hat, white cigar holder clamped between white teeth, a round face the color of Hershey chocolate, and two fantastic hands springing like crazy all over the keyboard, his white oxfords jamming all by themselves under the piano bench.

The Portrait

In the portrait, the writer tries to show the "whole" person, as Rembrandt would—the lights and shadows, catching both the inner and outer person:

The one word you think of when you hear George Probert's silver soprano sax sing out is: *soul.* Exciting to watch, and more exciting to listen to, George gets down in the dark music. Under his flashing fingers, the music ripples in beautiful patterns from his unique staccato tremolo to the clear treble and down into the mellow woody vibrato. The tone of his horn isn't like anything else in the world—a metallic, woody sound with a rich, mellow buzz that suddenly shrieks to a flutey whine.

George broods over the straight sax, the dark v of his hair a shadow over the triangular vein bulging across his high forehead. Standing, his big body slightly hunched, head shaking, dark eyes intense, Probert immediately impresses you with the delicate, finely balanced complexity of the real jazz musician. He has a master's degree from Stanford and is a film editor in addition to being a mainstay member of the Fire House Five Plus Two. In George, intellect, emotion, and fine musicianship fuse.

His voice carefully modulated, his conversation is always thoughtful, reflective, and searching. To George, jazz is jazz. All one warp and woof. Although one of the finest and best-known Dixieland musicians, he is quick to praise the moderns. Lighting his curved meerschaum pipe, he settles back into the leather cushions of the divan. "Charlie Parker was a genius, a far-out modern, and a great instrumentalist. But," he says, his dark eyes glowing, "I like traditional best, so I play it."

He drew at his pipe. "You know the real thing isn't whether one kind of jazz is outmoded or not; the real thing—to me, anyways—is to play jazz to entertain people. There has to be a rapport with the audience. If I have any criticism of the modern school, it's the attitude many new jazzmen have about 'doing the audience a favor.' I think there has to be a meaningful rapport between the music and the audience." His forehead ridged. "One of the great things I learned was when I worked with Kid Ory. Ory always felt the audience out, always asked himself, 'What do they want to hear played?' "

To George, entertaining is fifty percent of the business. Yet he is never the buffoon. He plays with the authority that is compelling to both the audience in front and the musicians on stand—and when "Big George" steps up to the mike, you hold your breath. He never disappoints you.

In this portrait, jazz is a device used to reveal character—the inner person. Dialogue, too, reveals the character's concerns.

Character by Dress

Clothing, of course, tells us a great deal about character. The way a character dresses reveals a basic attitude about life:

> Casual in his blue flowered Hawaiian shirt and a wide friendly grin in his lean, angular face rimmed by sandy hair and square hornrims, Charles Umnuss looks like a tourist bound for Hawaii, but he is a highly successful and sought-after Panamanian accountant.

Character by Anecdote or Incident

Often telling a story about the character reveals more than a lengthy analysis of personality would have done:

> San Francisco's "King of the Torts," Melvin Belli, says that going to court is like going to church: "You have to dress up for it." He won't let his clients wear weird suits, white shoes, message tee shirts, dark glasses. On the other hand, all of *his* suits have red linings, and his trousers hide his Western cowboy boots.

It would be easy to say that Belli is a shrewd, flamboyant attorney, but the delightful incident brings the traits to life.

Character by Dialogue

A nonfiction writer does not have the latitude to enter a character's mind and so cannot know what the character is thinking. But the writer can use direct statements which the character makes to reveal attitudes, beliefs, and concerns. This dialogue is important for delineating personality. The inventor Buckminister Fuller's beliefs and concerns stamped him as a great humanitarian. He warned that the world is in a race "between Utopia and Oblivion." Fuller went on to say:

> We now have the capability to take care of everybody or we have the capability to destroy ourselves. If we don't use our minds to make it good for everybody, we deserve … oblivion.

Character Through First Impression

Often a writer tries to convey to the reader the first impression the person made on the writer.

> Five foot six, nervously slender, John Finley looks like a kid who just blew in from San Antone—which he did. Standing straddlelegged and blowing, his head cocked over the taut arm fusing to his horn, the best of trumpetmen get hungry just watching him. Tremendously dynamic, his foot tapping, the wiry brown hair bushes straight out from his round kid face. Beer in one hand, trumpet in the other, he nods when he takes a number someone calls. He has a habit of whirling around to the drummer and then back to the mike, and leading off in clear brass at the same time.
> He found his first horn (a cornet) in a Texas trashcan when he was ten. It's the same dented horn he carries around in a paper sack. As one musician dryly quipped, "He's the only musician in the business who *steps* on his horn when he wants to change the tone." John often plays an expensive, dentless trumpet for the purists; but in spite of the dings, he still pours his best numbers out of the old cornet.

In this characterization sketch, an unusual incident (finding a cornet in a garbage can) accents the description of an unusual young man.

Character Through Metaphor

Sometimes a metaphor gives a dynamic quality to a characterization sketch:

> John Finley is a tornado in brass.

Metaphor catches the reader's attention and is more emotional than straight prose.

Showing Character Through Generalization

The writer can use a generalization to lead into a revelation of character:

> *Some men think big.* Bucky Fuller was one of them. Norman Cousins recalled

that once Fuller approached him excitedly, "his eyes shimmering behind the glasses like watermelon seeds in oil. Before he said hello, he said, 'Something wonderful has happened! I've just discovered the coordinates to the universe.'"

Character Through Other People's Remarks

Sometimes a montage of remarks made by people who are authorities in their field create an interesting composite that reveals complexity of character. For example, consider these remarks made about a successful businessman.

A destructive force.
A tremendously astute guy.
A big-stakes gambler.
A corporate raider.
An engagingly youthful businessman who relishes publicity.
An interesting, successful man but a tough bargainer.
Past the point other people would say the hell with it, he goes on.

By using quotes of this kind, made by other people, the writer can write an otherwise objective article and let readers make up their minds as to what the character is like.

Character by Achievement/by Background

Occasionally, a character is introduced by the mention of an interesting background or of some startling achievement:

Raymond Kurzweil, son of a conductor, is an electronic whiz. He devised a software package for statistical analysis by age 13 that was distributed by IBM; he won 7 national awards by age 16 and, more recently, he has invented a reading machine for the blind and predicts he will have within two years a typewriter that will turn the human voice into written words without hands touching keys. (Reuters News Release)

Summary

Successful characterization in the article does not have to be done in long blocks, but it demands a sensitive eye to catch distinctive details. Remember that it is not enough to merely give height, weight, and color of hair and eyes to establish character. Traits, too, need to be skillfully delineated. But don't feel satisfied because you have described a character as "soft-spoken," for a murderer and a minister may share this trait. You will, of course, note all these things; but they should blend to create a distinct, unique personality who feels, thinks, and speaks in a particular way.

ELEMENTS OF CHARACTER PRESENTATION

1. Always mention the character's name, occupation, and reputation.
2. Describe character physically and psychologically, revealing central traits.
3. Show character in action.
4. Modes of character presentation are:
   a. one-word description emphasizing trait
   b. one-sentence description
   c. established through exposition
   d. "the photograph"—external emphasis:
      i. zeroing in on trait
      ii. using series of traits
      iii. using a mannerism
      iv. emphasizing a physical feature
      v. emphasizing character in action
   e. "the portrait" (combination of inner and outer individual)
   f. by dress
   g. by anecdote or incident that reveals the character's beliefs, philosophy, attitudes, lifestyle, and actions
   h. by dialogue—using direct quotes from the character that support the points you are making, either about the character or about a particular subject
   i. through first impression
   j. through metaphor
   k. through other people's remarks—those of friends, relatives, business acquaintances
   l. through a generalization
   m. through interesting achievement or background

Exercises

1. Show your character through a one-sentence description.
2. Develop your character through a portrait.
3. Show your character through "the photograph."
4. Establish your character through a paragraph of exposition.
5. Establish your character through a trait (a mannerism) and show him or her in action.

17

The Interview Article

The success of such magazines as *People* illustrates that people like to read about celebrities: how they became famous; what they think about life; how they met their wives, husbands, or lovers; what kind of lifestyle they lead.

Celebrity articles can be broken into two categories: the personality sketch and the profile.

The personality sketch focuses on the celebrity's character, his or her viewpoint of life, and his or her basic philosophy. On the other hand, the profile focuses on the celebrity in relationship to career. More and more, however, most editors are calling both types of articles the profile.

Interview Procedure: How to Start

If you have an interview subject in mind, you have already achieved step one. But if you don't have anyone in mind, often a small news item in your local newspaper will supply a valuable lead. Movie stars, famous athletes, outstanding educators, successful businesspeople, well-known artists and writers, and politicians are good subjects. A man who has just won $300,000 in Las Vegas is good, too. Even though he is an average man, his lucky jackpot makes him a fantasy figure—wow, winning $300,000! How does he feel now? What's he going to do with the money?

People who do unusual things also make good copy. For example, a news story about a group of veterinarians who have formed a small jazz band might make an excellent human-interest article. Why are they doing this? Where did they meet?

People who attempt extraordinary feats make good articles—a man who sailed around the world singlehandedly in a small boat, or a man who is bicycling or jogging around the world.

You may also know of some unsung hero in your own neighborhood—a man who has been a "big brother," a woman who has been a "big sister," for many years. Some people have projects that they carry out singlehandedly—supplying clothes to a Mexican orphanage, nursing possums and various wildlife, adopting hundreds of cats and dogs. Professional people, such as psychologists, who specialize in the fields of child abuse, divorce, or battered wives also make interesting feature articles.

Once You've Decided on a Particular Person, What Then?

You can arrange the interview by:

1. phone (the quickest way and often the easiest)
2. letter (which usually takes longer, and sometimes you run the risk of not getting a reply)
3. telegram (often surprisingly effective because it catches a person's attention)
4. calling in person (however, you may have to get past a secretary or security guards)
5. a letter of introduction that allows you to set up a later appointment. You will probably have to approach the celebrity's agent as a preliminary.

When You First Approach the Celebrity, What Do You Say?

First of all, don't be afraid. Many celebrities are eager to be interviewed, appreciating the publicity; and frankly, many are flattered. On the other hand, it is true that some *extremely famous* celebrities will simply not let an unknown writer interview them. These celebrities have been in the news for so long, and have been misquoted for so long, that they are very selective about just whom they will allow to interview them. Generally, they either know the interviewer and his or her work, or the magazine that has sent the interviewer is very prestigious and very reputable.

You will find, however, that the average celebrity will be eager to speak with you. When you make the initial contact, be sure to pronounce the celebrity's name correctly and come right to the point, saying: "My name is _____ , and I'd like to do an article on you for _____ magazine." Even if you do not have a commitment from a magazine or newspaper for the article, you might say something to the effect: "I think the *Los Angeles Times* would be very interested in an article on you." If your article is about a particular subject, such as Japanese gardening, then you should mention that you have sought out this particular person because of his or her expertise—in this case, perhaps landscape design background.

In your conversation, try to indicate that you know a great deal about this person, that you have a personal interest in his or her career. The key in an effective contact is communicating your special interest in this person—otherwise, why would you be doing the interview?

You want to get five things across in your initial contacts:

1. who you are
2. the name of the magazine to which the article will be submitted
3. the focus of the article (celebrity's career, philosophy, awards, personality, recent events in life, some controversial situation or viewpoint)
4. whether photos are available or, if not, if you can take them
5. need for specific statistics (birthdate, important years in the celebrity's life, when the celebrity first became famous)

What to Do If the Celebrity Turns You Down

If you are turned down, it is still possible to write an article about the person by compiling information from other articles and books. Sometimes the celebrity will send you publicity releases that you can incorporate into the article. And this material is often good background. But the best articles result from a live interview, from the personal remarks that are never seen in publicity releases.

Another way of obtaining information from a celebrity is through sending a questionnaire with a letter. However, only four out of ten people reply to questionnaires.

One old pro insists he has a foolproof method of getting a celebrity to respond. He sends the celebrity a letter saying he has just completed an article about him or her and asking if the celebrity would like to read it before it is published. He swears that in every case the celebrities have given him interviews.

Do Your Homework Before the Interview

Before you go for your interview, make sure that you have read all the available magazine articles and books written about this particular person. Try to talk to as many people as possible who know the interviewee so that you see the interviewee in the framework of his or her life. Sometimes, knowing of a particular event and mentioning that event during the interview will cause the interviewee to retell the story and perhaps add new material that no one else knows about. Or sometimes you, as interviewer, can ask how he or she feels about the incident *now*, and the interviewee may reveal a totally new attitude.

When the Interview Date Is Set, Send a Confirming Letter to the Interviewee Shortly Before the Interview

Celebrities are very busy people and generally accept many engagements that they may or may not put on their calendars. They may agree to something over the phone and a day or two later forget about it. If you don't confirm the appointment, you may make a long trip for nothing, ringing the door of a house where no one is at home.

Arrive at the Specified Time

Promptness is a courtesy. Remember that celebrities are very busy and that they have probably rearranged their schedule to be able to give you this time. Arrive on time and, if you have agreed to a specific length of time, leave when it is up. On the other hand, if the celebrity seems to be enjoying the interview and obviously wants to keep talking, you may wish to stay longer. Let the celebrity give you your cues. If he or she is continually checking the time or mentioning other appointments, be as brief as possible. Once, an interviewee asked me to meet him at a restaurant where he was holding court with several of his friends. After a very interesting interview that lasted more than an hour, I stood up to leave and was greeted with "Oh, no, you're not going to leave now?" I was so genuinely pressed into staying that I did and was able to get some excellent material and enjoy myself at the same time.

Relax and Enjoy the Interview

Good interviewers usually enjoy talking to people and finding out how a particular person thinks, feels, and lives. If you are uncomfortable, you will make your interviewee uncomfortable. One of the best attitudes you can have as an interviewee is that you really like this person and have looked forward to getting a chance to talk to him or her.

It's a good technique to take a few minutes before the interview—out in the car, perhaps—to sit quietly and close your eyes to relax yourself.

Think about the person you're going to interview as an old friend; really try to *feel* friendliness and good will toward this person. Also, as you sit quietly for a few moments, you may find yourself thinking of some question you had not thought of before. Then, in this relaxed state of mind, ring the doorbell or walk up to the secretary's desk, whichever it might be.

Be Sure to Dress Neatly

Remember that how you dress affects the interviewee's first impression of you, and your appearance may have a direct connection as to how comfortable the interviewee feels with you. Be neat, your clothes freshly laundered and pressed. The more comfortable the interviewee is with you, the more chance you have of his or her feeling at ease and confiding in you. Besides, you don't want to be mistaken for the local bag lady or the neighborhood rapist.

Inasmuch as appearances are concerned, take heed from a very funny (and true) Hollywood story about a leading actor who interviewed for the part of a producer. A friend told him to "dress like one." Accordingly, the actor showed up unshaven and wearing a torn, dirty tee shirt. The interviewing producer was shocked, and, needless to say, the actor did not get the role. The moral of the story is that even though *you* think your interviewee is very casual, he or she may not be—or he or she may expect something different from you. It's always safe to be neat and well dressed.

Know the Slant of Your Article
Before You Begin the Interview

You should know the direction of the article before you actually meet the interviewee. Take a celebrity like Elizabeth Taylor, for example. You might want to deal with the men in her life, or actress as mother, or Elizabeth as gourmet cook and her favorite recipes, or how she fights her weight problem. Once you know the "slant," you will have specific questions in mind. As time is so valuable, you don't have time to ask general questions; rather, you want to zero in on your particular focus. Otherwise, you may leave an interview and discover that you never asked the really important questions you needed for your article's particular emphasis.

Make a List of Questions
You Would Like Answered

While you should be aware of the specific questions you need for your article, don't try to dominate the interview by reading from a long list of questions and requiring the celebrity to respond to them. If you do, you will kill the interview and the spontaneity that gives life to your article.

If you can, memorize your questions so that you have them clearly in mind. Then you might ask the celebrity an important leading question. As he or she talks, wait for opportune times to work in some of the other questions—but do this conversationally, so that things seem to "flow" along. The more comfortable the conversation, the easier the flow, the more the interviewee is apt to confide in you.

If you mechanically read your questions, one by one, the interviewee will tend to give you a straightforward answer, perhaps even a yes and no, and you will not get the colorful anecdotes that would have enlivened your article. Also, you may not see or be able to capture the interviewee's personality.

Be Polite and Tactful

Remember that the interviewee has graciously given you his or her time. If you are insulting, the interviewee will freeze, and you may not get the material you want. If you know that certain things will anger the interviewee, be careful. Don't just blithely proceed into dangerous territory; rather, approach the area as delicately as possible and allow the interviewee to bring up the subject and discuss it.

Is a Tape Recorder Necessary?

Yes, tape recorders are invaluable, but if you bring one along, ask the interviewee for permission to use it. The advantage of a tape recorder is that it captures every statement the interviewee makes—often, you can't write everything down fast enough and so may occasionally lose valuable bits of information. On the other hand, if the interviewee sees a tape recorder he or she often freezes and doesn't say anything. When I first started writing, I interviewed a Montana cowboy known for very colorful talk, and I was particularly interested in capturing some of the colorful expressions. But as soon as he saw the tape recorder, he lost his spontaneity and humor. All he would say was "Yep" and "Nope." That lesson taught me to keep tape recorders out of sight.

Do invest in a *good* small tape recorder that can be put in an over-the-shoulder bag (for both men and women). Then, after the introductions are over, say casually: "I'd like to tape this if I can, so I won't miss anything important." If the interviewee indicates that's fine, then turn the tape recorder on and put it in the open bag. Usually, the interviewee will forget about the tape recorder, and the interview will proceed normally.

What About Just Writing Things Down?

Again, remember that it's hard to have an animated conversation with someone who's holding a pencil and writing everything down. If you must use one, the trick is to keep the pencil and paper as unobtrusive as possible. A good interviewee tries to memorize as much as possible and to write down only key remarks. Granted, this procedure has to be developed, and you will get better at it as you do more interviews. Ultimately, you will develop a sixth sense for jotting down crucial remarks—and do take them down accurately, for you don't want to be sued for misquoting. Of course, if you have recorded the interview you will have an accurate source of information—provided the tape didn't break (every journalist's nightmare)!

Breaking the Ice

Nothing is worse than you looking at the interviewee and he or she just looking back at you. The first task you have is to put the interviewee at ease. The best way is to try to discover the person's special interest. It may be a particular hobby, a love of cats and dogs, or a love of plants. If you have done some homework, you may know these things. For example, Doris Day is noted for her love of dogs, so a good opening remark might be a commendation for all her work on behalf of animals. Even better, if you can find a common interest, one that you and the interviewee share, he or she will often open up—and the information gained may be the exact thing you need to personalize your article.

I remember facing one very important man who was staring at me rather coldly, and I remarked that my eighteen-year-old cat had just died and I wasn't at my best today. He changed immediately; he had three cats that he adored—and the interview was off and running. A nice addition to this seeking to find a common interest is that often the interviewee becomes a friend, and then the art of interview is able to provide you with a richness in your life that goes beyond a journalistic job.

On the other hand, don't go on and on about your on personal problems with an interviewee. After all, you came to get an article. And if even your interviewee does become a friend, you do have to maintain your objectivity as a writer.

Don't Let the Interview "Get Away from You"

No matter how much you enjoy the interview, you will have to keep in mind the slant of your article and your purpose in writing it. When the interviewee veers from the subject too much, you will have to gently and tactfully bring him or her back. Always ask yourself: *Why is this person worth reading about? What do my readers want to know? What do **they** care about?* On the other hand, some information you receive may be so striking that you may decide to change the entire slant of the article. Of course, if you've presold the article, you will have to check with your editor to see if the editor will accept the new idea.

Be a Responsible Reporter

One thing you should definitely avoid is tricking the interviewee into saying controversial things or *twisting* the interviewee's remarks to agree with your own philosophy or bias. Many celebrities refuse to be interviewed because they have been misquoted or put in a bad light by interviewers. As an interviewer, you have a responsibility to be a good reporter and to report what is true. In a sense, you are invading this person's privacy, and you have been given a privilege that you must not abuse. Be fair, be honest, and write an article that is true—one which both your interviewee and your reading audience will enjoy.

Copyrighting an Interview

If you write an interview article, certain parts of your article can be copyrighted:

1. your own introduction
2. your own selection of material
3. your own arrangement—"format"—of ideas
4. your own editorial comments
5. your own conclusion

Summary

1. Read your local newspaper daily. It is an excellent source of celebrity profiles.
2. When you decide on a particular person, arrange the interview by telephone, by letter, by telegram, by calling in person, or by forwarding a letter of introduction to either the celebrity or his or her agent.
3. Before you meet with the celebrity, do your homework. Read as much as you can about this particular person in magazines, newspapers, and books.
4. When contacting the celebrity, be sure to pronounce his or her name correctly.
5. Tell the celebrity the name of the magazine or newspaper for which the article is intended.

6. Tell the celebrity *why* you want to write this article, and explain the focus of the article.

7. Ask if photos are available or, if not, if you may take them.

8. If statistics are necessary, explain the need for them.

9. Assure the celebrity that you will submit a final copy of the article and photos (if any) to him or her for approval before the article is published.

10. When the interview date is set, send a confirming letter to the interviewee shortly before the interview to confirm the date.

11. If the celebrity turns you down, and you still want to write the article, ask if promotional material is available. You can still write the article by researching other articles and using promo material.

12. On the specified day of the meeting, be punctual.

13. When you meet the celebrity, be poised, confident, and dress neatly.

14. Relax and enjoy the meeting. Remember that this person is (probably) someone you admire.

15. Break the ice by referring to a common interest.

16. Always keep the slant of the article in mind as you interview the celebrity. If he or she continually veers from the subject, tactfully bring him or her back to it.

17. Have specific questions in mind and do make a list of questions beforehand—but don't read the questions off one by one to the interviewee.

18. Keep tape recorders and lists of questions out of sight.

19. When writing information down, try to be as unobtrusive as possible. Concentrate on key phrases, rather than on trying to catch each word.

20. Be polite and tactful. Insulting the interviewee will usually terminate the interview.

21. Strive for a relaxed, casual attitude.

22. Do not overstay the interview time allotted unless the interviewee specifically requests that you stay.

23. Be a responsible reporter; don't twist the interviewee's statements to support your own bias. To the best of your ability, write a factual article.

Exercises

1. Select a friend or classmate to interview. Set a time limit of thirty minutes for the interview. Let your article emerge *from the information you've gathered*.

2. Select a friend or classmate to interview. Have *a specific focus* in mind for your article. As you interview, try to keep your interviewee in perspective with the article you already have in mind. Don't let your interviewee veer too far from the subject. Set a time limit of thirty minutes for the interview.

18

Whom Are You Writing for—and Why?

In the case of new writers, a book usually chooses them, while more seasoned writers generally choose the books they will write. That is, most new writers feel compelled to write about things that emotionally involve them—no matter if those subjects interest anyone else or not. But pros realize that they are capable of writing many books; therefore they try to assess how "marketable" a subject is.

An important fact every writer must face is that most books take anywhere from six months to two years to write. That's a good chunk of time to take out of your life. Most people today do not enjoy "working for free"; in fact, few people would consider writing a book that has no chance of being published. Most new writers dream of their finished book selling wildly at the bookstores, their names emblazoned on the book jacket. Fame, money, an exciting life, all are part of the desire to write books. A writer may be a storyteller who loves spinning yarns or who wants to share a great message with society, but all writers want and need an audience.

Consequently, if you're going to spend your life energy writing a book, you should be practical about its publishing possibilities. A couple of important questions you need to ask are: Who will read this book? Why should they read this book?

The Average Reader

According to a recent UPI poll and a BIGS (Book Industry Study Group) consumer study, the average reader in the United States is a young, educated (some college) white female who reads primarily for pleasure and secondarily for knowledge.

Does this mean that a senior citizen, for example, has to try to write about subjects that are meaningless to him or her? Not at all. But being realistic, the older writer should try to touch on subjects that are timely and pertinent.

Be Timely

Your book must be current and must relate in some way to the experiences of current readers. Not long ago, a famous scholar mentioned that Tolstoy's *Anna Karenina*, one of the great novels in world literature, had become incomprehensible to young readers. They couldn't identify with or even understand Anna's problem: She was married to a man she didn't love and was suffering over her passionate affair with her lover, Vronsky. From a twentieth-century perspective, however, she could have gone off and lived with Vronsky. The problem was soluble. However, in Tolstoy's time, few women divorced, and so his readers could empathize with the character's dilemma. The point is that times change, and so do readers. The writer has to be aware of those changes.

Be Aware of Today's Reading Level

If a book is to be successful, it must be written at the reading level of its intended audience. A sobering thought is that today's reading is largely at the junior high school level. Therefore, showing off your vocabulary can seriously hinder you from publishing. Obviously, it's good advice to write "simply." However, many great writers have always advocated using simple language. As mentioned earlier, both Mark Twain and Ernest Hemingway advocated "four letter" words.

Test Your Audience

Certainly in fiction writing, being able to communicate to as wide an audience as possible is a prerequisite for writing a **best**seller, as is consciously directing a book to the largest possible audience. Recently at a west coast writer's conference, a highly successful western writer revealed the secret of his many bestsellers. He said that before he began a new novel, he made a list of ten ideas he would like to write about. He then showed that list to a diverse group of people: his mailman, the corner policeman, his wife's beautician, the checker at the supermarket, his family physician, his dentist. When one of the ideas interested all of them, he wrote that particular book. Remember, all of those ideas were ones that he enjoyed, ideas with which he was emotionally involved. He was not "prostituting" himself. Rather, he was capable of writing many novels; however, he wanted to be sure that the one he wrote would be well received.

Sell the Publisher on Your Idea

While successful writers have a knack for "psyching out" current reader interest, they also have to "sell" the publisher on their ideas. Publishers are necessarily wary of new book ideas because of the huge amounts of money they have to invest to publish the book. They know, too, that the public is fickle and that its likes and dislikes change overnight. Ask publishers what they wants, and the inevitable answer is: "A book that sells." Is the book that "sells" a *good* book? To the publisher, a book that does not sell is a bad book, no matter how well it is written. While the writer's concerns are writing a "good" book, the publisher is concerned with making money. Publishing is a business, while writing is an art and a craft. Don't get the two confused.

Avoid Hot Subjects

Many national publishers tend to be leery of current popular subjects because they may be highly salable now but may not be by the time the book is published or, if it is, not for very long afterward. Also, many hot topics are exhausted by other media, making it even more difficult for a publisher to put out a profitable book on the same subject. Then, too, at the time of a catastrophe, publishers may put out an "instant" book that deals with the event. Some hot topics to avoid are:

1. disasters (floods, fires, tornadoes)
2. death of any well-known person (it's better to write his or her story while that person is alive)
3. limited political conflicts
4. seasonal sports victories

Another reason these subjects are not all that salable is that people tend to forget about them.

Avoid Subjects That Have a Limited Readership

An important point about reader interest, too, is that some fields are limited to the very few. For example, less than 2 percent of the people in the world are interested in jazz; therefore, a jazz novel would promise a very low readership. In fact, some publishers say they will not consider a jazz novel for that reason—no matter how well it is written.

Salable Subjects

Irving Stone's advice on the subject of reader interest is to write about people "who can never be eradicated from history." While Stone advocates using historical personages as subjects for a novel, writers such as Harold Robbins and Jacqueline Susann became famous by writing about thinly disguised celebrities whom everyone wants to read about. Certain elements continue to fascinate people: the famous, sex, violence, money, politics, the occult, how-to, and religion. It's a pretty good bet that these things will always be the hottest recipe for the bestseller.

Should You Write for Money?

On the other hand, to consciously set out to write a book solely to make money may be a mistake. It's a pretty safe bet that the book will probably not be successful. Writing itself is a magical act; whatever the writer is thinking and feeling most deeply is inevitably conveyed in his or her prose. If a writer is experiencing joy, sadness, or love as he or she writes—so will the reader, too, experience these things as he or she reads. Good writers are storytellers who truly enjoy spinning a good yarn, and it is this infectious zest that produces a good book. Simply, good writers love what they're writing about.

How Do You Know if You're a Writer?

Most writers tend to be solitary people, given to daydreaming, but their daydreams are more real than life itself. If you spend most of your life socializing or lying on the beach, you'll probably never be a writer. A real writer spends lovely summer days in a stifling cubicle, acting out fantasies on a clacking typewriter or a silent word processor, or perhaps curled up in a chair and writing feverishly with a pen. Writing is a lonely discipline. Yet the dreams writers write are often more lovely or powerful than any true-life experience—and these are the dreams that cheer the monotonous life of the working world.

Writers live a very "mental" life, writing their fantasies. They read voraciously and often love the magic world of theatre, TV, and cinema. Books and dramatic media productions are schools for the writer. From current novels, movies, and TV scripts the writer gets a feel of what is current—the pulse of the world. The writer is also able to "pick up" on new and otherwise striking techniques which already-published writers are using. It's a truism that you can't write a book unless you've read a great many of them. Writers, of necessity, need a good vocabulary—which is often gained through reading. They also have to know what subjects have been written about so they won't waste their time writing the same kind of book.

Is It True That Some Writers Hate to Write?

Most writers like to write. It's true that almost all writers will tell you that they try to do everything *but* go to the typewriter when it's time to write. But the reason is not that they don't like writing—it's because they know they have to rewrite. Everyone loves the soaring flights of imagination, the reliving of an exciting experience, the creation of a loved fantasy as the first words are put to a blank piece of paper. But that's only the beginning. After the words are down, the artist/editor part of the self must craft the words into the final shape so the writing is alive, vital, flowing easily—so the work becomes an exciting real-life experience that makes every reader an "Alice in Wonderland." To most writers, rewriting is work as exacting as that of Michelangelo's chipping away at granite. Yet, as does any good sculptor absorbed in his or her work, a writer too derives satisfaction in "chipping" away at words to bring dynamic life to his or her creation.

Should You Take a Writing Class?

Yes, you should take a writing class! But, isn't this book enough? It's true that this book will give you all the basics you need to publish, but in a writing class you usually have the opportunity to hear your work read and to see firsthand the impact your writing has on other people. An advantage of a writing class is that it's composed of readers, the type of person for whom you are writing, and if your work is well received by the class, it's a good sign that it will be well received by a publisher too. Also, a good writing teacher can pick out your weak spots and help you to strengthen your writing. Then, too, because writers tend to be solitary people, it's rewarding to have the camaraderie of other writers who are working on projects. In such an atmosphere a "cross-fertilization" of minds occurs, for every writer is a teacher to another writer.

People Who Rarely Can Help You

It's equally important to point out that a close friend, a mate, a lover, or a relative is rarely a good critic. Each will invariably assure you that your writing is fantastic! But, just as invariably, that person has no experience either in editing, writing, or publishing.

People Who Can Really Help You

Your most professional critiquing will come from a teacher, a writer, a good editor, or a professional literary consultant. These qualified experts can save you years of trial and error. The next question, of course, is how to find such a person.

How to Pick a Good Writing Teacher

Good writing teachers are known by reputation. Look in your local college or university catalogue and see who is teaching writing classes. Often, professional writers teach part-time or evening adult education classes. Take time to read some of the instructor's books, articles, or short stories. Inasmuch as publishing is concerned, if a teacher hasn't published it isn't likely that he or she will be able to teach you how to publish. On the other hand, an unpublished teacher is usually working seriously at writing and is often able to pass on to you some valuable information. This type of teacher usually prepares you for a more advanced teacher, usually a well-known writer. It's good advice, though, in any field, to "go to the top" when you're ready to publish. Also, a good writing teacher generally knows one or more agents and will usually recommend you to one when you're ready to publish.

Will an Editor Help You?

While a good writing teacher often opens the door to a writing career, a good editor often polishes the fledgling writer into a professional. Again, however, to attract an editor you must have good writing skills. Editors are hard to get to know because they are usually behind closed doors, working with authors who have been assigned to them. Generally, you meet them when your book has been accepted for publication. Sometimes you may be lucky enough to meet an editor at a writing conference or at a cocktail party. By all means, push through the crowd at the editor's elbow and tell him or her about what you're writing. If the editor expresses any interest, follow up the conversation by mailing a proposal or synopsis to him or her. Be sure to have the name spelled correctly—and never, *never* mail a manuscript to a publishing house without addressing it to a particular editor. Invariably, a manuscript that is addressed only to a publishing house is returned unread.

How Much Time Should You Set Aside Each Day to Write?

Once you have determined to write your book, set aside a particular time each day to work at it—even if it's only half an hour. Pull out the phone jack or turn on the answering machine. Make your resolution clear to everyone around—your spouse or your lover, the children, your parents, your roommate, the cat, the dog—you are not to be disturbed. This is your time to write. Stick to your principles, and everyone in the household will understand that you mean it.

Don't wait until you get the urge. Frankly, you may never get the impetus to begin writing. If nothing comes, write something anyway. Sometimes the pages you seem to force will turn out to be very good, and often they'll fill in later parts of the book you're writing. It's not uncommon for a chapter in the middle of a book to arrive this way. The point is, start with a half hour and gradually work up. It's also a good idea to stop working when you're just beginning a new concept, when you know what you're going to write about. But if you finish a chapter and you don't know what next to write about, you may waste a lot of time sitting at the typewriter before an idea shows up.

Do You Need a "Writing Room" to Write?

Should you pick out a particular location in which to write? Not really, provided you always use the same location. We are all like Pavlov's dog, which learned to salivate when a bell rang. Similarly, writers train themselves to start writing when they are in a suitable place that allows their creative juices to flow; for many writers, just putting their fingers on their typewriter keys starts the creative process. For others, curling up in a comfortable chair and holding a favorite ballpoint pen initiates the process.

Mario Puzo wrote for years on the dining room table. When he became more successful, his long-patient wife convinced him to build a study in which he could write his novels, and Puzo did. But he was so used to the dining room table that he had to return to it. Hemingway in his later years wrote standing up, on a fireplace mantel. Thomas Wolfe also wrote standing up; he used the top of an icebox for a desk. The novelist Wirt Williams has to have a fan going in his writing room, the soft *whirr* stimulating ideas. Dostoyevski wrote feverishly into the wee hours of the morning, while other writers prefer to rise early and write, feeling that they are freshest then and so have the most energy to put into their work.

Where Do Writers Get Their Ideas?

If you wonder where writers get their ideas, you will probably never be a writer. Writers see stories in everything. Most of them draw richly from their own lives; however, the daily news is probably the greatest catalyst. Interesting events often tick off good story situations. It's important to point out, however, that few writers use their whole life as the subject of a novel. They may invent a character who has some of their own qualities and perhaps would react to a given situation as they themselves would react. The danger of writing one's own life story is that too often one loses the artistic focus of artfully dramatizing key events in a harmonic structure. Simply, the writer is too close to his or her own life story. It takes a little distance to really see the meaning in a story and to artistically shape a structure to fit that meaning. Unfortunately, life is not "art"; rather, life is a hodgepodge of events. It takes an artist to shape that "material" into a story.

Can You Use People Around You in Your Book?

Few writers will admit to using any one person as a main character in a novel. It generally takes three to four people of one's acquaintance to make one real literary character. It is not uncommon to invent totally fictional characters and events to "fill out" a real-life situation that the writer has experienced. If a writer actually writes a story exactly as it happened, it's a safe bet that the story or novel will be hopelessly dull.

Why Not Keep a Journal?

Many of the events that happen in one's life can be a springboard to a good story, novel, or script. For this reason, it's a good idea to keep a journal and record the powerful experiences that occur in your life, as well as your internal and external reactions to those situations. When you're in love, when a close friend or relative dies, when you're fired, when you achieve a great success, when you break up with a lover or spouse, when you feel angry at another person—all these things are the material of fiction. If you write your feelings down as they occur, you will have a rich source of material on which to draw. Often we pass through certain situations in life, and it's difficult to recapture those emotions later. But remember, you will not use these events exactly as they occurred; rather, you will draw from your journal to give the freshness and vitality of life to your imagined story.

Another important use of the journal is to record precise descriptions of particular trees, clouds, the exact shade of grass and flowers. Somerset Maugham was noted for keeping a card file, and when he was writing a scene and needed to describe "the sky," he sorted through his file and selected a description that he had written previously. Hemingway usually wrote in the morning and then went to outdoor cafés in the afternoon, recording his sensory impressions in his journals. When he worked out at the gym he later recorded the exact sound of his fists hitting the punching bag, the smell of resin, and the way he felt. This taking time to look at objects and then writing what you see and feel results in "freshness" in a writer's work. In fact, Joseph Conrad once said:

> My task which I am trying to achieve is, by the power of the written word to make you hear, to make you feel—it is, before all, to make you see. That—and no more, and it is everything.

So start a journal or set up a card file and record your impressions while you're riding on the bus, standing in a cafeteria line, browsing at the library, or eating alone. Draw portraits of people in words. Try to catch individual pieces of dialogue. You will become aware that there are hundreds of types of ears, noses, eyes, and legs. Try to determine exact colors of things, plus the various shades and hues. Record unusual situations that occur around you, and other people's responses to those situations. The one common thing about writers is that they have a highly developed gift of observation, and they usually ask the question "What if?"

How Long Does It Take to Write a Novel?

In the event you're wondering how long it will take you to write a book, there's no easy answer. The time varies for each writer. Balzac could write one in six weeks. Barbara Cartland, the romance queen, reputedly can turn out a book every eighteen days; and Erle Stanley Gardner (author of the Perry Mason books) turned out a book every two weeks. Isaac Asimov, who writes one every month and has for six years, has published more than 200 novels and writes ten hours a day, seven days a week. However, in contrast to these paragons of industry, the average writer takes anywhere from one to three years.

How Many Times Does the Average Writer Have to Rewrite a Manuscript?

The average nonfiction writer rewrites a manuscript three times, while the average novelist rewrites a novel ten times. Flaubert spent years rewriting *Madame Bovary*, and every line is considered perfect from a literary standpoint.

Yes, writing is work, but it is also wholly absorbing—and fun! It is the closest thing to playing God there is. You can create worlds and destroy them. You can create hundreds of characters and manipulate their lives—though sometimes your characters will have a life that goes beyond your pen. They become closer than your own children; and when a book is over, you will feel as sad as if a friend had died.

What Should You Write?

A question that plagues most new writers is: What should I write—articles, TV scripts, short stories, plays, novels? What am I best at?

When you're just beginning to write, it's a good idea to take some classes in each of these writing fields and try to write something in each discipline. You may discover that one of these types of writing is more enjoyable to you than another. But don't make up your mind on just one or two attempts. Too often new writers think that just because they happen to write good dialogue, obviously they're scriptwriters. Before you make up your mind what you will be best at, learn the craft of various types of writing.

Learn to characterize; to write good images, good settings; write some short stories, even some poetry. Short-story writing is excellent training for writing the novel. It also helps you develop excellent groundwork for scripts. The advantage of a short story is that you can gradually increase your length until you have a novel or a long script. If a writer who is unsure of his or her skills begins a long work, he or she tends to become discouraged and often bumbles along only to produce a mishmash that is unpublishable.

Once you have learned your writing skills, you may find that while you thought you were a scriptwriter, you're really a novelist—or it could be vice-versa. The point is, we tend to feel more comfortable when we can do something well; but by learning other things we discover that we do those things well too. Frankly, it may take a year or longer for you to finally discover what you really want to do.

Summary

So what does it take to be a writer? The professionals say that you must write for the sheer pleasure of writing and not money alone; you must write what you enjoy, and you must write it well. If you feel this way, you have all the instincts of a true writer. But do remember these vital things:

1. Be aware of your reading audience, their age, their interests.
2. Be current.
3. Test your market before writing; poll your friends and bookstores about the ideas you want to base your books and articles on.
4. Remember, publishing is a business; a proposed book is looked at from the perspective of "will it sell?"
5. Avoid current hot topics that the media exhaust.
6. Rewriting is an absolute necessity.
7. Writing classes, seminars, writing teachers, editors, and literary consultants can teach you many important things and save you time.
8. Seek an agent only when your writing is of publishable quality.
9. Write every day, if only for a half hour. Gradually increase your writing time.
10. Keep a journal and record all your impressions—but remember that life is not art, though it provides the material for art.
11. Don't be impatient—writing takes time.
12. Try as many fields of writing as you can until you discover your true specialty.

Most important—don't give up! If you're wondering if editors are really looking for new writers, the answer is *yes*. They're just as eager to discover you as you are to be discovered. In fact, the secret dream of every great editor is to be the one who discovers a Thomas Wolfe or an Ernest Hemingway. However, an editor can discover you only if you know how to write—and if you have written something that is publishable.

Exercises

1. Keep a daily journal of your impressions. Record what you see, how you *feel* about things.
2. Put ten of the ideas you want to write about on an index card. Poll your friends as to which idea they like best.

19

How to Approach a Publishing House

If you are a nonfiction writer and have finished your proposal, you are faced with marketing it to a publisher. Should you immediately send your book or proposal to any publishing house, without knowing of an editor, in the hope that you will immediately be recognized as the next Hemingway? The answer is an unqualified no. The odds of your book's being purchased "over the transom" (unsolicited) are approximately three in ten thousand! In fact, most editors can't even remember buying an unsolicited book (one that is not addressed to a specific editor) in their entire career. The majority of unsolicited manuscripts are returned to the author unopened. How, then, can a writer get a manuscript read? Is there some definite plan a writer can follow to cut down the odds? The answer to this question is an unqualified yes.

Select the Right Publisher

Whether you're writing a novel, a textbook, or a how-to book, you must take the greatest care in selecting the right publisher for your book. You can locate publishers that specialize in your type of book in *Writer's Market* and in *Literary Market Place* (known as the *LMP*). Remember, too, that many companies have specific divisions that specialize in manuscripts written for special-interest groups such as nurses, contractors, accountants, lawyers, engineers, and others. In nonfiction the trade book is written for the lay public, the technical book for professionals.

Remember: Publishing Is a Business

One problem with new writers is that they do not understand the world of publishing, so they often write books that have little or no market value. Don't forget that while writing is an art and a craft, publishing remains a business and not a charitable activity.

Certainly, editors would like to read every manuscript that comes in, but no publisher makes money reading manuscripts—especially unsolicited ones. Money is made only when a book is bought, published, and *sold at a profit*. Therefore, most editors, whether they like it or not, are forced to make publishing decisions based primarily on a book's marketability. Why? The majority of books published today do not make money for anyone. For this reason, publishers are tending to look more to "name" authors and professional writers with good track records to help publishers make a profit.

This marketing emphasis forces the new writer to be professional not only in writing but also when dealing with a publisher. One of the first lessons a writer must learn in order to publish successfully is to "write a book about a subject that everyone wants to read about." Unfortunately, a book may be beautifully crafted but may still have little chance of being published if it does not appeal to a large enough reading audience.

Should You Contact an Editor?

It is imperative to use any type of "in" to open the door to publishing. Use any method you can think of to get your work read by an editor: friends, relatives, acquaintances, teachers, someone who "knows" someone, colleagues, bookstore managers, perhaps even a publishing house sales representative. Why do you need such an "in"? It's simply to overcome your anonymity, to "flag" your proposal so that it's noticed by the editor, and to convince someone to look at your manuscript. This first contact is critical. The whole point is that you look like a professional and not an amateur.

But what if you don't have such a contact, what then? Again, don't be afraid to try a gimmick. Editors are creative people and enjoy a good scam. One editor likes to tell the story of a letter he received from a writer who had shared a wayward plane trip with him—the plane rerouted to Alaska, then Hawaii, and what marvelous drinks they had had and women they had met. The editor knew the whole thing was a fabrication, but he could hardly wait to read the manuscript of such an inventive writer.

If you're not up to such artful "mendacity," as Tennessee Williams liked to say, probably the easiest thing to do is to call the public relations department of the publishing house you've selected and make up a less creative story—how you met an editor at a cocktail party, a dark-haired woman, slender (there's always somebody like this at a publishing house), and she told you to get in touch with her, but embarrassingly you forgot her name, though you'd know it in a minute if you heard it—and when the reply is something like, "It sounds like Karin Lapham," say: "That's it!" And it is. Now you have a name.

Who Exactly Is the Editor, and What Does an Editor Do?

From the writer's viewpoint, an editor is a collaborator who helps the writer develop a book when the book has been purchased before it has been completed. In nonfiction, a manuscript is often bought on the basis of a proposal and a few chapters; the editor, then, is very important to the writer. On the other hand, in fiction, editors rarely work at developing a novel with the author because the novel is generally completed prior to submission. The novelist shouldn't anticipate kindly editors' rewriting or salvaging a manuscript that needs work. In the world of fiction the closer to perfection a manuscript is, the more salable it is—unless your name is Harold Robbins or James Michener. They can get contracts on ideas.

The old legend of that great editor Maxwell Perkins' complete reconstruction of Thomas Wolfe's long, rambling novel *Look Homeward Angel* is today a modern fairy tale. As one weary New York editor put it succinctly: "Maxwell Perkins is dead—and they ain't no mo' like him." In other words, the nonfiction writer will often have a closer relationship with the editor who oversees the completion of a nonfiction project. To the freelance nonfiction writer, it is the editor who is the psychiatrist, father/mother confessor, who is a phone call away. An agent usually takes that role with the struggling fiction writer.

In a sense, the editor is a double agent. The editor represents the writer to the publisher and the publisher to the writer. The editor is employed by the publisher and is committed to the writer. Too many times, his loyalties are divided by this situation.

What Should You Do if Your Book Has Been Rejected?

In the event of a rejection, don't respond immediately to the editor or agent until you've had a cooling-off period, until you've had a chance to become more objective about your manuscript. Don't call and argue with or write to the editor about it. The editor has rejected it for his or her good reasons. Put the review or rejection letter away, at least over the weekend—some pros recommend a month—then take it out and study it carefully. You may find the editor right on, or you may still feel that the manuscript is excellent the way it is. If so, get it back in the mail to another editor.

In nonfiction, the editor's comments are generally relevant and based on those of several reviewers. In fiction, rejections tend to be more subjective. Granted, however, the manuscript may just not be written well—the cause of most rejections. Be honest in this respect; the manuscript may definitely need to be rewritten. If the manuscript is written well, and if—after the necessary cooling down—you believe in that manuscript as it is, then mail it out again.

The important thing is: Don't lose confidence in yourself. Editors reject manuscripts for many reasons. They may have just published a book like yours, or, let's face it, the editor just may not be drawn to your idea.

One of the main things not to do is to go into a nose-dive when your book is rejected and gloriously hurl yourself into the "hamster" syndrome: running around the wheel of your self-guilt. (You should have done better, you knew there was something wrong, you'll never write again, why did you ever think you were a writer?) But then, don't go hopping to the wheel of self-defense. (It was a good book, the editor was blind, the reviewer was stupid.) All this is a waste of valuable time and energy. When faced with the hamster syndrome, take the weekend off and go fishing or get out into the garden. But the main thing is to get back to writing as soon as possible. The longer you pout and sulk, the longer it will be before you come to grips with the typewriter.

How Should One Evaluate the Language of the Rejection Slip?

A rejection slip does not mean that your manuscript is unpublishable and without merit.

If you've received printed rejection slips, and a lot of them on the same manuscript, accept that there just isn't enough interest in the book from anybody. Editors will usually try to encourage an author if they see any talent showing.

If an editor says something to the effect that he or she likes the book and would be willing to look at it again if it were revised, then do revise the book—if you have the time and the inclination. On the other hand, you don't want to be revising the book at each editor's whim. If your book has been to some fifteen houses or so and no one has bought it, then take a hard look at it and think about revision. Look for a pattern in the negative responses. Remember that the average book has been revised at least three times and perhaps as many as ten. Rather than commit suicide—rewrite! After all, the book may turn out to be a bestseller—and then look what you'd have missed. Pay attention to the editors' comments. Editors do not have enough time to write you a detailed letter on your book; they read many books and book proposals per day. Because they see so many manuscripts, they have become highly intuitive as to *why* a book sells; and when they dash off a remark to you they often put their finger on a weakness in the book. If several editors make the same remark, it's a good idea to rewrite that particular area of the book before submitting it again. Yes, a book can be resubmitted again if it is rewritten, and many many books have been rewritten and then sold.

What the Rejection Is/What It Is Not

The rejection is a flat statement from the editor that the material you have submitted is, for a variety of reasons, not suitable for his or her publishing house. The editor is not putting you down deliberately, is not saying that your book is rotten and that you should never write again, or saying that you are certainly stupid to think you can write at all. Publishers are in business to make money; they are merchandisers; and, like any other business, they need products to sell. It's up to you to come up with the right product. If you can accept this frank, bottom-line assessment, you'll find it easier dealing with rejections—and you'll use those rejections that offer good advice and discard the stupid ones.

So what do you do about rejection slips? Evaluate them, learn from some of them, ignore the stupid ones, and get back to your typewriter. You have books to write—and contracts to sign ... when you write the book an editor wants to buy.

How Often Should a Manuscript Be Sent Out Before It Is Rewritten?

This is a difficult question. *Love Story, All Things Bright and Beautiful, Jonathan Livingston Seagull, The Godfather,* and *Watership Down* all received twelve or more rejections prior to being bought by a publisher. Six rejections are average for a novel.

Reasons for Rejection Letters

The most common rejection letters say that the market for which you've written this manuscript is too limited—for example, a subject like jazz appeals to only 2 percent of the population, too small a percentage to interest a major publisher—or your book does not fit the house's publishing program, a common occurrence for a writer who sends a novel to a publishing house that publishes only nonfiction. Also, a genre writer can expect a rejection slip from a house that publishes only mainstream or literary projects.

Rejections occur because:

1. In a genre field—such as romance and adventure—you may not have created your story according to the rules. (It's a wise idea to send to the publisher for tip sheets giving genre requirements; most publishers supply tip sheets upon request with SASE).
2. The publisher has recently put out a book like yours.
3. There are too many other books like it in print.
4. You have written a novel that reads as though Hemingway or Faulkner wrote it—your style is too much like that of another famous author.
5. The concept is "tired," that is, not fresh and original.
6. The idea is not believable the way you have written it.
7. The characters are dull, boring, or unbelievable.
8. The manuscript lacks life—it's loaded with passive verbs and flat writing.
9. *Nothing is happening*—you don't understand suspense and plot.
10. The book is confusing. You don't understand viewpoint, and you're jumping into all the characters' minds, destroying the unity of action.
11. You have too many characters, and the reader won't be able to identify with any particular one.
12. You haven't motivated your characters properly.
13. Your manuscript sounds *dated* in style, subject, or in the way you have handled your material. Simply, you have not kept abreast of what is happening in your particular fiction/nonfiction area. For example:
    a. you can't write like Dostoyevski or Tolstoy in the twentieth century
    b. a subject hot in the 1930s, sex before marriage, isn't that grabbing to today's reading audience
    c. you can't write a book in the long, leisurely fashion, as Henry Fielding did
    Be timely. Read the latest bestsellers, see the latest movies. Try to understand what subjects interest today's reader, and note the newest ways of writing. Many novelists are borrowing heavily from screenwriters, and so cinematographic techniques are influencing today's writing.
14. The subject has been thoroughly exploited by the media.
15. You have used inappropriate material that will offend the average reading audience—sexually, politically, graphically (brutal scenes).
16. You've been didactic (preachy) in long, narrative passages or arrived at simplistic conclusions.
17. The editor is not interested in your subject, your theme, or your characters.
18. The editor likes your book but doesn't think it will sell—remember that if the editor acquires and publishes a flop, the editor's job could be at risk.
19. The book is too long, paper is expensive, and the editor just doesn't want to risk it—especially if you're a first-time novelist without a recognizable name.

20.   You've published three or more books that flopped and the editor knows it.
21.   The editor hates your style.
22.   Your mechanics are unforgivably bad, and your typing is a disaster.
23.   The editor is tired and wants to go home, and your book is unlucky enough to fall into his or her hands at the end of the day.

Summary

It's important for you to look like a professional when you submit your manuscript for publication to an agent or editor. *Don't* mail your manuscript in to a publisher without addressing it to a particular editor. Check the *Fiction Writer's Market* to be sure you're sending your manuscript to a publishing house that handles your kind of novel or nonfiction work. If you don't know the name of an editor, call the publishing house and ask who the fiction editor is, who the nonfiction editor is. If your book is rejected, let your manuscript cool for a few days and then look at it again. If the editor has rejected it for a particular reason, try to look at the manuscript from the editor's viewpoint. If the editor's point is valid, then rewrite the problem areas: plot, characterization, scene structure, dialogue. Don't call the editor and argue with him or her. If you feel you've solved the problems, you might resubmit the manuscript to the editor with a cover letter, saying you've reworked the novel according to the editor's suggestions. If you feel the editor was off base, send the manuscript to another publishing house; after all, the editor might be wrong. Be objective about your rejection slips. Some of them have good advice, some of them are stupid. Feel free to paper your bedroom with them. After you've sold your novel, you'll have a good source of many laughs.

20

How to Develop
the Nonfiction Book
Query and Proposal
and the Novel Package,
Including the Synopsis

Why Is the Proposal Necessary
for Nonfiction Book Writers?

If you are a nonfiction writer with an idea you wish to develop into a book-length manuscript, you need to prepare a query letter and then a proposal for the editor. To begin a book that could take several years to write, without any market or reimbursement in sight, is too big a risk—in time and money. Consequently, the nonfiction writer should always prepare a complete proposal for an idea.

The proposal contains many elements that will help your book when you submit it to an editor or an agent. The reason for a proposal is to increase the chances of getting published and to reduce the risk of rejection by giving information that supports the validity and salability of your novel. As competition becomes more acute, the writer with a good, solid proposal is more likely to get published than a writer without one. While some writers argue that "an agent takes care of all that," agents need all the help they can get to sell your book. The factual ingredients of the proposal provide valuable documentation for the agent and editor when they are reviewing you and your potential book project.

Why Is the Novel Package Necessary for the Fiction Writer?

If you are a fiction writer and are going to submit a novel to the agent or editor, you need to submit a "package." A package consists of a query letter, a blurb—a dramatic one paragraph condensation of your novel, a one to twelve page synopsis, and three chapters. Most agents and editors prefer to see the first three chapters because they want to see how the characters are introduced and if a significant problem is established. However, if you have a particularly good chapter later on in the book you might want to include it along with the first three chapters. A chapter with a major sex scene is an important one to include in the package.

Why Is a Query Letter Necessary?

Query letters save time. Agents and editors work with many authors and are busy reading *solicited* full-length manuscripts. They have little time to read unsolicited manuscripts. A query letter stating what you have to offer and asking the editor if he or she is interested is the quickest way to determine if your proposed nonfiction idea or your preferably completed novel manuscript can be published. The query letter *opens the door to the editor or agent.* It's an introduction, a way of getting the agent or editor to read the manuscript.

The query letter tells the agent about the book and gives the author's background and writing credits. If the book is on a subject that does not interest the agent, or if the agent judges your writing credits not sufficient, you have saved postage on a full manuscript plus the valuable time it took for him or her to receive the manuscript and return it to you.

Occasionally, a well-directed phone call to an agent or editor can act as an abbreviated query. It often promotes a quicker reading and evaluation of your novel package.

For the nonfiction writer, the query letter keeps the author from writing in a vacuum. It's better to "waste" a few hours on a query than two years on a book that has no chance of being published. Also, the input the editor makes on a proposed idea may reslant the direction of the book to a format in which he or she is much more interested, or the editor's input may result in a more salable book with a wider readership.

For the fiction writer, the value of the query letter plus the synopsis is that the package can be sent to many editors at the same time, which achieves a multiple submission of the synopsis. More editors will see your manuscript in a shorter time and you have a chance to choose the best offer. On the other hand, if you are submitting your package to a well-known agent, you are better off to submit the novel to him or her alone so that the agent has an "exclusive" on the book. No agent will want to put a great deal of work in on selling a book and then have another agent sell it.

If you're a first time novelist, you should have a completed or almost completed manuscript ready to send when you receive an affirmative response. A more established novelist with a good track record can submit a synopsis and three sample chapters of a proposed book to an agent or editor without having completed the novel. It is said that Harold Robbins can sell a novel on a phone call. Editors, however, are not prone to offer a contract to a new writer on the basis of a partial novel because, very simply, the new writer may not be able to finish the book.

The real value of the query letter is that it can produce a quicker sale. Most editors and agents answer queries within days. The nonfiction writer is usually luckier than the novelist for most nonfiction publishers will negotiate a contract on the basis of a complete proposal. Today, few publishing houses are willing to read complete manuscripts without being queried first. Reading a complete manuscript from the beginning to end takes too much time—and the book idea may be one that really doesn't interest the house anyway.

What Is the Query Letter for a Novel and How Is It Written?

The query is a one-page letter that sells your book idea and you. It must point out in easy-to-understand language why your book will be better than any other book on the subject. It is generally composed of four to five paragraphs and should include the following:

A NOVEL QUERY

1. *Tell the agent or editor the title of the book, its genre, and the time and place in which it takes place.* For example: "Dear _____ , I am submitting my novel, *The Conspiracy,* a contemporary suspense novel that takes place in Los Angeles, California.

2. *The second paragraph should be an exciting paragraph that describes your plot and characters.* A sample blurb might be:

   Ten men control the destiny of the world. They control nations and their leaders. They are planning a world-wide stock market crash that will plunge millions of people into povery and starvation. Only one man can stop them. But will he succeed in time?

3. *Give your special qualifications for writing this book.* Include your writing background and experience with the subject matter.

4. *Point out the market for your book.* If your subject deals with a particular historic event, such as the sinking of the *Titanic,* and *Titanic* clubs throughout the

United States will be interested in your book, mention this possible market. Capitalize on the interest shown in space travel, terrorism, the Civil War, World War II. Perhaps the book deals with a coming event, a visit by the pope or a state's centennial. Your suggestions may pique an editor's interest.

5. *State your desire to submit your already completed manuscript for review.* If you only have three chapters, tell the agent or editor how long it will take to complete the manuscript. End with a firm closure: "I look forward to hearing from you. Cordially."

Should a Fiction Writer Submit a Chapter Outline to Accompany the Query Letter?

In most cases, it's better to submit a synopsis—a dramatized condensation of your novel—written in your most exciting style and using some dialogue—although some synopses use an attached outline. A chapter outline is good to use when you're developing the novel. When laying out the action of the book, divide the novel into twenty chapters. Then write *one line* that describes what is going to happen in each chapter:

1. Chapter One. John Tracy, a sixteen-year-old boy, wants to be a jet pilot, and an airforce major takes him up in a jet plane.
2. Chapter Two. John goes motorcycle riding and a woman motorist runs into him, crushing his legs.
3. Chapter Three. At the hospital, the doctor tells John he will have to amputate his legs.

After the one sentence outline is complete, expand each of the sentences into a paragraph.

By breaking the book into chapters, the writer is forced to organize the major action or events of the novel. The writer should also work out a complex plot diagram (the W diagram) mentioned in the first chapter of the book. When the chapter outline is finished, it should be compared with the W diagram; the writer is then able to visualize how the scenes in each chapter work in the major plot outline—whether they are part of the initial action or the reversal or the resolution. Because the novel is so lengthy, one of the pitfalls is rambling and getting nowhere. It is far better to give some thought to the action (events) of the novel before starting to write it. The outline is generally for the writer's use alone, though some writers have submitted working outlines to editors on books in progress so that the editor can understand the design of the book. It is also important to remember that the outline will probably change as the book is written. New scenes will occur that were not planned, and some scenes that seem important as the book is being conceived may not be necessary when the writing actually takes place.

What Exactly Is the Synopsis?

A synopsis or treatment is very similar to a short story. It is a dramatized condensed version of your entire novel. It should *not* be a flat, boring presentation, and it should not be broken down into headings with Roman numerals. The first paragraph should give the time, locale, and some of the background. Is the novel contemporary, occurring in the past, in the future? Does the novel take place in New York, Atlantis, Egypt? What is the *problem* of the book? The main character should be introduced as quickly as possible, described, and seen in action in accordance with his or her main traits. Carefully select some of the novel's best scenes and artfully weave those scenes into the narrative, using dialogue, tension, and conflict. The synopsis should generate the same excitement as a good short story. You should work very hard to achieve a powerful, compelling treatment.

Remember that the synopsis is a showcase of your work, displaying all of your talents as a writer. It is meant to titillate the editor, making him or her eager to read the entire book. Much time should be spent on developing the main character in the synopsis, for the intent is to get the editor involved in the character's problem.

Most editors prefer a short synopsis. If your synopsis is longer than fifteen pages, you run the risk of boring the editor. After all, at any length the synopsis is never as compelling as your own work. Some editors refuse to read more than six pages of a synopsis. If you have a very long, complex book, however, a longer synopsis may be acceptable.

It's very difficult to give a definitive synopsis because agents and editors have different tastes. Examine the samples at the end of this chapter and determine which synopsis is most applicable to your book. More and more, though, there does seem to be a trend of editors' preferring the shorter synopsis, probably because they have to read so much material.

The synopsis is usually double-spaced and done in the present tense. It should have wide margins for easy reading, and it should not contain any spelling or punctuation errors. It should have a title page (see title page sample at end of this chapter) and should be put in a plastic jacket with a slide fastener, similar to that used on a college term paper. Do not staple, paper clip, or punch holes in the synopsis.

The Nonfiction Book Query

1. **Describe your book.** The first paragraph of your query letter must get the editor's attention and pique his or her interest. The first paragraph of the query for this nonfiction book was:

At last there's one complete handbook that shows how to write and publish both fiction and nonfiction. *A Complete Guide to Writing Fiction and Nonfiction, and How to Publish* is a reference guide for all writers, beginning or professional, interested in serious or commerical writing.

2. **Explain in substantive terms why you think your book should be published.** Emphasize the need for a book in your subject and how you're going to fulfill that need. For example: How is *your* book going to be better than other books on the same subject? Will it be more comprehensive, more detailed and easier to understand? The second paragraph of our query, which included author credentials, was:

> Besides being a reference handbook and a complete writing and publishing text, this book reveals why so many manuscripts are rejected—a subject of vital interest to every writer. But what makes this writing text different than any other? It's simply that the authors—a literary consultant who is also a prize-winning novelist and a teacher of writing at a California college, teams with a senior editor at a major publishing house—to reveal what editors look for in selecting manuscripts for publication. They speak directly to you as editors, showing you the difference between a well-written manuscript and one that is not well written.

The key to this paragraph is that the authors wanted to write a book about why manuscripts are rejected and how to cut down the risk of rejection.

3. **Give your special qualifications, your expertise, for writing this book, including your writing background.**

4. **Point out the market for your book.** Ask yourself, who are your readers? Are they a small select group—like neurosurgeons—who will pay well for the latest highly technical information—or does your book have mass appeal? Other questions you should consider:

1. What are the age and maturity levels of your intended audience?
2. For what educational level are you writing? Is the language suitable for this group?
3. Does your book/idea relate to the identifiable interests of this particular audience? Writers will also help themselves if they can suggest some specific marketing outlets for their books: Some suggestions are:
   a. trade bookstores
   b. newsstands
   c. specialty bookstores (such as occult, religion)
   d. college bookstores
   e. computer stores
   f. book clubs
   g. direct mail
   h. organizations and associations (specify)
   i. foreign market (specify)
   j. rights sales

Considering the reading audience at which this book is directed, how much do you feel your reader will pay to buy this book? Will the book be more salable in paperback or in hardcover? What is the approximate size of your reading audience? Be honest with the editor. Is this a limited or an unlimited market? Is it a new market? Is it a dying market? Is it a hard-to-reach market? Remember, you're the expert. Say what you think, but don't try to snow the editor. The editor already has a pretty good idea of the answers to all of these questions. Nevertheless, your input can help the editor evaluate your understanding of the possible markets for your book. It is very important for both author and editor to understand and communicate with each other concerning the book's potential markets.

Again, using the query for this writing handbook, note the following paragraph, which achieves the "identification of market":

> The marketing possibilities for the handbook are extremely broad, including both trade and textbook potential. It can be sold through trade stores, college bookstores, computer stores, writers' associations, and through mail order. As a literary publication, it could be advertised in book sections of newspapers and in writer's magazines. An advantage of the handbook is that it can be a hardcover reference book suitable for mail order, a softcover college text, and a trade paperback all at the same time.

The more you can convince the publisher that a lucrative market for your book exists, the more you enhance its salability to him or her. Then, too, this paragraph reveals how knowledgeable you are about your field in regard to marketing.

5. **State your desire to submit your already completed manuscript proposal for review.** Be short and concise:

> I am ready to send you my complete manuscript proposal including cover letter, resumé, table of contents, preface, outline, and sample chapters. I will look forward to hearing from you as soon as possible.

Now you should have the editor interested! He or she knows you are not speaking of just an idea you've randomly thought about. You've really taken time to think through your concept and have a complete proposal ready for review.

In essence, if an author can produce a succinct query showing that the proposed manuscript fulfills a need; that a definite market for this particular book exists; that the author has the credentials to write the book and the ability to look at a specific field from a new perspective, supplying valuable expertise; and that the author can express that concept, the writer cannot help but attract the editor's attention—which is half the battle of selling a book.

But don't expect every editor to respond favorably to your query. The

Fuller Brush Company once reported that it took eight house calls to produce one sale. Some article writers say one in ten is a good percentage in querying. Remember that once an editor knows you and can rely on you, your percentage will get better in a hurry—and then you should receive an affirmative response to each query. The important thing is not to get discouraged. Try to look at breaking into writing as a game. Take your writing seriously, but look at the process of enticing editors as a challenging one—like playing Monopoly. If you take each rejection as an affront to your ego, you may end up committing suicide as did a recent prize-winning novelist whose book was accepted after his suicide—and it won a literary prize, too!

Editors reject many ideas for many different reasons, not necessarily for lack of merit. They may have just published a similar book; the book may not be suitable for their particular publishing company (it's surprising how many writers send romances to technical houses); this particular editor may simply not respond to your subject—all these reasons have nothing to do with the writing itself. A professional sends out many queries to editors, just as a fisherman baits a hook and waits. When the writer gets a good bite, he or she tries to land the editorial fish by immediately mailing out a good, solid proposal.

What Does a Nonfiction Manuscript Proposal Consist Of?

The complete proposal can have up to six parts:

1. a cover letter (a two-page expanded query letter)
2. a resumé reflecting your publishing and business experience
3. a preface, introduction, or prospectus
4. a working outline and/or table of contents
5. sample chapter or chapters

What Is Included in the Cover Letter?

The cover letter is really your query letter expanded to include the following new information: a brief discussion stating *why* you have chosen that particular publisher; the approximate length, in words, of your proposed manuscript; and any special features you plan to use. Also, you should tell the editor what book or books already on the market will compete directly with yours and state why your book will be better. In regard to word length, note that there are approximately 450 words to the printed page and approximately 250 to the typed page. In general, to compute the number of printed pages your book will have, divide your typed pages by two-thirds. For example, if you have a 600-page typed manuscript, it should equal a 400-page printed book. *Always give your estimated word length and not the number of pages.* When closing your cover letter, state that you're waiting to hear from this particular editor and that you will not submit the complete proposal to anyone else until you hear from him or her.

What Information Should Be Included in the Resumé?

The resumé includes facts about your personal/academic background that relate to the book, any and all previous publications, degrees if any (particularly valuable if you are writing a technical book), and business experience (again valuable if you are doing a "how to" business book). For example, if you're a fiction writer doing a Vietnam War novel, the fact that you were a colonel in the army and served in Vietnam would give you credibility. Editors do not like to have books bounced back in their faces because the author does not know what he or she is talking about. Also, if you have done extensive research on the background used in the novel, mention this too.

What Is an Introduction, a Preface, and a Prospectus?

The Introduction is usually written by the author and is concerned only with the content of the book.

The Preface is the author's account of the scope and purpose of the book and also how the book came to be written. The Preface can also include the acknowledgments if they are not extensive.

The Prospectus is an abstract of the book, a concise abridgement, that includes all market considerations. A Prospectus is generally expected with textbooks and technical books.

Why Is a Working Outline Needed in a Nonfiction Manuscript Proposal?

Developing a working outline forces the author to *organize* the material. It makes the writer place all ideas and topics in a logical sequence, and it leads the reader from the introduction of the subject to the conclusion of the stated purpose.

One way to start organizing yourself and your material is to get a pack of 3" × 5" cards. Then brainstorm your ideas and put *one* idea on each card. List any idea that occurs to you, and stop only when the subject is covered. Then flip through the cards and decide on their proper sequence by establishing chapter and/or major headings. Now, organize the chapter groupings by again brainstorming. Finally, rearrange the cards within the chapters to achieve what you feel is the best ordering of events.

How Long Should the Nonfiction Working Outline Be?

The outline can consist of one-paragraph synopses of each planned chapter. It can also mean a two- to six-page description of the book or a working outline of up to thirty pages long. Try to make your outline as detailed and as specific as possible. The purpose of the outline is to help reviewers and editors see how the author plans to develop the remaining chapters.

The outline should include:

1. headings
2. subheadings
3. sub-subheadings with explanations as necessary

Which Chapters Should Be Sent as a Sample in Nonfiction?

Believe it or not, if you are writing nonfiction, the first chapter may not be the one to include. Pick out the chapters you believe to be your best, most interesting, and if possible most innovative or different. Remember, they do not have to be in sequence.

Make sure that your writing is top quality. You don't want to apologize: "If I'd had more time I could have ..." The editor will answer, "If you want to sell me a manuscript, you should have taken the time to have achieved the effect you want." Do your best at *all* times. Once you have submitted your manuscript, it's very hard to change a negative impression.

When Should a Proposal Be Sent?

From the nonfiction point of view, a proposal can be sent at **any** time. Definitely don't wait until you have written the complete manuscript.

Why Is a Complete Proposal Necessary in Nonfiction?

For the nonfiction writer, there are many reasons why a proposal is essential. For one, it gives the editor the scope of the book and presents the material in a concise fashion that enables him or her to consider your book as a publishing venture without reading the entire manuscript. Remember, the editor is besieged with many books and proposals to read, plus meetings with various writers and other editors. Most important, the proposal gives the editor complete documentation—in your own words—with which to justify to his or her boss the possible purchase of your manuscript. If you have not submitted a complete proposal, chances are that the editor will not have enough information to defend your book as a *profitable* literary project. Some published authors try to get by with a one-page proposal, but they risk being passed over in favor of a writer with a more detailed proposal.

What About Multiple Submissions?

It's all right to *query* as many editors as possible, and if you are a fiction writer *do* make multiple submissions of your synopsis with the query. Do not make multiple submissions to agents, however. But if you are a nonfiction writer, send only one proposal to one editor at a time. For example, if you send out twenty-five queries and you get a favorable response from five, then you can select the most promising response and submit your proposal to that particular editor while assuring him or her that you will not send your proposal to any other editor.

How Long to Wait for a Response to Your Proposal or Novel Package?

Two weeks after sending in your complete proposal, send a follow-up postcard—something to the effect that you were wondering if the editor received the proposal and if he or she has any encouraging words. After another couple of weeks you should send a short note stating that you would like to hear from the editor as soon as possible. If the editor still does not respond, then send a copy of your proposal to the next editor on your list.

Agents, of course, do make multiple submissions of fiction manuscripts; but if you are submitting your own manuscript be aware that some houses do not like multiple submissions. Check your *Writer's Market* to see which ones those are.

Helpful Tips on Submitting a Manuscript

The one thing you should strive for above all else is **good, clean copy**—free of spelling and punctuation errors. Do not make a lot of pen or pencil corrections. Use the following checklist.

SUBMISSION CHECKLIST

1. Make sure your equipment can produce good, clean copy.
2. Use a good white heavy bond paper.
3. Do not use onion skin or erasable bond (it smudges).
4. Type on one side of the paper only.
5. Leave at least a one-inch margin on all four sides of your paper.
6. Double space the entire manuscript—no exceptions.
7. Leave one half page blank at the beginning of each chapter and the Introduction.
8. Number pages consecutively (1, 2, 3, 4, etc.).
9. Mark the last page of each chapter "End of chapter."
10. Don't send the same manuscript to six or eight publishers in a row without retyping tired pages. A *dog-eared* manuscript will not have the appeal of a fresh manuscript. It's psychological to say "No" to a soiled manuscript—obviously, it's been rejected by many editors, so why should *this* editor buy it?
11. Put your title and last name on the upper left-hand corner of the page; underline title: *The Dance Game*/Harris. Be sure that your name is on the title page, too.
12. Don't send a *copy* of your cover letter. Remember you are telling the editor why you have picked *his* or *her* publishing company.
13. Don't write on illustrations. Don't place illustrations in the manuscript. They should be clearly identified by figure number and placed in a separate folder along with a typed list of captions.
14. Don't use staples or paper clips on anything.
15. Use two rubber bands to hold the manuscript together: one vertical, one horizontal.
16. Use a good box (a typing-paper box is good, but better yet is a heavy cardboard mailer box; these can often be obtained at mailing stations). You may also enclose the box in a heavy, padded mailing envelope.
17. Always put your name and address on the inside of a box in case the outside label is lost.
18. Always mail material to a specific editor, not just a company.
19. Always send material UPS or first class and registered.
20. If material is unsolicited, *always send return postage.*

Having prepared your proposal or synopsis and checked it over carefully to see that it is good, clean copy, you are now ready to submit it. Be optimistic. You've improved your chances by being professional.

Mailing Tip Sheet

Mailing

Mail short manuscripts flat in an 8" × 10" manila envelope and **enclose a return envelope and postage (SASE).** Do not staple manuscripts. If you must fasten the manuscript, use paper clips. When you mail a **book-length manuscript,** put it in a typing paper box and then in a heavy mailing box which can be bought at a mailing station. Write a check for return postage (SASE) and clip it to your cover letter to your agent or editor.

Synopsis for Book-Length Manuscript

A synopsis, usually from one to twelve pages, and accompanied by the first three chapters of the book, is often put in a transparent plastic cover with a slide fastener (the type of cover frequently used on a college term paper—again, do not staple or in any way puncture the manuscript).

Your "Package" to an Agent or Editor
for a Book-Length Manuscript

Usually you will send a cover letter accompanied by a synopsis and three chapters to the agent or editor. If an agent decides to accept your manuscript, you generally then send the entire manuscript, plus specified number of synopses and chapter packages for multiple submission.

Title Page for a Book Length Manuscript

(Give genre if novel)
A mainstream novel   Words: 65,000

                              STAR WALK

                                   BY

                              LANE ABBEY

                                          1408 Willow Lane
                                          Bell, CA ZIP
                                          Tel. (714) 521-6488

Manuscript Format for the First Page
of a Short Story/Article/Novel Chapter

Dana Doe   2500 words
1561 E. Adams
Hollywood, CA ZIP
Page 1

TITLE OF STORY OR ARTICLE GOES HERE
FOR A BOOK SIMPLY SAY CHAPTER ONE

by

(Pen name goes here—but leave blank if you do not use a
pseudonym; also **leave blank for a book chapter.**)

(Leave 4 spaces.)

Begin your story or article, about halfway down the first
page. You may begin a novel chapter slightly higher. You do not
need to put the address on the first page of a novel, for the
address will appear on the title page. Left margin: 1 3/4 inches.
Right margin at least 1 inch. Use pica type. First page is
numbered left top, under name and address. Second page is
numbered on upper right-hand corner, numeral only. All pages
are numbered sequentially through whole book.

Word Count for Short Manuscript

Count words of first three full pages of short manuscript; take an
average. Then multiply it by the number of pages in the
manuscript. (If entering a contest, *every word* must be counted.
"A" counts as a word and so do abbreviated words.)

Word Count for Book Length Manuscript

Take an average of five pages and multiply it by the number of
pages of entire manuscript.

Be Neat!!

Be sure manuscript is immaculate. Type on 16–20# white bond
paper (do not use erasable bond—it smears). Use new typewriter
ribbon for final copy; be sure typewriter keys are clean. If any
pages look worn, retype. **PROOFREAD!**

Linda Voorhees
Address
City, State, Zip
Tel. #

WINTER SCHEMES

(1 page synopsis)

by

Linda Voorhees

A ski romance with humorous overtones.

Hallie had no choice; her ex-husband Dave was in serious trouble, and no matter what had happened between them she could not allow him to lose Rebel Ridge Ski Lodge as well. She agreed to provide the money he needed on one condition: "This is strictly a business proposition, no emotional ties."

Dave agreed to her demand, but could she do it? The reason she'd left him hadn't changed, and she discovered that her love for him hadn't changed either. At every turn he seemed to have caught her up in one of his schemes, which led to comical and unpredictable situations. And again, it seemed her life was out of control.

Longer Synopsis Including Cast of Characters

Winter Schemes/Voorhees
(synopsis)

WINTER SCHEMES

Hallie Hunter is an independent woman substituting work for the emotional void she feels in her life. Tall, with cinnamon hair framing intelligent blue eyes and a smooth oval face, she believes she would be willing to do anything to save Rebel Ridge Ski Lodge from financial ruin. But when her ex-husband David Hunter becomes her business partner, she finds the price may be too high.

Dave is a strong-willed man, who still holds a certain power over Hallie. Tall, broad shouldered, his solid build gives him an imposing figure. Dark blond hair frames the strong firm features of his face. He is intelligent and relentless when it comes to business, answering only to an internal code of morals and to hell with the rules of the rest of the world.

Hallie wants to rid herself of any association with him, knowing that if she is forced to work with him, the attraction will be too great and she will ultimately lose control. She refuses to allow him to enter her thoughts or influence her emotions, reminding herself of their past sorrows—and the painful secret which keeps her from ever fully loving again.

It is not until each of them is able to put aside their past feelings of betrayal which each harbors, that their love is able to fulfil the promise begun when they first met, and married, years before.

Setting

The rugged Northern mountains of Oregon, in the small ski resort community of Crestridge.

Main Characters

Hallie Hunter: A twenty-eight year old divorcee, with copper colored hair and piercing blue eyes, she is a strong-willed independent woman substituting work for the void she feels in her life after a tragedy, which led to her divorce two years before. She attempts to maintain a logical, emotionless existence, feeling that love is too high a risk.

Dave Hunter: A rakish, handsome outdoorsman whose dark blond hair is a crown of curls. Formerly Hallie's husband, he is intelligent and relentless—and he intends to capture Hallie's love through any means possible.
His brown eyes sparkle with provocative interest when he is near Hallie, and he is constantly devising schemes which create comical and not-so-comical havoc in her life.

Karl Voighlander: A practical-minded bank manager who desires a serious relationship with Hallie. He is obviously out of place in the small mountain community of Crestridge, Oregon, with his Ivy League looks and interests. He has crisply cut straight blond hair, tortoise framed glasses, and wears three piece suits that accentuate his attractive slim frame.

Victory O'Shay: A statuesque blonde who has an intense interest in Dave. She seems to be in his company at every meeting, and creates uncontrollable jealousy in Hallie.

Eugene Swedlow, Jr.: (Antagonist) Eugene threatens the security of the lodge by plotting various destructive events. He wants the land of Rebel Ridge so he can develop it into condominiums. He connives to get the land and destroy David Hunter in the process.

THIS COMPLETES THE FIRST PART OF THE SYNOPSIS. ATTACH THREE COMPLETED CHAPTERS TO IT. A CHAPTER OUTLINE SHOULD FOLLOW THE THREE CHAPTERS—SEE NEXT PAGE.

Winter Schemes/Voorhees

WINTER SCHEMES CHAPTER OUTLINE

CHAPTER 4: Hallie attends a masquerade ball with Karl Voightlander, believing her feelings toward Dave are under control. She is shocked to discover she is capable of intense jealousy when Dave shows up at the dance with Victory O'Shay. She and Dave have words, intensifying Hallie's anger.

CHAPTER 5: Hallie tries to control her feelings of jealousy, and concentrates on developing her relationship with Karl. She discovers that there has been an incident between Dave and Eugene Swedlow, from Fieldcrest Lodge, which has landed them both in jail. Although it isn't serious, it further alienates Hallie from Dave.

CHAPTER 6: Rebel Ridge challenges Fieldcrest to a competition, betting their snowplow against Fieldcrest's lift gear which is sorely needed by Rebel Ridge. The competition makes Hallie realize that Dave cares about her, and has protective instincts toward her.

CHAPTER 7: A celebration after the game is ruined for Hallie when Victory O'Shay appears on the scene, making it obvious that she intends to vie for Dave's attention. She also informs Hallie that Dave has been using and manipulating her for the purpose of saving the ski lodge.

CHAPTER 8: The lift gear that Hallie and Dave fought for has disappeared, and he needs her help to retrieve it. Against her better judgement, Hallie agrees to the scheme. The caper goes haywire, and they have an accident on the icy mountain road.

CHAPTER 9: Dave and Hallie are forced to spend the night together, isolated in the woods on a wintry night. They confront their feelings, and Hallie reveals the true reason behind the divorce—a miscarriage from which she never emotionally recovered. The feelings between them are intense, culminating in a fiery love scene.

CHAPTER 10: Their feelings toward each other appear to be resolved. They retrieve the gear, and are prepared for the Thanksgiving ski holiday. But a blizzard hits and all reservations are cancelled; they are faced with ruin.

CHAPTER 11: Their last chance to make a profit on the ski lodge is the Christmas break. But an avalanche destroys one of the buildings. Dave comes up with an idea to convert the remaining buildings into dorm-style quarters, which permits them to honor their reservations. Hallie sees Victory with Dave again, causing deep insecurities. She decides to make a commitment to Karl instead.

CHAPTER 12: Christmas Eve, another avalanche threatens the lodge. Hallie recognizes a Fieldcrest uniform on an upper slope and she and Dave go on a wild snowmobile chase to catch the culprit. When they finally catch him, it is discovered that the mystery man causing all the explosions on the mountain is Eugene Swedlow—Dave's competitor.

CHAPTER 13: Hallie and Dave make amends. It is New Year's Eve and they stand in the midst of a crowded lodge, toasting the New Year before a crackling fire. They make a lover's pact, a promise of a new life together, and a rekindled love that can now withstand the test of time and adversity.

Dorothy McMillan   Words: 125,000
Address
City, State, Zip
Telephone #

BLACKBIRD

(1 page synopsis)

She has the face and body of a childish waif, the mind of a brilliant scientist and the heart of an insane monster. She scatters death like a papal blessing. She is a BLACKBIRD—the most dangerous mass-murderer in history.

Twenty-two people at the wedding are dead—victims of a sudden and torturous—sixteen more are dying. When Warren Elliot, special investigator for the State of California, is brought into the case, there are few clues as to what has happened. Within two days the remaining sixteen people are dead.

Three days later the mystery deepens when death strikes again. This time twelve people are dead at the scene and five linger on for twenty-four hours before dying.

When a report from the U.S. Center for Disease Control in Atlanta, Georgia reports that the cause of death is an extremely virulent strain of bacteria, once considered for use in germ warfare, Elliot is confronted with the nightmarish realization that the deaths are cold-blooded murder.

Enraged by the obscene slaughter, Elliot follows the thread-thin clues which led him on a chase from San Francisco to Honolulu to Los Angeles and at last to the woman called BLACKBIRD, only to find she has condemned millions of people to die and he may be powerless to reprieve them.

Dorothy McMillan
Address
City, State, Zip
Tel. #

BLACKBIRD

(synopsis)

Pearl Regina Bassett poisons her pet cat and then, with complete detachment, watches it die. She is pleased—the toxin works perfectly. The next day she uses the toxin on her former fiancé, feeling no remorse or guilt at being the cause of his agony. "Poor John. Poor, dear John," she says coldly then smiles and turns away, leaving him lying in the grass on his back like some over-turned tortoise trying to right himself. After all, he's brought it on himself by breaking up with her to marry Susan. It doesn't matter to Pearl that thirty-seven people at the wedding die along with John Ballantine—after all, she hardly knows any of them.

Nothing in Pearl's appearance suggests her psychopathic nature. With her sleek cap of black hair, wide-set dark eyes and her rounded, rather pouty mouth, she resembles a child. Even her body is puerile, with short, slim legs, protruding tummy and only the slightest illusion of breasts. To add to the youthful illusion, she makes a habit of shaving off all her pubic hair.

A photograph, a grass stain, the sight of a yellow pencil—so many things trigger painful memories in Pearl—memories of how she always failed to please her mother, of violent and swift retribution, and of her mother's illnesses. She prays that her father will rescue her—that one day he will put a stop to her mother's cruelties. But instead, he remains a shadow, and by the time Pearl is ten years old he is dead and the strange and dangerous fragmenting of her personality has begun. Aggressive drives build inside her, waiting for that once incident that will release them.

John Ballentine is the "catch" that Pearl's mother has wanted her to marry. When he breaks off his engagement, three weeks before the wedding, the only solid, sane part of her world is gone. It's as if he took every ounce of her energy with him. She can barely get out of bed in the morning. It is a chore just to pull her clothes on. When she tries to walk, her legs become dreadfully heavy. She succeeds in getting through each day at work, but when she comes home she is trembling weak, her heart pounds and she feels nauseated. Every day she thinks it will get better, but nothing changes—not until the idea of the bacteria invades her mind. Her own bacteria! It would be just and fair. It was so cruel of John to leave her like that. It would be his own doing. The more she thinks about her idea the better she feels. She begins to plan for the materials and equipment she will need. As a microbiologist she will have access to most everything at the hospital where she works. It will take time and careful planning but she is certain she can do the job.

Her spree of mass-murder begins with the contamination of the food at John Ballintine's wedding. The monster has broken loose and will never again be contained.

When Warren Elliot, Special Investigator for the State of California, is brought into the situation it isn't as yet clear what has so quickly and agonizingly annihilated so many people. His main fear is that it may be contagious. The best he can hope for is a contained toxin—a controllable substance at least. His job, at this point, is to coordinate the work being done by both state and local agencies involved in the deaths.

Elliot, with his fan of black hair falling over his forehead and the white sweatband that has become his trademark, looks more at home on his boat, *The Green Latrine*, than he does in his tiny, dingy-painted office. A sharp, prickling pain still haunts his left side and a network of red scars sprawl across his belly from where Heywire Haywood blasted him with a shotgun. If he is smart he will forget this case, take an early retirement and pack his wife and son into *The Green Latrine* and head for Mexico.

After the deaths at the wedding are completed, Pearl carefully reviews her actions to make certain she hasn't made any errors. Her mother has taught her that errors are unforgivable. When things go wrong, you must do whatever is necessary to right them. Yes, her mother would be pleased with her perfection.

Pearl rushes to the rest home where her mother now lies, to whisper the news about her accomplishments. Ida Mae Bassett, propped in a wheelchair, a thick safety belt around her chest to keep her from tumbling forward, can only listen to Pearl's tale of horror. A series of strokes has stolen her ability to speak or to react except for blinking her hooded eyes. The old woman's hands, yellowy-white and waxy white at the tips, are folded quietly in her lap. Like an excited child, Pearl relates the macabre details to her mother and then, before leaving, she breathlessly relates, "I have to go, Mama. I have more to do. I have to be very careful, you know."

Warren Elliot finds his answer to the strange deaths—bacteria in the food eaten during the wedding reception—a toxin, thank God, not a contagious disease. Elliot is relieved but the health department is not. The bacteria is a common one they inform him—botulism. But, there is something disturbingly different about this particular bug. It appears to be a hybrid—possibly more dangerous than the original. The amount of regular botulism on the head of a pin can kill a thousand people! And the hybrid? It kills faster than the original, is more resistant and may possibly be unaffected by the anti-toxin. The scarey part is that it appears to be mixed with the Escherichia coli bug. E. Coli is in every gut in this planet. The thought of it being combined with botulism is terrifying. It wasn't something that could happen but it has. "Damn!" says Elliot. "I knew I should have taken an early retirement!"

It's amazing how easy the next episode is. Pearl doesn't hang around the University in San Francisco long enough to see how successful her work has been, but from the last time, she is positive it will be most effective. Professor Gary Howland won't be able to flunk any more students out of his class. He had called her paper—junk! Her paper had been brilliant! Always before, with other teachers, she could talk her way into or out of most anything. But Howland had torn her theory apart, ridiculed her, and demanded she do the paper over or he would refuse to pass her. Even now, four years later, she remembers the awful, crawling sensation inside her and the way her hands shook the day he had humiliated her. But now … she feels good. Real good!

When Elliot learns that the new cases of death are caused by the same hybrid bacteria that was seen in the wedding party deaths, he presses to find the connection between the two. Everything leads to a dead end.

Excited, a Health Office informs him that the unusual bacteria appears to be a result of gene splicing. The genetic information is all mixed up. Recombinant DNA. "Gene splicing?" Elliot asks. "You mean someone has manipulated it purposely?" How did it get out of the laboratory? Negligence? An accident? However, a check into every lab in the U.S. that handles biohazard material fails to turn up any work being done with such a deadly combination.

The only answer to the riddle is one Elliot hates to consider. They are talking about murder now—as science-fictionish as it sounds—it is alarmingly true that someone has purposely developed a bacteria that may pose a threat to millions of people. The specialist assures Elliot that anyone, with the right materials and a moderate level of microbiologic skill can perform hazardous genetic manipulations.

Elliot reviews both cases of deaths for a clue … anything that will lead them to the killer. The bacteria is so swift and deadly it leaves no witnesses that may have seen or known something. The only nagging item is a name written in tiny, pinched handwriting in the wedding guestbook—the name Lillian Blackbird. She isn't among the dead and they can't locate her among the living. Not much to go on, but the name Blackbird becomes synonymous with the killer.

There is still plenty of bacteria for her next trip. Bacteria seem to have been born to make more bacteria. With a small amount of protein broth she can develop enough deadly toxin to take out every man, woman, and child in the country. It is such an exciting sensation, she realizes, to know you have that much power.

In Hawaii she is much more thorough. The Oahu Greenbox Research Laboratory is isolated in the interior of the island and when the phone system is out, no help can be alerted. Once the employees are dead the fire wipes out any trace of the year she spent there.

On the plane home there is something intense about her. She is strung tight and vibrating. Her dark hair crackles around her head like an electric spray and her skin blooms with color. She has the urge to jump up, take the microphone away from the flight attendant and announce to the passengers what she has done. If they only knew how perfectly she had managed it all, they would applaud her. But of course, she cannot do that. They would put a stop to her activities and she isn't through yet. There is a great deal more to do.

After three mass-killings Elliot is furious because he feels so helpless. "There's a maniac out there with a deadly bug, and we're so damm impotent!"

What did they have as a result of all their investigation and fancy forensics? The name Lillian Blackbird—a name that belonged to no one, a few drops of blood from the telephone box in Hawaii—type B+, a shoe print in the red mud outside the Greenbox—a woman's size 3 sneaker, brand new, probably discarded as soon as the killer left. So, the killer is a woman, one-hundred pounds or less, with Type B+blood, and some training or skill in microbiology. Not much to go on.

Dr. Celton wasn't really one of Pearl's targets, but he insists upon being hostile to her. He makes such a habit of blaming her for everything that goes wrong in the research department of the hospital. If he had only let up, she might not have put his name on her list. His dinner party is the perfect occasion. Pearl is glad that no one from the research department has been invited. That would have been such a waste. They are all doing such good work.

At last, for Elliot, some puzzle pieces begin to fall into place. The connection between Dr. Celton and Parker hospital is the first. On the day of the Hawaii killings a car was rented in the name of Deborah Harris, a microbiologist at the hospital. Even though Harris was at work on the day of the killings and the rest of the hospital employees can also account for their day, Elliot is convinced there is a connection. Carefully, the material from all the deaths is gone over—the lab areas of the hospital meticulously examined—each employee interviewed.

Pearl is annoyed with all the tramping in and out of the police, health department, and special investigators. Such a disruption! She and Deborah spend several lunch hours discussing the situation. Deborah is shocked to learn her drivers license and name have been used. She expresses some fear, because the police were probably right, the killer may be connected with the hospital if he had access to her name and license number.

There are only a few people at Parker Hospital who fit the description of the killer. Pearl is one of these. She weights less than a hundred pounds, wears a size 3 shoe, and has type B+ blood. Even the cross-match fits. Her claim that she is with her mother at the rest home on the day of the Hawaii murders, is substantiated by an attendant. But Elliot feels there is a flaw somewhere. Hawaii is five hours away. It's possible she flew there, completed her work and took a flight back, perhaps seeing her mother before and after the trip. It might give the illusion she had spent the day with her mother. Elliot can't risk any more time. If Pearl Bassett is Blackbird they have to get her off the street as soon as possible.

When detectives arrive at Pearl's home they find her dead. It appears she had accidentally contaminated herself with the bacteria. She is found sprawled out on the bathroom floor, with signs of having been ill from the toxin.

Elliot, relieved that the case is about to close as soon as they tie up all the loose ends, sends his wife and son to ready *The Green Latrine* for a leisurely trip to Mexico.

A call from the coroner's office brings the news that the body is *not* that of Pearl Bassett, but rather Deborah Harris. Blackbird has had several hours to continue her deadly work.

Pearl is upset. "That man" she sees on the news and reads about in the papers, is getting closer. She wants to hate him, but realizes he is only doing his work, the way she is doing hers. Men are rarely effective—like her father, and John. But Warren Elliot is almost as smart as she is.

She finds herself tired, the way she felt when John first left her. Is there anything she can do to gain more time? It's getting hard to think. She only wants to lie down and sleep.

It's still unclear to her just how Elliot discovered her. She has been so careful! Now, her mother will know just how imperfect she is. No, her mother mustn't find out. Ida is an old woman but for some reason, Pearl knows that when Ida is gone, she will leave an empty space—the way a piece of furniture leaves a blank when it is moved.

At the rest home Pearl orders a cup of cocoa for her mother.

A drop of the solution will do. She only has a small amount left. How magnificent her bacteria is. So efficient. As she feeds her mother the cocoa she tells her all about the bug and how perfectly it kills.

When Elliot learns he has had a phone call from a woman, he is alarmed to learn that his associate has told the caller about his boat and the trip to Mexico. His associate has mistakenly thought that Elliot was already on his way.

Down on the bay where *The Green Latrine* is docked, Elliot arrives with a squad of officers. Seated with his wife in the small galley slowly sipping a steaming cup of coffee, is Pearl Bassett. "Dannie," he shouts at his wife. "Did you drink any of that coffee?" "Oh, you know I can't drink it this hot!" she tells him. "I just made a fresh pot for … oh, yes, this is Mary, she just bought *The Rebel* two slips down from us."

Elliot looks at the woman seated next to his wife. So, this is what the deadly Blackbird looks like—so tiny, almost a child. "I think we should take you to the hospital," he tells her. "Yes," Pearl agrees, wearily. "but I don't suppose it will help now. It works quite fast. Do you suppose it will be painful?" Her wide dark eyes look up at him questioningly.

For a moment he feels cheated. Yet, even if she goes to trial they would no doubt put her in an institution. It's better this way, he knows. But somehow, there is an echoing emptiness inside him.

After Pearl's death, Elliot makes a special visit to the morgue. He must reassure himself that she is really dead this time. My God! She looks like such an infant. How could anyone who looks so harmless cause such destruction?

end

Nonfiction Proposal

A sample nonfiction proposal which includes query letter, table of contents, foreword, and first chapter.

Mr. Robert M. Howland
President
HDL Publishing
702 Randolph Ave.
Costa Mesa, California 92626

Dear Mr. Howland:

At the recommendation of Richard Re, we would appreciate consideration for our book tentatively called, <u>MAKING IT HAPPEN</u>. Enclosed are: Marketing Plan, Table of Contents and Sample Chapters.

<u>Focus of Book:</u>

<u>MAKING IT HAPPEN</u> is strategic planning for the individual. It is designed for men and women at all levels of professional experience who want to make the most of the changes, trends and opportunities in today's rapidly changing world.

It addresses life's major issues approached from four growth stages: Desire, Discovery, Direction, and Doing. This enables each individual to deal with practical career goals as well as one's long-term vision or mission in life.

Using a breakthrough approach to life planning, the reader is encouraged to design a Roadmap (<u>LMS</u> copyright), a practical, step-by-step game plan. Once learned, this is a lifetime process.

<u>Market at a Glance:</u>

The Market niche is those people wanting to change careers/jobs … entering first time careers … re-entering work after a long absence … looking for a meaningful life after retirement. Along with these, there are a whole host of other changes, such as mergers, Chapter 11, restructuring, marriage/divorce, mid-life crises and family issues. Hence, the book will focus on helping the reader learn how to "shake hands" with change … most important, changing one's self.

The market for our book can be summarized as follows: general trade book market, professional organizations, retiree service organizations, women's organizations, colleges and universities, job retraining or outplacement organizations, career counseling centers, academic institutions, as well as corporations seeking to upgrade skills within management.

International Recognition:

LMS was founded in 1976 by Marilyn and Hal Shook. Since then, programs and workshops have been successfully designed and conducted for hundreds of organizations and thousands of people. Today, LMS has a subsidiary in Japan and enjoys international recognition.

The LMS course is cited among others in: Reinventing the Corporation by Naisbitt and Aburdene, What Color Is Your Parachute? by Bolles, Full Potential by Radin, Winning the Salary Game by Chastain, Successful Mid-Life Career Changing by Robbins, and Ki: A Practical Guide for Western Society by Reed.

Why Publish?

Here's why we feel MAKING IT HAPPEN will be of interest to you:

- With the interest in quality of life, life planning is most timely and has wide appeal for people in all walks of life.
- Each day is filled with an increasing number of changes, so there is a meaningful and rewarding message in "how to take charge of your life."
- Since life planning centers around mission and goal setting, the book brings the individual and corporate goals together.
- Progressive organizations are now recognizing that it makes good business sense to enhance the talents and skills of their people. Executives and managers will personally grow by creatively thinking about their own lives and their essential role on the management team.
- Our book is based on an extremely workable and yet unique approach which will set it aside from other publications and will be enjoyed for years to come.
- The principles and techniques outlined in the book have been tested and refined among thousands of people in our workshops and programs conducted since 1976.

A major source of sales will be the past, current and future participants in our

<u>LMS</u> workshops as well as the various organizations where we have conducted special sessions.

<u>Conclusion:</u>

We hope that you will look favorably upon this proposal and we enthusiastically look forward to meeting with you.

Sincerely,

Marilyn and Hal Shook

TABLE OF CONTENTS

SECTION THREE

Discovery: What Do I Have to Offer?

Chapter 8:   Self-knowledge: Who Am I?
Chapter 9:   Values: What Do I Believe?
Chapter 10:   Success Patterns: What Have I Achieved?
Chapter 11:   Personal Strengths: What Are My Talents & Skills?

Personal Power Profile

SECTION FOUR

Direction: What Is My Mission in Life?

Chapter 12:   Vision: What Does My Mind "See"?
Chapter 13:   Goal Setting: What Do I Want to Accomplish?
Chapter 14:   Strategic Thinking: How Does the Future Affect Me?
Chapter 15:   Targeting & Networking: How Do I Find the Right Opportunities?

Personal Power Profile

SECTION FIVE

Doing: How Do I Make It Happen?

Chapter 16:   Your F.O.R.D. ROADMAP: What Is My Plan of Action?
Chapter 17:   Rhythm & Harmony: What Decisions Will Balance My Life?
Chapter 18:   Peak Performance: How Do I Keep Up the Momentum?
Chapter 19:   Celebration: How Do I Live With Success?

Personal Power Profile

CONCLUSION: YOU HOLD THE KEY

Personal Power Index

THIS IS YOUR "POWER METER" SHOWING HOW MUCH YOU ARE
PUTTING INTO YOUR LIFE ... IT IS A "BENCHMARK" FOR
DOUBLING YOUR PERSONAL POWER ... GROWING FROM "YOU"
TO "DOUBLE YOU"

* * *

APPENDIX

Bibliography
Suggested Readings
Index

FOREWORD

MAKING IT HAPPEN!—AN APPARENTLY SIMPLE CHALLENGE, but one that carries a message which can change your life.

In this hard-hitting yet wonderfully humanistic book, Marilyn and Hal Shook open three windows which, collectively, give the reader profound insight. The first is a window to the here-and-now, the world as exists today. The second looks to the future—into the "New Age" of the Year 2000 and beyond. And the third window is the most exciting of all. It opens to you—who you are today, what you will become tomorrow, and how you can invent your own dynamic reality.

When John Naisbitt and I published Reinventing the Corporation in 1985, we stated that, on a corporate level, strategic planning is worthless without "strategic vision." Vision is the key, and Marilyn and Hal Shook have used it to unlock this powerful tool for each of us. They tell us: "The future is yours, it's in your hands, it's up to you to shape and direct it to your ends." It's a way of conveying the vital message that tomorrow belongs to us as individuals, that the responsibility is invested with each of, where it truly belongs!

In our book Megatrends, we picture the corporation as the analogue of change, the most sensitive and responsive indicator of the way the wind is blowing. The Shooks have used the individual as the ultimate analogue. They cajole and test us, push us to the limits, and result is a highly introspective yet practical, down-to-earth diary designed to provide each reader with a uniquely personalized record of self-discovery.

Our new "information society" is moving rapidly away from the era of smokestacks and assembly lines. As we look ahead we see a growing cadre of independent professionals. Naisbitt and I called them "leased professionals," who will possess many specialties and skills, and who will work under contract instead of on the traditional weekly payroll. We project that by the turn of the century there will be no fewer than 10 million in their ranks—a projection which gives Making It Happen even more currency. Many who read this book will be numbered among those.

The most valuable hard asset in our society is you. Each of us is challenged to invest our talents in the best possible ways, to continually shape new challenges, new heights of achievement. You and I—all of us—are the future of an ever-more vital world society.

<u>Making It Happen! is your personal passport. It allows you to transcend today's</u> <u>"limits" and become a dynamic shaper of a "New Age."</u>

So welcome to this exciting voyage of self-discovery. Long before you close the covers of this challenging book you'll see clearly just how vital your role is, and how to invest yourself creatively today, tomorrow, and beyond the visible horizon.

<u>Patricia Aburdene</u>
Co-author
<u>Reinventing the Corporation</u>

SECTION ONE

Falling in Love with the Future

IN THIS SECTION OF <u>MAKING IT HAPPEN</u> you'll take the first steps necessary to reinvent yourself—starting right here and now! We'll find out who's really in charge of your life and explore your priorities, options and—most important—the way you view yourself and your future.

If you're a bit confused, you'll quickly discover that you aren't alone. We're going to begin to lift the fog, to gain a sharply focused outlook, and to begin the job of marshalling <u>all</u> the resources you'll need break free and be the person you want to be.

You'll also study our snapshot of the "New Age"—what the world is going to look like at the turn of the Century. You may find it surprising, startling, maybe even a little scary. But we promise you won't be bored!

So turn the page, please, and begin a love affair with your future.

CHAPTER ONE

Reinvent Yourself—Now!

ARE YOU IN CHARGE of your life?

If the answer is yes, congratulations!—you're one of a small minority of Americans who have managed to beat the odds of chance and circumstance at home and in the workplace.

If your answer is no, take heart—you're among the estimated 80 percent of working Americans who, for want of a better word, are "trapped" by forces seemingly beyond your control, if not your comprehension.

If you're a part of the majority, what does this say about you as a person? Alas, most of us shy away from an answer because, quite simply, self-examination in the grip of a feeling of helplessness is a painful exercise. Few of us are ready to confess that we've contributed to the $1.5 billion spent each year on Valium. It isn't easy to accept that we may be among the 80 percent of the workforce that is tagged as "underemployed" by jobs that look good on paper but which in reality leave us unsatisfied, grumbling, passing the buck, cursing the infamous "they" who arbitrarily control our destiny.

More unpleasant still is the shadowy realization that "they" are more imagined then real, semi-plausible scape goats invented to take the heat of our own self-inflicted frustrations. What is truly amazing about this form of self-deception is that it operates at the highest reaches of professional and everyday existence. Sooner or later we are confronted by the truth: "We", not "they," have backed us into a corner. You may not find this the happiest of conclusions, but until we accept its validity the world will remain a hostile, unfair and apparently endless source of anxiety.

Nowhere is this more clearly seen than in the workplace. It's the great American battleground of the spirit, the place which defines us, nourishes us, challenges and engages us in a quest for more than a livelihood. This is the ideal. Strip away the hyperbole of idealism and what emerges is a field of conflict, bitterness, confusion, and a set of rules that have come to be known as "social Darwinism"—survival of the "fittest," which has nothing much to do with being either the best or the brightest.

We have our own special name for it: "Murder in the workplace." For now it's enough to recognize the mechanics of the process. The victims are those of us who, in good faith, believe that diligence and hard work automatically bring the highest rewards. We have faith; we trust the "system"; we allow ourselves to be guided by the notion that fair is fair, that "what goes around inevitably comes around" in the form of material rewards and personal gratification. And most of all the victims have (once again in the spirit of good faith) abrogated their power of self-determination. "They" will do the right thing by us. "They," like some ancient council of universal justice, will lead us to the Promised Land.

Unfortunately it doesn't work that way.

"They" are a myth. A crutch. A convenient delusion. In truth, "they" don't exist, never have existed, and, short of judgement day, never will exist. To praise or blame in the name of "they" is about as useful as imploring the ancient god, Zeus, to banish war and human conflict.

You are the all-important factor in the game of life and work. *You*—and no one else—are in charge. If you happen to be among the more than three million people who are annually seeking better, more rewarding and fulfilling jobs, your success or failure depends almost entirely on you and how you view your special place in the world.

BEHAVIORAL INFLUENCES

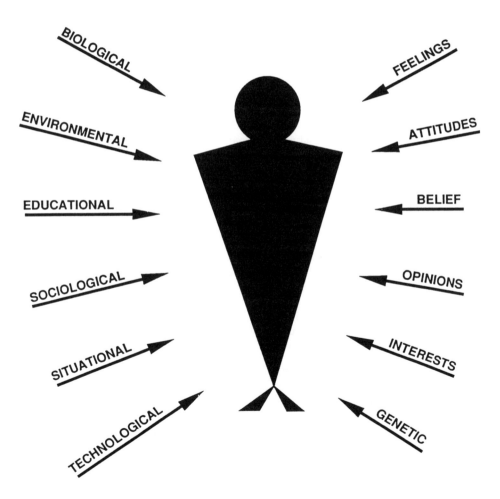

Magic in the Looking Glass

It takes courage to view one's self without excuses. Few of us are prepared to dismiss the concept of "they," since "they" make our frustrations so much more tolerable. But until you make this quantum leap and unload the debilitating psychological baggage you've collected over the years, the true vision of who and what you are, and the promise of what your future holds, will remain as bewildering and opaque as deep waters of the ocean.

This idea is as old as written history. It predates scripture. When the ancient Greek philosopher Heraclitus remarked that, "You can never step in the same river twice," he was saying that change is constant, inevitable, and that the one checkpoint of reality is you and your ability to make your way in an ever-transforming world.

The twentieth century philosopher, Beatrice Bruteau, gave us an updated version of Heraclitus. "We cannot wait for the world to turn," she wrote, "... for the revolution to carry us around in its new course. We ourselves *are* the revolution."

Hold on, you say. How does this apply to everyday life?

It applies very directly to those who feel trapped by circumstance (usually of our own making). They have a deep-rooted belief that one of these days the world will change, that a magical transformation of human values will occur, and when that day comes all that is wrong in our lives will be put right by an enlightened social ethic.

How wonderful life would be if only it were true. Unfortunately, such a belief amounts to another classic self-denial, a confession of impotence, and a sure-fire way to avoid the basic challenges of shaping your own reality. If you doubt it, consider the warnings of Thomas Kuhn, who in 1962 introduced us to what he called "the Paradigm Shift," which he defined as great leaps ahead in scientific and/or social knowledge. "You can't embrace the new paradigm until you let go of the old," he wrote, which brings us back to you—standing before the mirror without excuses or defenses, of accepting that you alone are the maker of today and tomorrow.

What comes next is up to you. Perhaps you want more out of life. Most of us do. But just what exactly do we mean by "more"? Can you describe it in 25 words or less? If so, you're ahead of the curve.

Joe Alexander, a career and life counselor who changed his outlook and career well past the age of 40, captured the essence of the issue in his book, *Dare to Change* (New American Library, 1984). Like many of us, the author discovered that events rather than will had shaped his destiny. It was a hollow feeling. Alexander saw clearly that he had been adrift most of his life, and that the drift had been the source of discontent. "I seemed to be caught in a cyclical trap and felt doomed to make the same mistakes over and over again," he wrote. "I wanted more out of life, but I didn't know what my 'more' was."

This realization forced Alexander to stand before the mirror and confront the real villians: his indecisiveness, his fear of change, his failure to take control of and full responsibility for shaping the world in his own image.

Suppose I Fail?

One of the most common excuses related to continued personal drift and frustration is the fear of failure. Richard Bolles, author of *What Color Is Your Parachute?* (Ten Speed Press, 1987) calls this the "rejection syndrome." In its simplest form the rejection syndrome is the reason why the cartoon character, Charlie Brown, is afraid to strike up a conversation with the love of his life, "that little red-headed girl." He forever views her from afar, dreaming, wondering constantly, "what if ... ?" If he tries to approach her she'll laugh at him, or so Charlie Brown believes. For more than three decades Charlie Brown has been mooning over this secret love of his, and so far he's no closer to gaining her attention than he was on the very first day his creator, Charles Schultz, published the first "Peanuts" comic strip.

To some extent, we're all Charlie Browns. The rejection syndrome holds us in place as powerfully as gravity. Viewed from the perspective of the workplace we see that while nearly every male and at least 50 million females will seek new jobs or career changes in the decade ahead, 95 percent of them will be derailed by their fear of failure. However, nowhere in this book will you find much sympathy for the self-made chains that come with the fear of failure.

In a study of great men and women, we have found that the one word missing from their vocabularies was (you guessed it!) failure. To Henry Ford, Madame Curie, Thomas Edison, Mary Cassatt, and many others right down to our present-day makers of commerce and culture, the idea of failure meant a "necessary mid-course correction." Failure isn't seen in the negative sense, but rather is a vital component of ultimate success. When our Apollo astronauts soared to the moon in 1967, their flight trajectory wasn't a simple straight line; it was an endless series of corrections. In shaping your own destiny, such corrections (adjusting for small and large "failures") is unavoidable and consistent with the job of arriving at one's desired destination. In short, we believe, failure doesn't exist except as a means to gain greater degrees of success.

Discussing the rejection syndrome in *When Smart People Fail*, Linda Gottlieb and Carole Hyatt (Simon & Schuster, 1987), say that when a person wakes up in the morning, looks into the mirror and sighs, "I'm an unemployed steel worker," that person is immobilized. But when he learns to say, "I'm a human being with options," he sees new opportunity instead of a dead end.

The real fallacy of the rejection syndrome is in the way we view success. Remember Vince Lombardi, the famous football coach? He was idolized by players and fans alike, but he gave us a self-defeating definition of success. "Winning isn't everything," he said. "It's the only thing." It sounds heroic, even profound. But the truth is that success, like football, is a matter of moving incrementally down a defined path toward a defined goal. When a certain play doesn't work, adjustments are made, plays are rerun, reshaped; each "failure" is an invitation to make necessary corrections. And there's another flaw in the Lombardi approach. If winning is everything, losing means you're dead. That isn't how truly successful people think or make decisions. Lombardi invented a slogan, not a useful tool of personal and professional mobility.

Wanting It So Bad You Can Taste It

You may know what it is you really want in life, but just how badly do you want it?

The "Great Negotiator," Herb Cohen, says you should never want anything so badly that you can't live without it. If you maintain this limit in some unspoken way, those on the opposite side of the negotiating table will always be slightly off balance.

> **IF YOU THINK YOU'VE GOT IT,**
> **YOU'VE GOT IT.**
> **IF YOU THINK YOU DON'T HAVE IT,**
> **EVEN IF YOU'VE GOT IT,**
> **THEN YOU DON'T HAVE IT.**
>
> *Herb Cohen*

It's great advice if you're negotiating. But life planning, the on-going process of invention and reinvention, isn't a game of thrust and parry. It isn't about someone else's life. It involves you at the most fundamental levels of being. Life planning is the outline of your very being, who you are and who you will become.

We ask again: How badly do you want it? And what will it take to get it?

Our position is that you must want your success so much that you're willing to bring it to life, to plan carefully and take a few risks to achieve it.

Hal Shook, one of our authors, first learned of the passion of achievement in a tough combat situation where achievement spelled survival. One of Hal's missions was to isolate Hitler's forces and prevent them from crossing the Seine river in France and regrouping on the other side. It was on one of these search and destroy sorties, in which 16 fighters were grouped together, that heavy flak flew up out of nowhere, exploding with a dull, ugly "whooomp!" He was no longer flying through air, but rather a screen of red hot metal and black smoke. It was the kind of flak they said you could "walk" on.

The fighters weaved and changed altitude, hoping to outguess the flak gunners and find the specific target. When the target was spotted, he rolled his plane over and pointed its nose downward for a straight-on bombing run.

Seconds later, flak ripped into the fuselage and the propeller. Instantly oil covered one side of the aircraft and spewed onto the windscreen. The author later recorded that life-or-death moment in his wartime diary:

> With one eye on my target, going nearly straight down, I put the other eye on the instrument panel to check my RPMs, which shouldn't have exceeded 2800; the engine was at 4200, and going higher.
>
> But I had a perfect bead on my target. I couldn't pull up now. So I kept on diving and punched off my bombs at the last minute, to get direct hits.
>
> Now what to do about my airplane. It was still running, but visibility through the windscreen was zero. It was a good plane; any other would have forced me into the Seine with a parachute. But it was pretty torn-up. I knew it couldn't last much longer.
>
> Locating a grassy strip along the French coast, I called a flight leader to land after me. Somehow the two of us managed to squeeze into his single-seat fighter and return to base.

The story is told here because it represents the most vivid goal the author ever wanted. Quite simply, the goal was to hit the target and make it back home alive. There was no compromise, no trade-offs. This was a goal—an achievement—that defied negotiation.

The author summed it up this way back in 1944:

> The urgent need to hit the target and to make it back in one piece, was such that nothing was going to stand in the way. I felt I could not be stopped, short of being completely wiped out!

Today our message is the same. Whatever it is you want out of life you must go for it with single-minded insistence. <u>You are going to make it. Period!</u>

21

Everything about Literary Agents

It's a fact. If you have written a novel, you will need a literary agent. Although there are a few well-known novelists who do negotiate their own contracts, most novelists are not really interested in the business of book publishing. They prefer to spend their time writing.

Why a Good Agent Is Invaluable to The Fiction Writer

The agent is familiar with marketing conditions and *knows* where to send all types of genre fiction.

Some publishers try to avoid categorizing fiction and say they consider all "adult fiction." Yet there *are* subtle differences between the type of material published by most publishers. These differences vary with the in-house editors. As these editors move to other publishing houses, the types of books purchased by those houses change accordingly. This is a factor that makes an agent's job even more difficult. It is for this reason that most good agents make it a point to know as many editors as possible on a first name basis.

If you are a novelist, you should do everything in your power to get an agent. In general, the fiction writer—because he works through an agent—

will not have as much control in selecting the publisher as the nonfiction writer does. Still, the fiction writer who knows his market can tactfully point out to the agent that the book was written for a particular publisher—a consideration which is of importance to many publishers. The writer should always emphasize that preference in the cover letter. It shows the publisher that the author has taken some time to look over the various publishers and checked out the desired publisher's background. It also achieves a slight psychological edge; and from the publisher's point of view, shows your "good taste."

Is a Big Name Agent the Best?

It's true that often a big name agent can get big advances. But it's also true that new writers have a very difficult time getting a big name agent to represent them. He already has a stable of producing writers and is very busy taking care of them. You will need a recommendation from a well-known writer or, perhaps, a teacher to attract the big agent's attention.

In fact, you may need a gimmick. Clive Cussler, who wrote *Raise The Titanic* had letterhead stationary printed, assuming an imaginary agent's name. He then wrote to a well known New York agent, saying they had met at a party and he still remembered what a wonderful time they had. Now he was retiring, closing his literary agency, and wondered if his good friend would like to take a look at two manuscripts (both Cussler's) which he thought were promising. The well-known New York agent bit on the scam, which started a profitable relationship for both Cussler and the agent.

On the other hand, a smaller agency may do more for a beginning writer than a big name agent. The advantage of a smaller agency is that it often offers the writer a chance to have a more personal, friendly relationship with the agent. Then, too, the smaller the agency the more time the agent has to work on the literary properties of each author. It is also true, though, that editors favor the larger agency because it is able to supply more literary projects. Some of the agents in the larger agencies do try to have personal relationships with their clients, too.

A well-known agent offers the advantage of having many contacts with editors that have been developed over the years; however, a younger agent just starting in the business may work twice as hard to sell your manuscript because he needs the money to live and is trying to build a reputation as an agent.

First Novels

Either way, don't expect agents to be overjoyed at a first novelist; they aren't. According to a recent *Publishers Weekly* poll, only about seven hundred out of one hundred thousand first novels will get published. Agents gamble on a new novelist knowing they will have to work very hard to place the new writer's manuscript. Without a name, without a track record, the new writer will rarely command much of an advance, which means that the agent will not get much of a commission. However, the agent will sometimes take on talented newcomers as a calculated risk in the hope of getting "new blood" for his stable.

What Commission Does an Agent Charge?

Most agents handle between thirty and forty clients, and charge an agent's commission from 10 percent to 15 percent of what the writer earns. In most cases the difference in the commission depends on whether you're a new writer or a proven pro with the ten percent being given to the proven writer.

The Ten Percenters

At this commission rate, reserved only for the pros, the agents can't afford to take the time to critique material and work with the writer, teaching him how to write, in the hopes that the manuscript will sell. The ten percenter will read a manuscript, or part of it, and if he feels it is not salable will shoot it right back to you.

The Fifteen Percenters

This commission rate is reserved for the nonprofessional writers. More and more agents have to charge fifteen percent now for new writers because it is much harder to place a book for a new writer and obviously it costs more in postage and phone calls, plus the time to convince a jaundiced New York editor that yes, this new writer has all the ultimate sales potential of James Michener.

Charging a Reading Fee

As a rule, there is a bad connotation to an agent charging a "reading fee" and frankly you shouldn't pay it unless you've checked to find out if the agent is a bona fide literary consultant. Don't be afraid to ask what qualifies him as an agent. Many of them have been assistant agents, former editors, writers, or teachers of writing. *Ask for recommendations.* A good agent will be happy to supply you with satisfied clients. In fact, a reputable agent is proud to honor such a request. If you have had difficulty in publishing and your book has been rejected many times, it might be very wise for you to seek out a critic agent and stop wasting valuable time on a "sick" novel when a good "doctor" is at hand.

What Exactly Is a Literary Consultant and What Is a Critique?

A literary consultant is often a well-known teacher, editor, or writer who is affiliated with a literary agency. He will undertake to work with writers who are close to publishing, but are not yet fully professional. The consultant will read the manuscript and will prepare an evaluation of several typed pages that is a blueprint of what needs to be rewritten to bring the book to a publishable state. The consultant charges a critique fee for this service and, often, for an additional fee will work with the author to create a publishable book.

If you decide to seek out a literary consultant, make sure, that he is well known in the field and has a track record. Don't be afraid to ask for the names of previous clients. A good literary consultant is proud of his clients who are in print. Call those clients and find out if they were satisfied with the services performed. Working with a good literary consultant can be one of the quickest ways to publish, for the consultant knows both technique and the elements of a publishable book—which a local writing teacher may not know. Also, the consultant works directly with your manuscript on a one to one basis—editing it, pin pointing weak areas, and helping you to rewrite those weak areas. The six months to a year spent on a one-to-one basis with a good literary consultant can easily save several years writing at home without instruction. In fact, usually the fledgling writer becomes a professional within a year—a process that is far quicker than even a good writing course at a local college or university.

There is a vast difference between getting ripped off by an unscrupulous agent who is more interested in collecting reading fees than selling your book, and a reputable agent who is recommending a literary consultant to help you. You can protect yourself by carefully investigating reputations of both the agent and the literary consultant.

What Are the Personal Advantages of a Good Agent?

An agent often is the author's best friend and father-confessor, encouraging the writer when writer's block hits, and sometimes pointing out weak passages that need to be rewritten in the manuscript. Generally, the agent will not edit a manuscript. He is too busy "selling" books.

The agent acts, too, as a buffer between the author and the publishing company during heated discussions and tries to keep both parties happy. A really important function of the agent is handling rejection slips. That is, the agent receives the rejection slips for the author and tries to diplomatically convey the editors' remarks to the author in such a way that the author is not emotionally shattered by the criticism.

The agent reads your manuscript, talks it over with you, occasionally makes suggestions that will make it more salable, and discusses the possible markets where it will fit. He is interested in you as a person, as a writer, and is vitally interested in developing your writing career. When your book is sold, the agent calls you and shares in your joy. In all correspondence the agent represents you as an outstanding writer to every editor and explains how all your special gifts and experiences relate to your novel.

Will an Agent Do Multiple Submissions?

Due to the long time it takes for the publisher to consider a book, it is very common for an agent to, selectively, submit multiple copies of an author's book. A publisher generally takes at least six weeks to evaluate a manuscript. Therefore, if an agent submits a copy of the book to three different editors, the book will have three separate readings in six weeks instead of one. The advantage of the agent is that he knows which editors will accept multiple submissions and which ones won't.

When Should One Seek Out an Agent?

You should not go to an agent when you are learning to write. You will only waste his or her time if you're a novice. Ninety-five percent of the manuscripts an agent reads are unpublishable. If you really write well, it is quite possible that you will find an agent who will try to market your book.

Where Do I Find an Agent?

Finding one is easy—but finding one who can really help you is hard. Most literary agents are listed in the *Writer's Market Guide*, the *Literary Market Place*, and the *Writer's Guide of American West*. When you find an agent that sounds good, call or query. Then, according to the agent's request, either send a synopsis and sample chapters or the complete manuscript. Be sure to send a self-addressed mailer box with return postage. Agents can also be met at various writer's conferences which are given by your local colleges and universities. Don't be afraid to go up to an agent and tell him about your book.

Before submitting any work to an agent, you should know something about him. Your first concern should be that he is reputable and well thought of in the field. However, this is often hard to ascertain because many of the best agents try to keep a low profile. They have enough writers to represent and only will take on an extremely gifted newcomer. Asking other writers what they think of a particular agent is usually helpful.

When you are seeking an agent to represent you, remember that agents often specialize in a particular field. For example, an agent adept in the romance line may not have any contacts in science fiction or men's adventure so that if you send in a science fiction book to an agent specializing in romance, he may not be interested in handling your book at all.

If an Agent Accepts You as a Client, Does it Mean You Definitely Will Publish?

If an agent accepts you, it generally means he feels your book is a publishable one; but no agent can guarantee you will publish. Even though you may have written a fine book, there are many variables in the publishing business—editors' likes and dislikes, a subject that has been written about too often, a subject that editors feel is not timely, and a subject that is not salable enough.

If a Publisher Wants to Buy Your Book and You Have a Contract, Should You Get an Agent?

If you're a novelist, yes. If you're a nonfiction writer, it may not be necessary. A novelist needs an agent to protect the many subsidiary rights, but a nonfiction writer usually isn't as involved with rights sales so the negotiation are not as involved. The difference between the deal arranged by an agent and that of the deal arranged by a knowledgeable nonfiction writer is probably nil.

Mistakes to Avoid in Dealing with an Agent

Don't send any bad material because the agent will probably remember you for a long time as a bad writer. Don't seek out an agent too soon. Make sure you are ready. Also, don't send short stories, poems, and articles because even if the agent could sell them the commissions wouldn't even begin to pay for the cost of handling the projects.

Summary

If you are a novelist, you definitely need an agent. Yes, he *will* take ten to fifteen percent of your earnings—but he will sell your book, negotiate the contract, protect your subsidiary rights, examine the accuracy of your royalty statements, give you advice on your book, and often will be the best friend you ever had. If your book is not publishable, the agent can't sell it, so do everything in your power to create a marketable manuscript.

22

Whee! You Received a Book Contract —Now What?

Book contracts have one universal side effect—they not only frighten new writers but old pros as well. Some writers have attorneys check and recheck a book contract to a ridiculous degree, writing in so many provisions to protect the writer that a publisher often refuses to go ahead with a project, while other writers blindly sign a contract without realizing what they've signed. In fact, though it may take years to write and publish a book, too many authors spend little or no time examining the contract.

What Does Signing a Book Contract Mean?

In general, signing a publisher's book contract means that you have agreed to write a book on a specific subject and have it completed by a certain date. The publisher, in turn, has agreed to publish your manuscript providing it is received in final form and content which is *acceptable to the publisher*.

When an Editor Says He/She Wants to Publish Your Book, What Does It Mean?

When an editor makes an offer on your book, he is saying that the publisher:

1. Would like to buy the *book publishing rights* to your book

2. Would like to *sell your book throughout the U.S.* and, if possible, throughout the world
3. Would like to *buy the rights to license* or sell any and all other rights
4. Will *pay you a royalty* on all books sold
5. Will *pay you a percentage* on all rights sold or licensed.

Does a Book Contract Favor the Author or the Publisher?

Most publishers do not set out to take advantage of an author, but they are in business to make a profit. The conditions established in the contract generally reflect the financial arrangements which most publishers feel are fair to both author and publisher. On the other hand, a writer should examine the contract carefully because there *are* certain changes which can be inserted that are more advantageous to the author.

Clauses Vary

While most publishers do not have multiple agreements, they do have a variety of clauses to add or substitute; and all agreements contain blanks to be filled in after author and publisher negotiations. The agreement itself may vary in length from fifteen to over one hundred and fifty clauses. If you're a first time writer, don't expect a perfect contract. You may have to compromise until you have proven track record. On the other hand, be aware that many parts of the agreement are negotiable.

What Are Your Liabilities After You Sign a Book Contract?

If for any reason you do *not* complete the manuscript by the due date, the contract is the publisher's only recourse to recover the monies advanced by you. Also, if the book becomes a best seller it may be that you would have liked a better percentage of the net or gross, but the contract holds you to the agreed percentage. For this reason, it is important that all authors study a blank draft of the contract prior to signing.

Some of the More Common Clauses Found in a Publisher's Book Contract

Grant of Rights Clause

Nearly all book contracts start out with this clause: The author grants to the publisher the exclusive right to publish, in English, in book form, in the United States and throughout the world a work together with such other rights as are set forth herein, for the entire period of any copyright.

In short, you are granting to your publisher the exclusive right to print and publish your book in English in the United States and throughout the world and also any other rights to be named later for the entire period of the copyright.

Copyright Clause

This is one of the most misunderstood clauses in any contract. All authors talk about copyright but very few really know what copyright means.

What is copyright? Copyright is a form of protection provided by the laws of the United States to authors of "original works of authorship." This protection is available, automatically, to both published and unpublished works. Copyright in the United States stems from a 1710 English statute known as the Statute of Anne. Following the American Revolution, most of the states enacted copyright laws generally patterned after this English act. The need for federal legislation, however, was soon recognized, and when the U.S. Constitution was drafted the principle of copyright was written into it. Article I, section 8 grants Congress the power "to promote the progress of useful arts by securing for limited times to authors the exclusive right to their writings." Thus, the primary purpose of copyright legislation is to foster the creation and dissemination of intellectual works for the public welfare; an important secondary purpose is to give creators the reward due them for their contribution to society.

The new copyright law—1978 On January 1, 1978, a completely new copyright statute came into effect in the United States. Some of the highlights of the new copyright law are:

1. **SINGLE NATIONAL SYSTEM.** The new law established a single system of statutory protection for all copyrighted works, whether PUBLISHED or UNPUBLISHED.
2. **WHAT IS COPYRIGHTABLE?** It is well established, by a long line of court decisions, that in order to be copyrightable a work must meet the following requirements:
   a. The work must be in the form of "writing," i.e., it must be fixed in some tangible form from which the work can be reproduced.
   b. The work must be a product of original creative authorship. That is, the author must have produced the work by his own intellectual effort, as distinguished from merely copying a pre-existing work.

An example of a copyrightable work includes but is not limited to a description, explanation, or illustration of an idea or system. However, it gives the copyright owner no exclusive rights to the ideas, method, or system involved. Suppose, for example, that an author copyrighted a book explaining a new system for manufacturing cars. The copyright will prevent others from publishing the author's text and illustrations and describing his ideas for machinery, processes and merchandising methods. However, it will not give him any rights against others who adopt the ideas for commercial purposes, or who develop or use the machinery, processes, or methods described in the book. In short, you can copyright the development of an idea but not the idea itself of an idea.

What is not protected by copyright? Several categories of materials are generally not eligible for statutory copyright protection. These include all titles, names, short phrases, slogans, recipes, facts, jokes, and outlines. Also, copyright protection is not available for: ideas or procedures for doing, making, or building things; scientific or technical methods or discoveries; business operations or procedures; mathematical principles; formulas; or any other sort of concept, process, or method of operation. Remember we are talking about copyright, not patents or trademarks.

Duration of copyright For works created after January 1, 1978, the term of protection starts at the MOMENT OF CREATION (not necessarily publication date) and lasts for the author's life, plus an additional fifty years after the author's death or the death of the last co-author. On works made for hire the term of protection is seventy-five years from date of publication or one hundred years from the date of creation, whichever is shorter.

The new law does not restore copyright protection for any work that has gone into the public domain, i.e., any material on which the copyright or patent right has expired.

Fair use The new law adds a provision to the statute specifically recognizing the principle of "fair use" as a limitation on the exclusive rights of copyright owners, and indicates factors to be considered in determining whether particular uses fall within this category. Those factors are:

a.   the purpose and character of the use, including whether such use is of a commercial or nonprofit nature
b.   the amount and substantiality of the portion used in relation to the work as a whole
c.   the nature of the copyrighted work
d.   the effect of the use upon the potential market for or value of the work.

One thing is very clear: no real definition of "fair use" has ever been established to date. No specific tests have ever been established to determine if a particular use is fair. Each case raising the question of fair use must be decided on its own facts.

Who should own the copyright to your book, you or your publisher?
For some authors this is a major decision. However, most authors, agents,
and lawyers say that the writer should retain the copyright. Yet, even if the
copyright is in your name, you still will not have one hundred percent
protection. Why?—because you will eventually have to *license, sell,* or *give*
some right to someone else, depending on what subsidiary rights are sold.
Many publishers will copyright a book in the author's name if the author
requests.

All articles, short stories, poems, plays, television scripts, *should* be
copyrighted in the name of the author; or the copyright should be assigned
to the author upon publication. However, many magazines will not allow
authors to retain their copyrights even after the magazine has run the
article.

Do you have to copyright your work? No registration or other action,
by the author, is required to secure copyright under the new law. **Copyright
is secured automatically when the work is created, and a work is "created"
when it is fixed in form for the first time.** Generally, "fixed in form" means
you have a material object from which a work can be read, such as a book. If
a book is prepared over a period of time, the part of the work existing in
fixed form on a particular date constitutes the created work as of that date.
**PUBLICATION IS NO LONGER THE KEY TO OBTAINING COPY-
RIGHT PROTECTION.** However, the definition of publication is still very
important to copyright owners. The new law defines publication as being
the distribution of copies of a work to the public by sale or other transfer of
ownership. The distribution of copies to a group of persons for purposes of
further distribution, or public display also constitutes publication. Remember, a public display of a work does not of itself constitute publication.

The copyright notice It is a good idea to use a notice of copyright on
all your work, especially your unpublished work, because it shows that you
are claiming copyright to the material and helps prevent innocent
infringement. *The notice of copyright includes the following three elements:*

1. the symbol c (the letter in a circle) or the word copyright
2. the date of creation
3. the name of copyright owner for example: (© 1983 John Doe).

No location is specified except that the copyright information must be
clearly visible and all of it must be in one location, usually in the front of
your work.

Copyright registration In general, copyright registration is a legal
formality intended to make a public record of the basic facts of a particular

copyright. However, even though registration is not a requirement for protection, the copyright law provides several inducements or advantages to encourage copyright owners to register their unpublished works anyway. Some of the advantages are the following:

1. Registration establishes a public record of the copyright claim.
2. Registration is necessary before any infringement suits may be filed in court.
3. Registration can make available attorney's fees and statutory damages which are not available under the automatic copyright protection program. *If you are planning to publicly distribute your work you must register your work with the* COPYRIGHT OFFICE, REGISTER of COPYRIGHTS, LIBRARY of CONGRESS, WASHINGTON, D.C. 20559.

The Manuscript Clause

The word count called for in the book contract is very important to the editor because many decisions are made based on the estimated length of the finished book. For example: the price of the book, the market, and in many cases the original decision to publish your book were all made based on your estimated length of the book. Don't guess. If you submit a manuscript of 120,000 words and the decision to publish your book and the agreement both call for an 80,000 word book, you are not only in violation of your agreement, you may have priced your book out of the market. Remember, that the word count *includes* illustrations.

Don't add illustrations to the number of words contracted for in the contract. For example, if your contract calls for a book of 80,000 words, or their equivalent in words, then send in a manuscript that contains approximately 80,000 words only if you don't have any illustrations. If, on the other hand, your contracted for 80,000 manuscript is going to be one half illustrations and one half words then turn in a 40,000 word manuscript and the equivalent in illustrations.

Why is the completion date so important? Besides word count the *date* you plan on completing the manuscript is very important. Many people connected with the publisher have to make plans based on that date: the production editor, the printer, the director of advertising, and the marketing director. If it looks like the writing of your book is going to take longer than you anticipated, and it almost always does, tell your editor as soon as possible and obtain an extension in writing. Don't wait till the last minute.

Your manuscript must be acceptable to the publisher The contract states that the manuscript must be delivered by the author to the publisher in *final form* and *content acceptable* to the publisher. This clause gives the publisher the right to reject your manuscript if the manuscript is considered unacceptable. For years this clause has been under fire from authors, agents, and lawyers as being unreasonable and unfair. Some reason editors give for rejecting manuscripts are:

1. It is poorly written.
2. It does not resemble the outline and or sample chapters on which the agreement was based.
3. The manuscript length is not in keeping with the length called for in the book contract. (It is too short or too long.)
4. The manuscript is completed well past the date called for in the book contract.
5. The reviews were very bad.

What recourse does the writer have if a publisher does not accept the contracted for and completed manuscript? If a publisher refuses to publish a contracted for book the writer should:

1. Try to determine exactly *why* the manuscript was unacceptable and correct it as soon as possible.
2. Talk to your agent or lawyer.
3. Try to find another publisher.

How many copies do you have to submit to the publisher? Another necessary specification in this section is that the writer deliver **two copies** of the manuscript, **retaining a third** for himself. It has happened that an author mailed in the original manuscript and a copy, both of which were lost.

Book Royalties Clause

Each time a book is sold by the publisher the author of that book receives money from the sale. This money is called a royalty. It is usually a percentage of the list price of the book for most fiction and some popular nonfiction and a percentage of the net price (actual cash received by the publisher) for all other types of books.

The Payments Clause

It is in this section that the "advance against royalties" clause appears. What is an "advance against royalties"? It is money paid to an author by a publisher in advance of that author's book earning anything. Publishers do pay professional authors an advance to help them with manuscript preparation costs for such expenses as: typing, photocopying, research, travel, and illustrations.

The advance is meant to help the author find time to write instead of consulting or moonlighting at another job. The advance is not a gift; it has to be paid back by the author if the book is not accepted by the publisher. If the book is published, the publisher then holds back all monies otherwise due the author until the advance is paid back. In other words, a book must sell enough copies to pay back the entire advance *before an author can begin to receive a royalty check.* If the book is put into production but does not earn enough money to pay back the advance, the author is still entitled to keep the entire advance.

The advance is paid in many different ways. The most common way is to pay one half of the total advance when the contract is signed and the final half when the final manuscript is accepted by the publisher.

The "Matter Supplied by Author" Clause

This clause deals with all the material supplied by the author *other than* the manuscript itself. The clause, as it is usually written, says that the author must supply at *author expense:*

1. Preface/Forward (if needed)
2. Table of Contents
3. All art work which includes:
   a. photographs.
   b. artwork—(rough draft is OK)
4. The index

The clause goes on to say that if the author does not supply the artwork the publisher will, and further that the author could be charged for the expense. The point is: the author is not only responsible for supplying the artwork, or at least a rough draft of it, but in some cases, if he or she has not made arrangements with the publisher beforehand, the author may have to pay for the artwork. Artwork is very costly. One page of it is far more expensive than a page of type. Be sure you know the *kind of artwork you and your editor want* and also the *number of pieces of artwork wanted.* Most publishers realize that an author is generally not an artist and that he or she is not able to *pay* for camera-ready artwork. Most publishers will accept a rough draft (hand-drawn) and then employ in-house artists or outside free-lance artists to develop the camera-ready art.

The "Author's Warranty Clause"

In this clause the author guarantees that:

1. He is the sole author of the book.
2. He is the sole owner of the right being granted to the publisher.
3. He has the right to sell the publisher the book.
4. He has full power an authority to copyright the book and to make his agreement.
5. The work does not infringe any other copyright.
6. The work does not contain any scandalous, libelous, or unlawful matter.

The "Copyrighted Material Clause"

It is the traditional and contractual responsibility of the author to obtain all the "necessary permissions" to use material from other published works. Every publishing house has standard permission forms on which the request should be made. All permission forms should be included with the final manuscript when it is sent to the publisher. It is also a good idea to keep a copy of all permissions for obvious reasons.

The Publishing Details Clause

The publisher's Determination Clause says that the PUBLISHER has the right to:

1. Publish the work in a suitable style as to paper, printing, and binding.
2. Fix and alter both the title and price if necessary.
3. Determine the manner in which the book is marketed, including *all* advertising and promotion.
4. Determine the first printing and publishing date.
5. Determine the book's format and dust jacket.
6. Decide if the book is to be a hard cover or a paper back.

If you, as author, have strong feelings about any of these points you should discuss them with your editor *before* signing the agreement.

Free Copies Clause

The actual number of free copies given to the writer varies from six to twelve copies. Most publishers will give you at least six copies of your book. These free copies are for the author's personal use. You can give them to family members and close friends.

If you need copies for promotion and advertising, the publisher will usually supply them free of charge. However, the publisher is not in the business of supplying free books for authors, so be realistic when you ask for extra copies.

Competing Work Clause

This particular clause gives rise to more author publisher conflicts than any other in the agreement. It says that during the term of this agreement you cannot agree to publish with any other publisher a book on the same subject that will conflict directly with the sale of this one. Common sense should answer nearly all questions concerning what conflicts and what does not.

The "Option Clause"

This clause, if left in the agreement, grants to your publisher the first option (refusal, choice) at publishing your next two books.

Nearly all agented authors delete this clause completely, whether fiction or nonfiction, for most authors feel they can do better on the next book regardless and they don't really want to be tied to a publisher. Another option to consider is to leave the clause in but cross out "upon the same terms" and replace it with "terms to be agreed upon."

The Agent Clause

When you place your agent's name and address in this clause, it empowers your agent:

1. To collect *all monies* due you under the terms of this agreement,
2. To deduct his percentage off the top and send you the remaining monies,
3. To act on your behalf in all matters concerning this agreement.

This clause, however, *does not* give your agent the power to sign this agreement on your behalf. Very few authors, even-well known personalities, ever give an agent the power to sign for them. Most publishers, when dealing with well-known personalities and co-authors, require the personality to sign the agreement as a measure of their involvement, especially if a promotion tour is deemed necessary by the publisher.

The Agent Clause, because it is part of the agreement, should in no way imply to the author that an agent is necessary or even recommended by the publisher.

The Changes Clause

Simply, this clause says that neither you, as the author, nor the publisher can change any part of this agreement without the written consent of the other.

The Construction Heirs Clause

This is a very common clause, found in all publishing agreements. It says that all legal disputes will be interpreted in accordance with the laws of the state in which the publisher is located. If you're concerned, check the laws of that particular state.

What about Signing The Contract?

Be sure to sign the book contract with your legal signature. If you're not sure what constitutes your legal signature, you should consult a lawyer.

Also, don't forget to enter your social security number. If there is more than one author, each respective signature and social security number must appear on the agreement. Be sure that an executive from the publishing company signs your agreement.

Any change from the printed agreement, whether it is an addition or deletion, must be *initialed* by both the author or authors and the publisher. The initial usually follows at the end of the clause and to the far right side of the page. The initial at the end of the clause will suffice for one or more changes within the clause.

Normally, most publishers require that you sign a minimum of three original contracts. One last thing to remember, it is just good business practice to require that your publisher send you an original contract, completely executed by yourself and your publisher for your records.

Summary

Authors do not pay enough attention to the agreement after the advance and royalty is decided upon. This is a major mistake. It takes years to write and publish a book, yet all too often writers spend little time on the agreement.

ALL AUTHORS, AND ESPECIALLY THE FIRST TIME AUTHOR, SHOULD TAKE HOME A BLANK OR ROUGH DRAFT OF THE AGREEMENT AND STUDY IT PRIOR TO SIGNING.

If you are a first time author, do not expect a perfect agreement. Compromise is in order until you can demonstrate a successful track record. Remember that many parts of the agreement are negotiable, while some are not.

Straighten everything out to your satisfaction *before you sign* the agreement. Good luck!

Index